AF428434

Finishing Strong Under the Sun

Finishing Strong Under the Sun

by

Kenneth W. Brooks

An Imprint Of
HAVEN HALL
PUBLISHING

ISBN 979-8-9885041-0-8

Printed in the United States of America

Published by Haven Hall Publishing

In memoriam,

G. Burcham

CONTENTS

Preface xi

Introduction xv

Part 1: My Journey

Chapter 1 21

Chapter 2 29

Chapter 3 39

Chapter 4 43

Chapter 5 47

Chapter 6 57

Chapter 7 63

Chapter 8 67

Chapter 9 71

Chapter 10 75

Chapter 11 81

Chapter 12 83

Chapter 13 95

Chapter 14 101

Chapter 15 105

Chapter 16   111

Chapter 17   117

Chapter 18   127

Chapter 19   131

Chapter 20   135

Chapter 21   145

Chapter 22   153

Chapter 23   159

Chapter 24   167

Chapter 25   179

Chapter 26   185

Chapter 27   195

Chapter 28   199

Chapter 29   203

Chapter 30   213

Chapter 31   219

Part 2: My Beliefs

Chapter 32: Creation and the Light of Jesus   227

Chapter 33: Who Is God?   231

Chapter 34: The Holy Bible   237

Chapter 35: Eternity Versus Time Under the Sun   245

Chapter 36: God's Foreknowledge Versus Man's Free Will 249

Chapter 37: Once Saved, Always Saved?   255

Chapter 38: Second Chances, Exceptions, God's Will   265

Chapter 39: God Is in Control   275

Part 3: Redemption

Chapter 40: Adam's Fall to Abraham   291

Chapter 41: God Calls Out Abraham   295

Chapter 42: The Exodus and the Law   301

Chapter 43: The First Coming of Christ   307

Chapter 44: The Church Begins   315

Chapter 45: An Invitation to the Gentiles   323

Chapter 46: The Impact of Peter's Vision   331

Chapter 47: The Beginning of Paul's Ministry   337

Chapter 48: The Mysteries Revealed to Paul   345

Chapter 49: The Cross Changed Everything   353

Chapter 50: Redemption and a Gracious Gift   361

Chapter 51: The Disciples and the Kingdom Message   365

Chapter 52: Defining the Gospel   369

Chapter 53: Impact of the Revelation of the Mysteries   373

Chapter 54: Let's Talk About Miracles   383

Chapter 55: The Tribulation and the Second Coming   387

Chapter 56: Flow Charts and the Bible   401

Preface

In the Fall of 2000, I was at a Christian men's retreat at Fall Creek Falls in eastern Tennessee. At daybreak, with just enough light for me to see, I was running along a winding trail. With a slight breeze, ducks flying overhead, squirrels jumping from limb to limb, and deer grazing in a meadow, I could barely feel my feet hitting the ground. You would be hard-pressed to find anything more peaceful and relaxing. But the silence was broken when I heard a voice say, "I want you to write a book." I used the word "heard" because at the time that was exactly how it felt—external. It was so crystal clear that I immediately looked around but saw no one. I still find myself questioning those few seconds. I tried to convince myself that it was just a thought in my mind, then decided if that was the case, it was not my thought—it got there without my knowledge or help. I know one thing for sure: I heard what I heard. If it was not a word from God—internal or external—then I have no answer other than it was certainly not from me. The thought of writing a book had never crossed my mind until that moment. Thereafter, I could not get away from it, no matter how hard I tried. And I tried every excuse known to man.

A few weeks before Christmas, I had a fatty tumor removed from my neck and had a reaction to a medication that put my life in danger. For over a week I steadily lost weight and progressively got worse. I finally prayed that if I lived, I would write the book.

It took about a year for me to write *Running with Angels*. I started with no outline, no title, and no idea what I was doing. To say I lacked experience would be an understatement. At the start of each training run, I would totally focus on the book. During each run, the next part of the story would kind of scroll through my mind. As soon as I finished, I would write it down by hand, which at times lasted well into the night. I would then spend time cleaning it up before my next run. I did this week after week, month after month. Once finished, I thought, "What now?" After a good amount of research and effort, I self-published *Running with Angels* as a hard-cover book, and I also have a Kindle version available on Amazon.

Most events that occur in the first half of *Running with Angels* were drawn from my own life. They were enhanced and molded to create the story line for the main character. Looking back, it is easy for me to now admit that I was being led to write a nonfiction book but I could not bring myself to do it at the time. I wrote the book as promised, but as a Christian fiction novel instead of a nonfiction novel about myself. It would have been too personal, and I just could not bring myself to go there. Over the last twenty years, as I steadily moved deeper and deeper into senior citizen status, I began to realize that one of my biggest regrets in life was when I decided to ignore the way I was being led and instead took the easier path.

Writing a book is a big commitment and far from easy. It takes long hours, late nights, and a sustained focus throughout the whole process. You better believe that every time I considered this idea of making amends for that decision, I would remember how difficult it was the first time. This worked for a while, but the regret was still there. During this same time period, there was another issue that would become involved in my desire to make amends. Right after publishing *Running with Angels,* I went on a tour of Israel with my church. The tour opened my eyes to the fact that reading the Bible regularly was a good thing, but it was not doing a lot to improve my understanding of the Bible. That's when I made the decision to no longer just read the Bible, but to take the time to study it as well. It took a lot of trial and error before I finally developed a study method that worked for me, which I will describe later in this book.

For many years this idea of "making amends" and my process of gaining a deeper understanding of the Bible were totally independent of each other. Slowly, I began to realize that writing a second book would require this deeper understanding of the Bible.

But I still had plenty of excuses to not get started, which far exceeded my sincere regret. One point I want to make clear: During all those years, I never felt I was being led or pressured spiritually. This was not like what happened in the Fall of 2000, at the Christian men's retreat. This feeling that I hadn't fully written my story was all on me, and I was doing an excellent job of not giving in.

But something happened on my son's fifty-first birthday on January 23, 2020, that shook me to my very core. A week later I made the decision to write this book.

Introduction

These are the only subjects that I rank myself "an expert": detailing cars, bacon, tires, flow charts, Fortran, Cobol, tomatoes, marathons, and finishing strong. And there is possibly one more: falling elevators. If you are wondering what this has to do with this book, you will understand if you read to the very end. There is one item on my list that weaves its way throughout, from the beginning to the end: marathons.

Two major factors influence a runner's ability to win a race: pace and endurance. For a short race like a one-hundred-yard dash, it is all about pace (speed), but the longer the race, the more pace takes a back seat to endurance. For a marathon, both are relevant, but endurance becomes the driving force for a successful finish. As I approached retirement, I began to realize how similar our life's journey is to running a marathon—from the start, to the middle, to hitting the wall, and then to the finish line. As an analogy, the start is our youth, the middle is middle-age, the wall is retirement, and then to the finish line. I have used this analogy throughout the book.

One of the things I want to accomplish is to show just how much God is involved in our journey, even though at the time we are so often unaware. My life offers the perfect example. I was a true believer at twelve and never wavered in my belief throughout my life. But it took me many years before even attempting to make God a priority, and at times my attempts would only get Him to second or third place. It seems I only made course corrections when I reached a spot where I needed God's intervention. But God is not just there during challenging times; God the Holy Spirit is with us 24/7. Just look closely at my life and you will see a pattern of me ignoring Him and yet God always being there. As I grew older, I slowly began to figure it out. It always works out better if you get God's opinion first, rather than having to depend on Him to bail you out, again and again.

Prior to my trip to Israel, I was in the process of reading through the Bible. Upon my return home, I soon reached Ecclesiastes. In the past when I read Ecclesiastes, I always stopped and pondered on how this strange book made it into the Bible. Then I would plow through Solomon's depressing opinions about life under the sun being pointless, useless, and meaningless. But this time as I read, a light came on, and I got very interested in what he was saying and why he was saying it.

Once I finished Ecclesiastes, I doubled back and actually attempted to understand how a man who had been blessed by God with everything under the sun could reach the end of his life so disillusioned, disappointed, and depressed. I stopped my Bible reading, focused on Ecclesiastes, and spent some time researching and studying this book. This is probably the first time I actually got a real taste of the difference between reading and actually studying the Bible. During my research, I found a poem specific to Ecclesiastes 1:1-5 that I am going to share below. I feel like it reflects Solomon's mindset toward the end of his life when he had drifted away from God.

Time Under the Sun – *author unknown*

When as a child, I laughed and wept,

Time crept;

When as a youth, I dreamed and talked,

Time walked;

When I became a full-grown man,

Time ran;

When older still I daily grew,

Time flew;

Soon I shall find in traveling on,

Time gone.

My eyes opened to the fact that I was nearing that same last stage of life and I did not want to go there with the mindset of Solomon. I did a lot of soul searching and realized that just because you are a true believer who could be blessed with a long life, that does not guarantee you will be able to enjoy each additional sunrise and sunset. We spend years planning and working toward financial security in our golden years. But what about our spiritual and physical health? In Part 1 you will see that I have always put in the effort to stay physically fit, but as for the spiritual health issue, not so much. I realized there were a number of things that needed to be changed spiritually in order for me to finish my life strong, both physically and spiritually. First, I planned to develop a method for studying the Bible that would work for me. More importantly, I would make it a priority.

This book is divided into three parts titled Part 1: My Journey, Part 2: My Beliefs, and Part 3: Redemption. Part 1 could be described as an autobiography or memoir. It gives an account of my life, but for me it is much more than that. Now over eighty, I have the ability to look back and revisit the events that shaped my life, and that is actually a great advantage. My short-term memory is fading fast, but my long -term memory is better than ever. Therefore, I can clearly see those experiences (and in some cases exploits!) that had a substantial influence on my life and faith—even though at the time, I had no clue. In Part 1, I follow a progression of specific events that defined who I would become. Some of these experiences were actually life changing and a few others were life threatening. Each one got my attention and strengthened my faith.

My hope is as you read these stories of "my journey," you will see how much God is involved in our lives even when we cannot make time for Him. You can know God and ignore God at the same time. For a number of years, I was very skilled at doing just that. But I can tell you for a fact that God never ignores us, no matter how far we stray from His will. As you read, you will see how my life forever was changing as my faith grew and as I moved closer to God. Without a doubt, learning to involve the Holy Spirit in each and every one of your life choices makes all the difference. Is there anything too big or too small for God? I don't think so! My hope is that when you finish Part 1, you will feel like you know me as well as you know your best friend.

There is one thing I will avoid in Part 1: I will not look around in my family's or friends' closets. As I was growing up, I learned a valuable lesson from my mother. She would say, "If you don't have anything good to say about someone, say nothing." If more of us could follow my mother's advice, it would greatly reduce a common activity: gossiping.

You can find the details that caused me to finally commit to writing this second book near the end of Part 1. To spur your interest as we begin, I am going to make these following three statements:

- I have never drank a beer or smoked a cigarette.

- No one has ever cut my lawn.

- No one has ever washed or detailed my vehicles.

Somewhere in Part 1, you will figure out which of these three is not totally true. In hoping you will not only enjoy but be inspired while reading this book, I will leave you with this thought: In all things, fear God, wait on God, listen to God, and above all believe God.

Part 1

My Journey

Chapter 1

I know there are "experts" who proclaim that a child does not have the ability to remember events that occurred early in life, but I beg to differ. My first memories are when I was very young. I remember riding on that train. I remember being pitched up into the air by the ice truck and landing on my head. I remember sitting in my mother's lap as we rode a bus to see a doctor. I remember looking at my father's hand and asking him, "Does it hurt?" All of these occurred within a week's time.

My father was a tire builder at the Firestone Tire plant in Memphis, Tennessee, prior to WWII. As the war continued, he enlisted in the Army on August 21, 1943. After basic training, he departed for overseas on February 23, 1944, and was assigned to the U.S. 7th Infantry Regiment, which was part of the 3rd Infantry Division that was fighting German forces in the Battle of Anzio, as part of the Italian Campaign. The Battle of Anzio was a four-month stalemate during which British and American losses totaled 7,000 killed and 36,000 wounded or missing. The siege of Anzio ended on May 23, 1944, when the Allies launched a breakout offensive that led to the capture of Rome on June 5, 1944.

My father was wounded on May 22, the day before the siege ended. He had his first surgery on May 23 and another on May 25. On September 1, 1944, he returned to the states and was admitted to a VA hospital in Alabama. At that time, my mother did not know how to drive; in fact, she never learned to drive until after my father's death. She took me and my older sister, Joyce, by train from Memphis to Alabama. This must've been a challenge, since I was only two-and-a-half, and Joyce was four years old. She rented a small house, and we visited my father daily at the hospital as they worked through his rehab and all of the paperwork required for his release from the Army.

Our rented house had an icebox, and an ice truck would deliver a block of ice every morning. The driver would leave the truck running while he placed the ice in our icebox. The truck had a big tarp covering the ice and a chain hanging across the opening at the back of the truck. If I jumped, I could hang on the chain, which I did. Unfortunately, the driver did not see me hanging onto the chain, and I did not see the driver get into the truck. When he took off, I flew up into the air and landed on the slate gravel road. A sliver of rock lodged in my face about a half-inch below my eye. My mother was afraid to pull it out, fearing I would bleed to death before she got me to a doctor. So, she pressed a damp washcloth against the wound as we took a bus to see a doctor. After a few stitches, I was fine; I still have the scar today. As far as visiting my father at the hospital, I remember little to nothing, but I do remember looking as his scarred, twisted hand and asking him if it hurt. I don't remember how the four of us got back to Memphis, but I know for sure it was not by train.

My father returned to Firestone and started drinking. My mother would read her Bible and pray. We began walking to a small Baptist church that was close to the house, but my father stayed home. Our family grew when my parents had my brother, David, and then my youngest sister, Nita. My father's drinking grew worse. He always drank alone; sometimes at home and sometimes at a bar. When at a bar, he would sleep in our car until he felt sober enough to drive home. At times, he would lose his temper for the slightest reason, and I slowly started to fear and hate him. Although he never hit my mother, I feared he would totally lose control and hurt her, my brother, or my sisters. We never knew when or what would set him off. He would overturn the kitchen table while we were eating our meal with none of us understanding what had triggered it.

My whole family became professionals at walking on eggshells. I told my mother that I hated my father. She told me to never say that again, and that I should pray for him. She said something happened during the war that caused him to drink and act this way. She said my father was a good man who had been badly hurt during the war—and not just from his wounds. I asked her countless times what happened, but she would never reply. I hated him anyway.

Every Sunday morning, we walked to church, and I paid no attention to the sermons. But there were those rare occasions when my father would drive us to church. Sometimes, after being sober for a number of weeks, he would decide to attend church with us. On the way home, he would start singing "Blessed Assurance," out of the blue.

Blessed assurance, Jesus is mine;

Oh, what a foretaste of glory divine!

Heir of salvation, purchase of God,

Born of His Spirit, washed in His blood.

Perfect submission, all is at rest,

I in my Savior am happy and blessed;

Watching and waiting, looking above,

Filled with His goodness, lost in His love.

This is my story, this is my song,

Praising my Savior, all the day long.

This is my story, this is my song,

Praising my Savior all the day long.

My father had a beautiful baritone voice. I have never in my life felt more at peace and safe than during those occasions as we drove home from church. To this day, that is my favorite gospel song—and the one in second place is not even close.

An event occurred that had a compelling impact on my relationship with my father. It was so significant that it probably altered the very direction my life was heading. It dealt with my father's half-brother, Calvin, who came for a visit right before Christmas. Since I devoted a chapter to this topic in *Running with Angels*, I am going to insert a part of that chapter, which was totally true (nonfiction) and occurred pretty much as written. I did enhance the severity of the storm, and since at the time I was a little kid, I described the stitches in Calvin's head as numbering in the hundreds. Now looking back over seventy years, I can just say there were a lot of stitches—but probably not in the hundreds, as I thought at the time.

****

<u>*War in the Front Yard*</u>

Calvin called and said he was in Los Angeles working as a bouncer. He asked, "Can you pick me up at the Greyhound bus station? I'm coming to visit during the holidays."

The first week went well. Calvin spent hours talking to me about his football career. I grew more determined to be a football player. Two days before Christmas, the weather turned unusually warm. Short-sleeve weather in late December – this was strange. But as the day progressed, the skies darkened and the wind picked up, blowing cold air straight out of the north. The spring-like day was about to collide with "Old Man Winter," and that meant trouble.

As thunder rolled in the background, Calvin and my father began drinking. Both were well on their way to intoxication when the liquor ran out. Calvin said, "Let's drive to a bar." "No, we'll need to sober up before driving the car," my father said. I was sitting in the kitchen, watching them through the doorway to the dining room. The keys to our Ford sedan were hanging on a hook near the doorway. Calvin jumped up, grabbed the car keys, and headed out the front door with my father right behind him. I followed them outside. Calvin climbed into the car and put the key in the ignition. My father reached through the open window and took the keys. Calvin's face grew bright red. "I'll beat you to a pulp if you don't give me back those keys," he yelled. My father replied, "Stay in the car, sober up, and then we'll go to the bar." I watched him go back into the house. Calvin got out of the car, still red-faced, clearly looking for a fight. My father came back into the yard, with our rifle in one hand and a fist full of bullets in the other. "Calvin, get back in the car," my father said, but Calvin would have no part of it. Someone grabbed my arm from behind, and I looked around to see my mother. She pulled me across the street into our neighbor's house. While my mother was dialing the phone, I sneaked out onto the front porch. My father was telling Calvin to get back into the car, but Calvin was headed straight for him. There was plenty of time to load the rifle, but he threw the bullets on the ground. Just as they met in the middle of our front yard, my mother grabbed me and pulled me back into the house, then returned to the porch with our neighbor. I went out the back door, circled the house, and crouched where I could see our yard without being seen by my mother. Both my father and Calvin were covered with blood. The rifle stock was broken. My father hit Calvin on the head with the barrel, knocking Calvin to his knees.

Finally, the winter storm broke. Icy rain pelted down, instantly soaking my clothing. Lightning illuminated the dark sky overhead. Calvin pulled himself to his feet and hit my father directly in the face with his fist. My father sprawled on the ground with the rifle barrel still firmly gripped in both hands. He jumped to his feet and hit Calvin on the head with the barrel, knocking him to his knees. I watched as they continued fighting. First Calvin fell to his knees, and then my father was knocked clear off his feet. Over and over, like instant replay, this scene repeated itself. The wind blew, the lighting flashed, the thunder roared, and the icy rain poured down in sheets as, wide-eyed, I watched every blow fall. As the distant wail of sirens grew louder, both stayed down. My father sat in the mud in the middle of our yard. Calvin crawled toward our house.

Two sheriff patrol cars and an ambulance came flying up the street. My father stood and held out his arms. Two officers spun him around, handcuffed his hands behind his back, and shoved him into the back seat of one of the patrol cars. Another officer with a clipboard approached my mother. I dashed across the street and ran up to the patrol car. My father was leaning forward, head bowed. His face was cut and swollen. Blood dripped from both his upper and lower lip and puddled on the car's carpet. Speechless, I stared into his bloody face. My whole body felt numb. I wasn't sure if I was numb from the cold wind and rain, or from what I'd just witnessed. "Hey, we need a rope," a medic yelled. I turned as an officer carried a coil of rope toward our house. Were they going to tie Calvin up? I sprinted after the officer. Calvin lay under our front porch. Blood oozed from deep cuts covering his head and formed a pool on the ground. Surely, he was dead, I thought, but then I saw the movement of his chest as he breathed. Watching the two medics tie the rope around his waist, I realized Calvin was stuck underneath the porch. The medics tugged Calvin free and took him to the hospital, and the officers took my father to the county jail. It took over 150 stitches to close Calvin's head wounds.

They kept my father in jail for three days, but when Calvin refused to press charges, he was released the day after Christmas. After his release, the three of us went to see Calvin in the hospital. My father and Calvin apologized to each other and then to my mother. A few days later, Calvin was released. We took him directly from the hospital to the bus station.

****

As I stared into the patrol car, watching the blood drip from my father's face, I felt like I was seeing him for the first time. I now saw his suffering and pain. My feelings of hate were replaced with feelings of compassion. I saw a man who was broken, and he did not know how to put himself back together. I saw a man who feared nothing except his memories. I never felt hate toward him again. From that day forward, I changed. He did not. But he would stop drinking for a while. He would go to AA for a while. He would even go to church with us for a while, and I started listening to the sermons. He never stopped trying until the very end. There were even times when we felt like a normal family.

Chapter 2

Not long after the episode with Calvin, my mother got sick. It started with a persistent cough, fatigue, and night sweats. For the first couple of trips to the doctor they treated her for a cold. But she did not get better, so they thought maybe she had the flu. They ran more tests, took x-rays, and finally tested her for tuberculosis (TB). The test came back positive for active TB, which was highly contagious. She was kept under quarantine at a hospital in Memphis as arrangements and paperwork were completed for her to be transferred to Oakville Memorial Hospital, which at the time was a TB sanitarium for Shelby County, near Memphis. We were allowed to go see her one time before she was moved to Oakville Memorial. We were not allowed in the room, but could see her through a glass partition.

At this point, things happened fast. It was a foregone conclusion that my father could not work and take care of us. That is not even taking into account the drinking. Three of my mother's relatives agreed to take one kid each. I ended up being the one left over. It was decided that I would stay at Porter Leath while my mother was being treated at the sanitarium. Being the oldest son, I agreed with the decision. Porter Leath was an orphanage in Memphis at the corner of Chelsea Ave. and Manassas St. Although it was named Porter Leath Orphanage, all of us kids living there called it Porter Leath Home. I think it is still there to this day, but with a different name. The next morning, after my brother and sisters were gone, my father took me to Porter Leath. As he was leaving, he promised to come on Sunday mornings and take me to church as often as he could. This was my mother's only request, that last day we visited her in the hospital. He kept his promise, but there were times he looked pretty hung over. We would walk together to a small Methodist church that was about two blocks away. I continued listening to the sermons. We always stopped at a drug store coming back. I would pick out a comic book and have a chocolate shake.

There are two incidents from my life that I still remember in minute detail: the fight between Calvin and my father, and my first day at Porter Leath. Each had a lasting impact on my life. Here's a chapter from my book, *Running with Angels*, called "Don't Like Your Looks," which discusses my first day at Porter Leath. Prior to starting, I want to answer a question you will have after reading this segment: To this day, I still do not have any idea where the hammer handle came from.

****

<u>Don't Like Your Looks</u>

My first glimpse of the orphanage frightened me. Why was that huge, old, brick building so far from the road? Why was the chain-link fence so tall? And was the barbed wire to keep strangers out or to keep the kids in? All these thoughts whirled through my head as we made our way up the long drive. We arrived at the orphanage around noon, when all the kids were at school. Two administrators showed us the grounds and ended the tour in a spacious room on the third floor of the main building.

The room contained row after row of small beds. Each bed had a gray wrought-iron headboard that looked old enough to be classified as an antique. A large metal chest rested at the foot of each bed. Clothes hung on rods within small, open compartments on the front and back walls. I counted the beds as my father put his questions to the administrators. Six rows of ten beds each—sixty beds. As I turned my attention back to my father, I saw the two men walking away.

My father scooped me into his arms, held me against his chest, and told me to be strong, like a man, and everything would be okay. Then, all too quickly, he was gone. I stood, fighting back tears, trying to be a man, but I still felt like a little boy.

A woman pushing a large dust mop entered the room from another door. She stopped and regarded me. "Now, who do we have here?" she asked. "My name is Mark Matthews," I replied. "So, you're the new boy. Well, you can call me Marie." I looked at the dust mop. "Are you the maid?"

"Don't you be calling me a maid. I'm the third-floor matron for the second shift. Worked this floor for the past twelve years and seen many a boy come and go." With that said, she showed me my bed, helped put away my clothes, and took me for a tour of the floor. I gaped at the huge bathroom. Everything was in the open—no privacy there. Another large room on the floor, about half the size of the dormitory, contained only a wooden bench that ran around all four walls. Above the bench, shelves held games, a can of marbles, cards, dominoes, and more.

Marie sat me down on the bench and said, "Boy, no need for you to worry; our Lord is in control, and you're going to be just fine. Those kids will be back from school around three -thirty, and then you can make you some friends."

She sounded just like my mom. I watched her return to the dormitory to run the dust mop up and down between the rows of beds. It was one-thirty. I sat on the bench. Two o'clock came and went. I sat on the bench. Two-thirty. I continued to sit on the bench. I was ready for those kids to show up, but as the clock inched closer to three-thirty, I became uneasy. What if they didn't like me?

Too late—I heard them clamoring up the stairs. I anxiously scanned each one as he topped the staircase. Of varying heights and ages, the boys moved all over the room, but most mingled with their own age group. There were quite a few, but not enough to fill all sixty beds. I tried to count them, but they moved around too much. I guessed there were maybe forty. In fact, I learned never to keep count, because the number always varied. As Marie had said, "The boys come and go."

A small group spotted me sitting on the bench. As they headed in my direction, the tallest yelled, "Well now, look what we have here. What's your name?" "Mark," I mumbled. One after another, the questions came faster than I could respond. "How old are you?" "What grade are you in?" "Do you have a mother?" "Do you have a father?" "Then, why are you here?"

I attempted to answer each, but before I could reply to one question, someone was asking the next. The battery of questions continued until all had their turn. By now, the whole party had gathered around me. I continued to look them over. Suddenly, I realized I was the smallest boy in the room. This did not raise my comfort level. In fact, despite being in the middle of a crowd, I felt very alone.

A stocky boy rolled his eyes, looked me over from head to toe, and asked for the second time, "Are you really in the third grade?" For the second time I replied, "Yep, third grade." "You look too small to be in the third grade," he said. He backed off and stood watching me for a while, then stepped forward and said, "I don't like your looks."

It was many years before I finally figured out why he made that statement. Okay, I'd been staring at him, and he took exception to anyone staring in his direction. He was redheaded, but his hair was actually a bright orange color. Freckles covered every exposed area of his skin. He had no neck; his head sat right on his shoulders. But that wasn't what made me stare. It was his hair. It grew in every direction, sticking out at all angles. Some strands sprang straight forward at a multitude of angles, some straight back at other angles, and some to one side or the other at all angles. His hair was in such total disarray that it was quite beautiful, like a bulldog that is so ugly it looks cute.

Here he was, saying he didn't like my looks, while I was thinking, "Have you looked in the mirror lately?" The possibility that my staring had hurt his feelings never crossed my mind. I was not the first, nor would I be the last person who stared too hard at Carl. He finally said, "I think I'll beat you up."

Fear flowed into my bloodstream and pumped into all parts of my body. Carl was bigger, and he looked like he enjoyed beating on people. Then I heard Marie say, "You kids can go out to play before supper." Everyone started streaming down the stairs, including Carl. I tried to tell Marie I didn't want to go out to play, but she would have none of that. She herded me down the stairs with the other boys.

When I got outside, I realized the place was huge. I looked in every direction and didn't see that chain-link fence. As I searched the horizon for the fence, Carl headed toward me with a sour look on his face. I ran. Carl started running too, but I was faster. He chased me for a while, then rested, chased, and then rested. This was kind of fun. I ran slower and allowed Carl to draw near, and then I sped away. I let him get close, and then quickly changed directions. I looked back to see him trip over his feet. This was really fun! But Carl was getting madder by the minute.

As we were called to go inside and clean up for supper, I realized it might be a mistake, having so much fun at Carl's expense. When we reached the third floor, Carl could no longer contain himself. He pushed me down on one of the beds, jumped on top, and hit me repeatedly in the face with both fists. The first blows bloodied my nose. I was in for a beating.

I'd caught sight of a hammer handle lying on the bed as I fell back. It was not a hammer, just the handle. I extended my arm and with one sweeping motion, I gripped the handle. I swung with all the strength I could muster. It struck Carl on the back of his head with a loud thud.

He dropped on my chest like a dead weight. I struggled out from under him. Carl was out cold. A rather large knot grew on his head as I watched. Maybe I had killed him. After a few moments, Carl stirred. He's really going to be mad now, I thought. To my complete surprise, Carl said, "Boy, you're pretty tough for such a small kid. What did you hit me with?" "This hammer handle," I replied, hefting my makeshift weapon. I had just knocked out a guy with a hammer handle and made a friend for life. Go figure.

Carl and I talked for hours that first night. His full name was Carl London. He was also in the third grade. I'd assumed he was at least in the fifth grade. As we talked, he revealed that he had failed the third grade the previous year. When he was three years old, he told me, his parents were killed in an automobile accident while he was with a babysitter. He had no brothers or sisters, and since none of his relatives wanted him, he ended up at the orphanage. No one came to visit; he was on his own. After hearing this, I didn't feel so bad. I had both a mother and father, and I'd be at the orphanage only until she got well. Carl was a permanent resident.

The next day I went to Guthrie Elementary with Carl. The school had two third-grade classes, but as luck would have it, I ended up sitting next to Carl. My life at the orphanage had begun.

****

Thinking back, if I could choose one word to describe how I felt that first day, it would be abandoned. That first night in a huge room with so many boys sleeping all around me, I felt so alone. But, as weeks went by, I made friends and fell into a routine. My mother would write, and I would answer her letters as best I could. Time slowed down, and it seemed like I was there for years. I remember being there for only one Christmas and two summers. During the summer, we were taken to the Memphis opera once a week. I remember going for two summer series. The first summer, I hated going—but by the next summer, I actually looked forward to each visit (even though I did not understand one word, since all the singing was in Italian). Therefore, I believe I was there about a year-and-a-half to two years.

None of the medical treatments worked on treating my mother's TB. The last resort was to remove the infected part from each lung. After the surgery, the medicine started working, and the TB became inactive. Not long after, she was released, and we were back home together as a family. I say "home," but we never owned a house while my father was alive; we only rented.

During my time at the orphanage, I will admit my spiritual journey took a direct hit. Even though I was still intently listening to the sermons, I began questioning why this happened to my mother. Why could my father not stop drinking? He tried so hard. Why God? There was much I did not understand.

For the next few years, I remember little that I would consider significant. My father continued to work at Firestone. He continued to drink. During the week he would drink, but stay sober enough to work. On some weekends he would drink until he passed out. He always drank alone. At times he would stop drinking, go to church with us for a while, and even attend a few AA meetings. But we all knew that the next thing could set him off into another drinking binge. We all continued to walk on eggshells. It was our way of life. But mother would never speak an unkind word about him, so neither did we.

There is one important point I forgot to mention. It held true, from the time he was released from the VA hospital in Alabama until his death. It was something that the whole family understood was off limits. Do not, under any circumstances, ask him about the war. And if a war scene came on the TV, change the channel quickly. Sometimes, when he was not drinking, he would take us to a movie. I don't remember my mother ever going with us. There was a new action/adventure movie showing at the Crosstown movie theater in midtown Memphis. We begged him to take us. About half way through the movie, there was a part that flashed back to a WWII battle. My father got up and headed for the exit. We all knew the reason. We sat, looking at each other. Finally, I said I would go check on him. I found him sitting in the lobby. Before I could speak, he said to finish watching the movie and he would wait for us in the lobby. We never would have asked to see the movie, if we had known it had a war scene. He avoided anything that dealt with the war, right up until his death.

The next noteworthy event occurred when I was in the sixth grade, so I must have been twelve. We had been attending church regularly, and at times my father would go with us. The more sermons I heard, the more I wanted to understand. So, after each service, my mother and I would discuss the sermon. I had many questions. My mother would patiently answer each one, as best she could. Finally, after I had just asked a question about salvation, she told me to read the four gospels: Matthew, Mark, Luke, and John. For a twelve-year-old, that was a lot to read and even more to understand. Looking back, I can now see she had a plan, and it worked. If she could just get me interested, I would not turn loose until I understood.

So, after some time, we were sitting toward the back of the church in the middle of a pew. Our pastor finished his sermon and gave the altar call. This was a Baptist church, so if there was a sermon, there would be an altar call. For the last couple of weeks, I wanted to get out of my seat, march down the aisle, and accept Jesus as my Lord and Savior. But this was something I would never be able to do. Every person in the church would be looking at me. We had altar calls, week in and week out, without a single person leaving their seat. So, it was not as if I would be among a crowd marching down the aisle. It would only be me.

I sat there and made the wise decision: not this week. But in slow motion, I felt myself standing up, at the same time as I was trying my hardest to stay down. And to make matters worse, I was stepping on my sister's feet as I made my way toward the center aisle, saying "excuse me" along the way. Once I cleared the pew, it was clear sailing as I headed to the front of the church. Every single person watched each step, with many nodding their approval, and our pastor waited in the front with open arms. This was my first of many encounters with the Holy Spirit, and over the years I have grown to understand and appreciate the term "the power of the Holy Spirit."

Chapter 3

$\mathbf{T}$he next event dealt totally with my mother. It made me realize just how much I did not yet understand. Allow me to give some background. I remember exactly when it occurred: during the summer between tenth and eleventh grade. We had rented a house on North Dunlap St. about the time I started high school. It was close to Firestone and actually within blocks of Porter Leath and Humes High School. So, I ended up going to the same school as the kids from Porter Leath. I did not know any of them, which was no surprise, since there was so much turnover at the orphanage.

By the time I was in tenth grade, I had figured out that if I was ever going to own a car, I would have to save the money to buy it. Therefore, I needed a part-time job. It took a while, but before the end of the school year, I got a job washing tractor-trailer rigs on the weekends. I had to work Saturdays and Sundays, and this meant I would have to stop going to church. My mother did not like this at all, but my constant begging won out. The owner of the truck-washing business was named Hess Hall. Surprisingly, I still remember his name. He usually kept three crews, and each consisted of an older team leader and three teenage boys. One crew worked the trucking firms in and around West Memphis, Arkansas, right across the Mississippi River. The other two crews worked at trucking firms all around Memphis. I never worked with the West Memphis crew.

I don't know which of the following will shock you more. I

made exactly one dollar an hour. I washed tractor-trailers starting toward the end of the tenth grade and worked into my second year of college. I worked weekends during the school year and seven days a week in the summer. I did make an effort to get off on Sundays, whenever possible. I saved every dollar I made. When I graduated from high school, I had saved $1,800. My father helped me find a car. I paid cash for a 1955 Ford sedan. Looking back now, I find it hard to believe, myself.

On a Sunday during that first summer, my crew had just arrived at our work site when Mr. Hall showed up. He talked to our crew leader, then came over to talk to me. The West Memphis crew was two men short, and he wanted me to work with them. He drove me to West Memphis and dropped me off. The trucking firms were always closed on Sundays, but our crew leaders would pull the rigs up to where they had a water outlet. I normally climbed on the top of the trailer and used a long-handled brush to wash from the top down. Another would do the same from the bottom up. The third would wash the cab. The crew leader would wash the wheel rims and clean inside the cab. This day, we were still one short, so we had to make do. We worked until 4:30 p.m. The crew leader said Mr. Hall would pick me up, and that they were taking off. I said, "Okay," but I was thinking, "Maybe you guys should hang around a few minutes until Mr. Hall arrives." I was in the middle of nowhere, in a different state, and did not have a penny in my pocket. I waited for about an hour before I decided no one was coming. I started walking toward the Mississippi River Bridge. I figured it was at least ten miles to the state line, which is in the very middle of the bridge. I crossed the bridge at around 8:00 p.m. I figured, at that point, I was beyond halfway home.

Normally I was home from work by 5:30 p.m., at the latest. After I was an hour late, my mother started getting worried. After another hour, she was pacing the floor and praying. By 8:00 p.m., she had talked my father into driving to find me. At 8:30 p.m., I was walking down a dark, empty road through downtown Memphis, and I saw a car driving slowly. As it neared, I realized it was our car. My father was driving, and my mother had her head out the window. I yelled, and they saw me.

As I got into the car, I asked my father how he knew where to look. He said, "I didn't. Your mother told me where to drive." So, I asked her. She said, "The Lord knew you were in trouble and where you were." That answer was not good enough, so I asked her again. She gave me the same answer. I was about to ask again, but my father was looking hard at me, and although he had not said another word, his look clearly said, "Leave your mother alone." I gave up.

The next day, I did not go to work. I was still upset about being abandoned and was still worn out. My father was at work, so I tried asking my mother again. It was as if we were not speaking the same language. Now, as I look back, it is clear to me it was a faith issue; I had faith smaller than a mustard seed, and she had faith the size of a mountain. The best I could get from her was, "I didn't know where you were, but somehow knew when to turn." To some, this might not seem significant. But for me, this had a tremendous impact on my life. It helped me understand how and why my mother stayed with my father to the very end. And it made me realize how little faith I had, compared to hers.

There is probably one point I need to clear up: Why was I left to walk home? In fact, this was the first thing I asked my crew leader. The West Memphis crew leader thought Mr. Hall would pick me up; Mr. Hall thought the West Memphis crew leader would take me back to my crew leader; and my crew leader thought Mr. Hall had taken me home. It was the perfect storm, and I got caught right in the middle of it. Everybody felt really bad, but that was not good enough. I let them all know: Don't expect me to ever work in West Memphis again. They had no problem with that.

Chapter 4

The next event dealt totally with my father, and although it most certainly had an impact on me, looking back, it may have impacted him more. Before I go there, I need to assure you that I have never considered myself to be smarter than my classmates, coworkers, friends, or family. As Albert Einstein said, "It's not that I'm so smart, it's just that I stay with problems longer." I made all A's in ninth, tenth, eleventh, and twelfth grades, graduating with a 4.00 GPA. Firestone had a scholarship program for their workers' graduating high school seniors, offering one scholarship per region. My father worked at the Firestone plant in the Southeast region. The four-year scholarship, which covered tuition, books, housing, and meals, could be used at any college in the Southeast region.

I cannot think of a time when I ever saw my father so excited as the day when he brought home the Firestone scholarship application. It was full of forms—some we had to fill out, and some my high school had to complete. It took some work, but after everything was finished and signed, my father turned it in. Around a month later, my father came home even more excited. The scholarship committee had their list down to two finalists: a department manager's daughter and me. I can't remember the department manager's plant; just that it was in the Southeast region. The plant manager had come out to my father's tire machine to tell him the good news. I will admit; now I was excited. I had already decided I wanted to go to Georgia Tech and study engineering if I won the scholarship. But, now for the bad news: I came in second and received a $250 savings bond.

Sure, we were disappointed, but my whole family, including my father had accepted the fact I had come in second. Unfortunately, that was not the end of it. The plant manager came down to my father's tire machine again. He was upset about the results. He said that I had the better grades and GPA, but the girl had taken some pre-college courses, and the committee took that into consideration, thus placing her first. I know our plant manager meant well, but it would have been better if he had kept that information to himself. My father asked me, "Does Humes have pre-college courses?" All I could say was, "No." I had never heard the term, but figured they were special types of classes used to prepare a student for college.

He did not fly into a rage or go on a drinking binge, but I could see he took it hard. After that day, he still had his highs and lows, but the lows were lower and the highs were also lower. Looking back, I think the reason he took this so hard was because he had to quit school and work before he even learned to read or write. When my mother met him, he signed his name with an X. After they were married, she taught him to read and write. She once told me he was an intelligent man in an uneducated body. I think he wanted me to get the education he was denied.

The good news is that I did end up winning a scholarship. Some weeks later, I received a letter from Southern Boiler Maker, a local company in Memphis. They were awarding a two-year, pre-engineering scholarship to Memphis State University that would pay for tuition and books to the person who made the highest score in the state on the science portion of the SAT—and that was me. But you probably need to know the reason I won. About three months before we were scheduled to take the SAT, I asked my old science teacher how I should study for the science portion of the exam. He reached in his desk, handed me an old copy of our chemistry book, and said, "Read it cover-to-cover before taking the test." I did—but the more I read, the more I thought, "information overload." It took me forever, but I stuck with it until I finished. In the end, I won the scholarship. My mother was elated, but my father? Not so much.   He could not turn loose of the way the Firestone scholarship had been decided.

Chapter 5

After I finished the two years at Memphis State, a series of events occurred that had a huge impact on my life. Looking back, I have come to realize that losing out on the Firestone scholarship turned out to be one of the best things that ever happened to me.

Memphis State did not have an engineering department. They only offered a two-year, pre-engineering program, which consisted mostly of math and science courses required for engineering degrees. I took a number of math and physics courses during those two years, but then I had a problem. There was no college near Memphis that offered engineering degrees, and living on a campus would be too expensive. Even if I found a part-time job, I would not be able to afford the tuition, books, meals, and housing costs. My mother had a younger sister who had married and moved to Dallas with her husband. After much discussion, they came up with the idea that I could stay with her and her husband and go to University of Texas – Arlington campus (UTA). UTA had an excellent engineering department and was located half way between Dallas and Fort Worth.

My aunt and uncle lived in the suburbs of Dallas in Oak Cliff. They were renting the bottom unit of a two-story duplex. When I arrived in the summer of 1962, my aunt and uncle greeted me with open arms. My plan was to work full-time for the summer and hopefully part-time once I started going to UTA in the fall. My uncle helped me look for a job, since he knew places that were hiring. I filled out a number of applications. When I went to apply at Decker Meat Packing Company, they said the position had just been filled, but they would take my application anyway. Two days later, Decker called and offered me the job. The other applicant did not work out. When they told me the starting salary, I thought they must be kidding. Who would pay that much? I soon found out their workers were members of the most powerful meat packers union in the country. On the first day on the job, I was encouraged to join, which I did.

My first day was a twelve-hour shift on the dock unloading frozen mutton from a boxcar. A two-man crew was assigned to each boxcar waiting to be unloaded. When I looked into the boxcar, I asked, "How much do those boxes weigh?" The guy I was assigned to work with replied, "100 pounds." I noticed the mutton came from Australia. You may be curious why a meat packing company would be using frozen mutton from Australia. I am sure you have eaten hot dogs or bologna, and you may have noticed there are usually two kinds sold: all beef and all meat. The mutton was an ingredient for the all meat, but on occasion, it might end up in a run of all beef—even though there was a federal inspector working full-time at the plant.

On the second day, I began a week of training as a utility man for the bacon-packaging department. About halfway through the shift, my supervisor said, "Well, I didn't think you would show up today." I asked, "Why?" He told me the other guy quit after four hours on his first day. Later on, I found out that all new hires work a twelve-hour shift on the unloading dock their first day. If they come back the next day, they start their training.

The bacon-packaging department was on the third floor, along with all the offices for management. The smoked meat department was on the second floor, and the shipping/ receiving department was on the first floor.

Railroad tracks ran alongside the unloading dock at the back of the building. All meat to be processed came in refrigerated boxcars, and after being unloaded, it was taken to the second floor for processing. All cooking, smoking, and packaging was done on the second floor, and then the meat was moved to the shipping area on the first floor.

Each morning, Decker trucks would back into the bays, load their orders and deliver them to restaurants and grocery stores in the Dallas and Fort Worth area, with some of the trucks traveling as far as Texarkana, Arkansas.

There was one exception: bacon. It was smoked on the second floor, then moved to the third floor, where it was hung on metal trees, which were hung on rails that crisscrossed the ceiling in a huge, refrigerated room. The trees could be pulled all over the room and out into the bacon-packing area. Each tree held thirty-six slabs. Prior to hanging, each slab was weighed and separated into the following weight-groups: eight to ten pounds, ten to twelve pounds, twelve to fourteen pounds, and fourteen to sixteen pounds. Each tree was loaded by weight-group. The quality and cost of bacon is determined by the weight of the slab. The lighter the slab, the leaner the bacon. The heavier the slab, the more fat in the bacon. Therefore, you will not find bacon from eight to ten-pound slabs in grocery stores; it is only sold to restaurants.

The bacon-processing area consisted of a bacon-slicing machine, a conveyor belt, a bacon-wrapping machine, and finally the packaging area. The slicer, our supervisor, and myself were the only men who worked in the department. I remember the slicer's name was Walter, but I do not remember the supervisor's name. Twenty women worked along the belt—ten on each side—separating, weighing, packaging, and stacking the boxes of bacon on a large, four-wheel cart. Our department had one shift, from 8:00 a.m. to 4:30 p.m., but they only ran the line for seven hours. It was shut down for a thirty-minute lunch and then at 3:30 p.m. The last hour was used to clean and sanitize the equipment, which was all stainless steel. The federal inspector had to check the line and give his approval before the line could be restarted.

Since Decker had such a large union presence, all openings

were filled based on seniority. When an opening occurred, workers applied for the opening, and the position went to the one with the most seniority. Then, workers applied for his previous position, and it cycled down. This is how I was hired as a utility man. An opening occurred and was filled, and this rippled down to the bottom of the pay scale to the position that required constant activity: the bacon-processing utility man. But for me this was perfect. I was used to working hard, and I would have worked for half the pay. For those working on the bacon line, it was an altogether different matter. They were at the top of the pay scale and were the only workers in the plant who could earn a bonus. Each day when the output exceeded a specified amount, everyone working the line that day, including Walter, received a bonus. The bonus varied, since it was dependent on how much the production exceeded the specified amount. I was the only one in the department who did not earn the bonus, since I was not actually part of the line.

After the week of training, I was on my own. My job entailed replacing the loaded cart with an empty one, taking the loaded cart to shipping, stacking the boxes of bacon, then returning the empty cart to outside the bacon-processing area. I also had to keep all of the supplies required for each run stocked along the line. Each run might require different bacon trays and boxes, depending on whether it was being branded as a Decker product, or for a large restaurant or grocery chain. The final part of the utility job was helping Walter. The trees of bacon had to be taken from the cooler to a staging area for Walter. The timing of staging the bacon was critical. If the slabs were not quite thawed when Walter needed the tree, the slices would be brittle and break up. If slabs were too thawed, the slices would stick together. Either case was bad; the women on the line would throw a fit (that's a polite way to say it). This would prevent them from earning a bonus for the day, and I do not know the words required to express their displeasure.

Walter was nearly seventy and was the oldest worker in the plant. He had been operating the bacon-slicing machine for over twenty-five years. He taught me how to time-stage the bacon and how to operate the machine. The line workers would take two fifteen-minute breaks a shift. The women would stagger their breaks, since the line kept running. Therefore, I soon was slicing the bacon while Walter took his breaks.

After about a month, I had developed a routine and was feeling pretty good about myself. Then, something happened. Looking back, I kind of question having to admit this, since it might sound a little crazy. First, I have to tell you that it did not take twenty women long to fully load the cart. Second, my trainer had told me that if I got behind, I could unload the cart outside the bacon-processing area and move the bacon to shipping during lunch or after the line shut down at the end of the shift. I did not like that idea at all; it created double work. So, I worked very hard to stay caught up. But on this day, I got a little behind, and when I got back upstairs, the women had loaded the cart a little more than normal—maybe more than a "little."

Our plant had two elevators: one for the workers, and a service elevator for moving product between floors. I was going from the third floor to the first floor on the service elevator. The elevator started slowly, as normal, but then started picking up speed, making a whining noise, and was soon in a free fall. My first thought was, "This is not good." By the time I hit bottom, I had braced myself against the cart. It still knocked me off my feet, and I found myself on the floor, covered in bacon boxes. Right before I hit bottom, it felt like the fall slowed down somewhat. Later, I found out there was a coil spring built into the bottom of the elevator shaft, which was supposed to reduce the impact for moments like this. I would like to say this was the first and last time it happened. That would not be true. Looking back now, I am aware this sounds crazy, but remember, I was only twenty years old at that time. Crazy or not, I risked a possible fall in order to keep from having to do double the work. And I need to point out, falling from the third floor to the first floor is only two floors, not three. During my time working as the utility man, I fell twice more. After the first, it was not nearly as frightful, since I knew what to expect.

There was one other time when—for a brief moment—I just knew a fall was coming, and it had nothing to do with an overloaded cart. When I showed up for work that particular morning, my supervisor introduced me to a man who looked like "a big man in a little suit." He was going to follow me around all day to time-study the utility job. Until we were on the elevator with the first load, I had not even thought about his weight. I had a normal load on the cart, but as I pressed the elevator button, a thought flashed through my mind that nearly caused me to yell out, "Hang On!" But I did not, and thank goodness, we did not fall. The whole morning, the man slowed me down; he could not keep up. Then, after lunch, he was nowhere to be found. I asked my supervisor about it, and he said my time-study man had gone home sick. I never saw him again. There are two things I learned from falling two floors in an elevator three times: First, your mind will tell you to brace yourself, hold on, and that lying on the floor is not an option. Second, no matter how well you brace yourself and hold on, you will end up sprawled out on the floor.

I worked full-time throughout that first summer. In the fall, I asked management if I could work part-time, so I could go to UTA full-time. The answer was no. Decker's policy was for full-time positions only. I was in a pickle. I was going to have to pay out-of-state tuition, which was significantly more than in-state tuition, and I knew I would never be able to find another job that paid like Decker. My supervisor requested a meeting with management so we could try to come up with some type of compromise. My supervisor brought Walter with him, and Walter brought our union rep. I knew that going to school full-time was no longer an option, if I wanted to continue working for Decker. After much discussion, it was agreed that on the three days I attended class, I would work seven hours instead of eight. This one hour might not seem like much, but it really was a blessing for me. I started going to UTA part-time in the fall. I only took engineering courses at UTA, since I had pretty much completed all my electives.

After that first semester at UTA, something happened at Decker that had a dramatic impact on me, and it dealt with Walter. Walter was amazing; at his age, he did his job so well. The line made their bonus, day after day. A breakdown was about the only thing that would stop their streak. Walter was not fast nor quick. He was the model of efficiency, with no wasted motion. He was a storehouse of information. I loved talking to him. He taught me how to time-stage the bacon, and how to adjust the pace of the line based on the weight of the slabs being cut. I not only asked him questions about the job, but everything else under the sun.

It all started the day Walter told me he was going to take off the next Monday. Up until that point, I had only run the bacon slicer during his fifteen-minute breaks. I was very nervous that Monday morning. I did not want to cause the line to lose their bonus. But everything went smoothly, and we made it. A couple of weeks later, he told me he needed to be off the next Monday. This time, I asked if everything was okay. He said, "No problem. Everything is fine." The same thing happened again. I no longer worried about running the bacon slicer, but was becoming concerned that Walter was keeping something from me. A few weeks later, Walter missed another Monday, then on Tuesday morning, there was still no Walter. On Wednesday morning, Walter was still out, and instead of starting the line, our supervisor called a departmental meeting. I knew it was going to be about Walter. But, little did I know.

Walter was retiring and moving to Austin to live with his oldest daughter. He had been having cancer treatments on those Mondays he missed work, but without a lot of success. He was scheduled to start a new type of treatment at a hospital in Austin. Everyone in the room was asking the same question: "Why didn't Walter tell us?" The best we could get out of our supervisor was, "Walter did not want us worrying or feeling sorry for him."

His job was posted, and I was assigned to run the bacon slicer until it was filled. The man with the most seniority of those who applied was assigned the position. After a week of training, he was on his own. It was a train wreck or a total disaster—whichever you prefer. I knew it would be. This was not a job he could have learned in a month, much less a week. The union contract allowed for one week, so that's what he got. The women on the line were not kind. He requested to go back to his old job.

The job was posted again with the same results. There was a meeting attended by management, the union reps, and the women from the line. I was not asked to attend, but after the meeting, the union reps told me to apply for the position and told everyone else not to apply. At first, I thought everyone would think I had received special treatment and would give me a hard time. Thank goodness, that was not the case. No one wanted the position; they did not want to incur the wrath of the women on the line. So, after less than six months on the job, I went from being the lowest-paid union employee to the highest. If I could remember, I would include the amount I was making. I cannot, but I do know that it was a lot more than the amount I was making as a utility man. Now looking back, I think Walter knew this was exactly what was going to happen. And that was why he put so much effort into my training and waited until the last minute to tell management he was retiring.

There is one more event that occurred while I was working at Decker. Since I remember not only the date, but also the hour, I guess it should be considered significant. On the other side of the railroad tracks at the back of Decker was a seven-story building. At the time, I did not know the name of the building, but I did know it dealt with lots of books. I had seen them stacked on pallets on their back dock that first day when I worked the twelve-hour shift. Soon the whole world would know that on November 22, 1963, at 12:30 p.m., a sniper fired a shot from a sixth-floor window of this building, the Texas School Book Depository, mortally wounding President John F. Kennedy.

We had just finished our thirty-minute lunch break. I had just restarted the bacon-slicing machine. A faint sound of sirens grew louder and louder. The loudest seemed to be coming from the back of our building, but suddenly they seemed to be coming from everywhere. We had all left the line and were looking out the back windows when someone rushed in shouting, "The President has been shot!" Someone else asked, "What president?" Then, "President Kennedy." I did not know President Kennedy was in Dallas. Everyone began talking at once. Then our supervisor came in and said, "They want us to evacuate the building." Someone asked, "Who wants us to evacuate?" Our supervisor said, "The Secret Service."

We came out of the building and found men in business suits, carrying rifles, waiting in our parking lot. When it came to my turn, my car was searched, and I was told to go home. No problem, the sooner the better, as far as I was concerned. But that was not the end of it. Our duplex was on Ninth St., which ran parallel to Tenth St. then West Jefferson Blvd. The Texas Theater on West Jefferson Blvd. was two blocks from our duplex. As I crossed West Jefferson Blvd., I saw a number of police cars in front of the Texas Theater. I continued home. As soon as I walked in the door, my aunt began telling me something, but she was so excited, I could not understand what she was saying. She slowed down and said she had just heard on the news that the man who shot the president had been captured at our movie theater.

Before this happened, I could have told you who our President was, but probably could not have told you if he was Republican or Democrat. It took some months for all of this to sink in, but once it did, I realized how little I knew about our government. I was twenty, and old enough to vote, but was clueless as far as politics was concerned. It did not happen overnight, but I did make the effort to become more informed, and later on became a registered voter.

I can now look back at those two years at Decker and see how it influenced my life. It had nothing to do with bacon processing, but was all about relationships, trust, and the respect I developed with everyone in the bacon department. At that time, my family relationships were subjected to constant stress because of my father. My relationship with

God was in its infancy and growing quite slowly; it was like I was still in diapers and learning to crawl.

Chapter 6

I have thoroughly covered my two years working at Decker, but I have another story to share about why losing out on the Firestone scholarship turned out to be the best thing that ever happened to me—and, at the same time, caused me to commit a robbery. Bear with me as I try to explain.

On the day I moved in with my aunt and uncle, they introduced me to the family living in the upstairs duplex. It was a family of five: a divorced mother; a fourteen-year-old daughter, Linda; a twelve-year-old daughter; a ten-year-old son; and a four-year-old son. Linda's mother worked a full-time job, plus some part-time jobs. That left Linda in charge of the cooking, cleaning, and taking care of her three siblings—besides going to school. No matter how hard she tried, it was not good enough to keep her mother from belittling, berating, cussing, and screaming at her. My aunt wasted no time in sharing her eyewitness accounts. It did not take long for me to witness it myself. Before meeting Linda's mother, I honestly thought all women "walked on water." I quickly realized that was not the case.

All through high school and during the two years of college, I never had any close friends, much less a girlfriend. In fact, I spoke to no one unless they spoke to me first. I attended church, school, studied, and worked. My mother said I was just shy. That's probably true ... but there was more to it than that. I never, and I mean never, brought any school friend or classmate to my house. My home was not really a place where you would want to bring a friend—or maybe not even an enemy. I could not risk them meeting my father. Looking back, I know this was wrong, but that is the way I felt.

Linda was the first girl I ever met and got to know. In fact, this was probably the first time I ever had a lengthy conversation with a girl. She told me about how hard it was, living with her mother. In turn, I told her how hard it was, living with my father. And there was something else we had in common. When Linda was twelve, they rented a house that was across the street from a Baptist church. Linda started attending by herself. After some months, at each altar call, she wanted to go down the aisle and be saved, but could not get out of her seat. Then, the week came when she had again decided, "I can't do it," but found herself up and headed down the aisle, just like me.

Once I started that first fall term, I stayed so busy with work, school, and studies, we talked mainly on weekends. Time seemed to fly, one semester after the other. I was still going to school part-time and working full-time. I had completed the summer session and was about to start the fall, when my old Ford sedan started breaking down. I decided to buy a newer used car, so my uncle and I went to the Ford dealership. Looking back, I still find it hard to believe what happened. We walked into the dealership showroom, looking for a salesman. Right in the middle of all their new cars was a 1958 baby blue and white Thunderbird. This car even had baby blue and white leather seats. With the help of my uncle, we settled on a price with trade-in. I used most of my savings and paid cash. At the time, and still now, I know it was wasteful—but I had fallen in love with the car on first sight.

At the end of the Spring semester, I decided to go home to see my family. This would be my first time to see them in two years. My oldest sister had married and moved to another state while I was away. Everything else was mostly the same, except my father had lost something. He was still going to work each day, but it felt like he was giving up. I don't remember how many days I had been home, but do know it was May 26, 1964. That morning, I went to check on him in his room and found he had died in his sleep. In two weeks, he would have been forty-six. No family is prepared for something like this, but we were totally unprepared. We all took it hard, but my mother especially. Somehow, we got through it. He had a military funeral and was buried in Memphis National Cemetery. The autopsy showed the reason for death was excessive alcohol in his bloodstream. The doctor said no one could live with more than ten percent alcohol in the bloodstream. His was greater than ten percent. To this day, I do not think this was intentional. I think the amount of alcohol required to put him to sleep finally reached that ten percent breakpoint.

After the funeral, I realized I was going to have to make a drastic change of plans. My family was more important than college. I called Firestone and asked if they were hiring. They said whenever I was ready, a job was waiting. I called my aunt, told her my plans, and said I was going back to tell Linda goodbye before I started working at Firestone. She said, "You know Linda is going to be broken-hearted." I replied, "No more than I."

This is what caused me to commit the robbery; I robbed the cradle. At least that is what I have been told, over, and over, and over. I admit it, but with no regrets. Linda was now sixteen and had just finished tenth grade. I was now twenty-two. For two years, we had talked about everything under the sun except marriage. Well, that is not totally true. We thought it was something we would consider once she finished high school and I graduated from college.

When I called Linda to tell her my plans, we talked, and talked. Then, out of nowhere, Linda said, "Why don't I just ask my mother? What would it hurt?" To this day, I am still amazed that her mother said she would give her okay, if we promised that Linda would finish high school. We gladly promised, and although that was far more difficult than we imagined, we kept our promise. With her mother's permission, I was about to marry this tender-hearted teenage girl, who was wise beyond her years. From the day I met Linda, I would refer to her as "The Princess," and after fifty-nine years of marriage, I still call her "The Princess."

On Tuesday, June 16, 1964, we were married in Garland, Texas. We drove to Memphis the next day, and I starting building tires the following Monday. The Memphis Firestone plant had more than 3,000 employees, and every one of those employees' seniority was greater than mine. The first shift was 7:00 a.m. to 3:00 p.m.; the second was 3:00 p.m. to 11:00 p.m., and the third was 11:00 p.m. to 7:00 a.m. My father had always worked the first. I will let you figure out my assigned shift.

There were so many things we had to work through; I will spare the details. But, foremost, we had to learn to co-exist. We quickly sold the Thunderbird and bought a used Volkswagen. The first few months were hard on everyone, but somehow we figured it out and made it work. My mother found a job downtown and rode the bus to and from work. It was many years before we could talk her into learning how to drive. Linda started going to Humes in the fall with my sister Nita. After her first year at Humes, someone asked what she hated most about being married and having to attend high school. Her quick response caught me completely off guard. She said it was the fact that I was the one who had to sign her report card. But I knew immediately where she was coming from. Every time I signed, I would say something about her grades to the effect of, "The Bs are good, but the Cs don't make sense." Looking back, that was a terrible thing for me to think, much less say. I have no excuse, except it is now obvious: I should have taken some sensitivity classes.

After my brother graduated from Humes, he was soon married, and shortly after, began working at Firestone. It did not take long for me to realize that, no matter how hard I worked, he could build faster. We were paid a set amount based on the union scale, plus a fixed amount per tire; in other words, the more you built, the more you made. I was working through my breaks trying to keep pace with him. I probably would have worked myself to death, except a pipefitter, who was making some fine-tune adjustments to my tire machine with his sledgehammer, said, "Hey, little buddy, is building those tires harder with you being left-handed?" With his perceptive observation, he opened my eyes. Every tire machine in the plant had the control panel on the right-hand side. I had to reach across my body with my left hand to operate the machine. From that day forward, I took my breaks along with everyone else.

That first year was not easy, but we kept our promise, and Linda graduated in 1966. I was not there for the graduation. Since I was no longer attending college, I became eligible for the draft. During our second year of marriage, I received a draft notification. I had one overseas tour, but not to Vietnam. Linda stayed with my mother while I was overseas. As soon as I finished my tour and returned home, we started looking for our own apartment, and I went back to building tires on the third shift.

Chapter 7

It had been over four years since my father died, and Linda and I were now in the process of moving to our very own apartment.

I had been wanting to have this discussion with my mother many times, but would back out at the last minute. I knew it was now or never. I cannot recall exactly how I asked the question, but it amounted to something like this: "I want to know what happened to my father during the war." She calmly sat down and told me in detail. First, she explained how she had promised to never discuss the war. But now that he was gone, she would tell me everything, as best as she could remember.

He was fighting somewhere in Italy near a small town. They had been stuck there for some time without making any headway. He was the machine gunner for his platoon. His assistant gunner, who helped feed the rounds, had been with him since basic training. On the day he was wounded, they had gained some ground. Later that day, the Germans pushed back, and his platoon was forced to pull back. My father and his helper had stayed in their foxhole and were laying down cover fire as their retreat began. Both were hit at about the same time. My father was wounded, and his buddy was killed. They lay together in the foxhole as the Germans overran their position. She thought it was the next morning before the Germans were forced to pull back, which allowed the medics to find my father still alive. He had lost a lot of blood and was in bad shape. Later that day, he had surgery in a field hospital, and two days later, he had a second surgery at another hospital. Many years later, Nita contacted the Department of Defense and the VA and obtained documents that confirmed my conversation with my mother, but with the specific dates and locations that I included in chapter 1.

My mother also told me he received the purple heart for being wounded. He was also awarded the bronze star for meritorious service in a combat zone. I knew he must have received the purple heart, but did not know about the bronze star. Then, she told me the reason it had taken so long for his return to the states: He was suffering from shell shock, so they kept him in a hospital overseas for treatment. Whatever the treatment, to put it mildly, he hated it. After his release, he refused help from the VA. Then, in the early fifties, while going through an extra rough spell, he agreed to the electric shock treatments they had been recommending. After the second treatment, he had enough. He told them it not only did not help, but was making him worse. From that day forward, he tried to manage it on his own.

I am aware that I have placed a lot of focus on my father, but it is now so obvious the impact he had on every aspect of my life. I can see a man with great character and integrity. While constantly fighting his demons, he still tried to be a good father, husband, and provider. Looking back, my greatest regret is that I failed him, my family failed him, the doctors failed him, the military failed him, and the system failed him. At the time, we just did not know; therefore, he had to live with it, day in and day out, without proper treatment or relief. Today, it is so apparent that he suffered from post-traumatic stress disorder (PTSD) or to be more politically correct now, post-traumatic stress syndrome (PTSS).

Below is a list of the symptoms:

Feeling upset by things that remind you of what happened

Having nightmares, vivid memories, or flashbacks of the event that make you feel like it's happening all over again

Feeling emotionally cut off from others

Feeling numb or losing interest in things you used to care about

Feeling constantly on guard

Feeling irritated or having angry outbursts

Having difficulty sleeping

Having trouble concentrating

Being jumpy or easily startled

Frequently avoiding places or things that remind you of what happened

Consistently drinking or using drugs to numb your feelings

Pulling away from other people and becoming isolated

He met every one of these conditions, with the exception of using drugs.

Below is a list of factors that can increase the likelihood of a traumatic event leading to PTSS:

The intensity of the trauma

Being hurt or losing someone you were close to

Being physically close to the traumatic event

Feeling you are not in control

Having a lack of support after the event

Lying wounded in a foxhole for many hours with the body of your comrade

Okay, I admit to adding the last one. It just seemed to fit right in with the other five. I have one more thing to say about my father: He never had a chance.

Chapter 8

After four years of marriage, Linda and I had our very own apartment. We still did not sleep together, except for weekends, since she slept during the night and I during the day, as best I could. I guess things worked out, because our son, Mark, was born on January 23, 1969, during our second year at Yorktown Apartments. I thought sleeping during the day was difficult, but little did I know that adding a baby to the mix would make it even more challenging. I'd like to make one point about sleeping during the day versus the night: The quality of sleep is not the same. And I should know, since I worked third shift for many years.

At this point, I need to catch you up on my spiritual journey (or lack thereof). The day of our wedding was the only time I stepped foot in a church while in Texas. Then, when I started working third shift at Firestone, night shift was my excuse. And then, out of nowhere, my mother not only changed churches, but also denominations. That gave me another excuse. She had started going to a little Pentecostal church, and I asked, "Why?" As normal, she sat down and gave another one of her simple but profound answers. She said, "Son, there is just not enough Spirit in the Baptist church." I had learned over the years that her first response was the best you were going to get, so I let it go.

This brings up a point I want to make about my mother. From my first memory, until her passing, I don't remember one time she ever addressed my brother or myself by our names. Anytime she spoke to either of us, she started her first sentence with the word "son." She called our two sisters by their first names, but for us, it was "son" this or "son" that. We accepted this as normal and never questioned it.

Looking back, her denominational change was just one of my many excuses. It was still a priority issue. I still thought about God—actually, quite a lot. I just did not make time for Him. This continued, right up until we were in our apartment. But this was about to change.

It was just another Thursday night on April 4, 1968, as I was driving to work for my 11:00 p.m. shift. I was coming from under an overpass when I heard a loud noise and felt the car shake. My first thought was I had hit something. I slammed on my brakes, jumped out of the car, and looked around. I saw nothing except some boys running from the overpass. It was dark, but I could see they were teenagers. I turned to get back into the car and saw a huge dent in the roof, right above the driver's seat. As I pulled off, I realized the windshield was cracked. It started at the top, near the dent, and ran at a slant to the bottom of the glass. When I got to work, I told everyone about what happened. That is when I learned about something else that happened that night: Martin Luther King Jr. had been shot and killed in downtown Memphis at around 6:00 p.m. I did not even know he was in Memphis.

On Saturday, I took the car to a body shop for an insurance estimate. I told the shop manager about the teenage boys throwing a big rock off the overpass. He looked at the car and said, "How fast were you going?" I estimated between fifty and sixty miles per hour. He looked at the car again and said, "That was no rock. That was a boulder." Then he said, "If you were going a second slower, it would have hit the windshield, and you would not be here today." As I drove home, I decided this matter of just "a second slower" was a wakeup call. That boulder had my name on it, and was meant to get my attention.

God had a plan, and it worked. Linda had been saying for a while that we needed to start going to church. I totally agreed, but kept letting my busy schedule get in the way. But after this near miss, my busy schedule did not seem near as important. We started visiting a number of churches and joined Bellevue Baptist Church, near downtown, at the corner of Bellevue and Court Avenue. We attended Bellevue regularly on Sunday morning and Wednesday night until we had to move away from Memphis. Our children, Mark and Mandy, were both saved and baptized there.

It took me many years before I understood the significance of that day in Memphis. Without a doubt, the assassination in Dallas and in Memphis had a tremendous impact on our country, and that impact still resonates today. And for me, personally, they both had an impact on my life. But it was many years before I connected the two. Me being in the middle of what happened in Dallas could be considered just a coincidence. But after my close call in Memphis, I saw neither as a coincidence. There is a limit to God's patience, and I felt I had exceeded that limit. I guess it took two tries (Dallas and Memphis), but it got my attention and altered the direction my life was heading.

Chapter 9

The next event was not only significant, but planned. During that first year of marriage, we would share ideas, aspirations, and goals for our future. That was no easy task, considering Linda was still in high school. Owning our own home and finishing college were at the top of our list. Renting was all either of us knew, and we both felt my college degree was still within reach, if we would just not give up. I also wanted the degree for my father.

During our early years of marriage, saving towards these goals was next to impossible. It was a number of years later before we reached our first goal. In 1970, we paid the down payment and closing costs on our first home. It was still in north Memphis, but a little further out from downtown. It had two bedrooms, one-and-a-half baths, and a small bonus room. As it turned out, we needed the bonus room—on September 18, 1972, our daughter, Mandy, was born.

Our house payment was only $120 a month, which was much less than the rent for our apartment. I am aware that sounds unbelievable, compared to today, but I guess working from age sixteen until twenty for $1 an hour also sounds like fiction.

In September of 1974, my brother and I had been at Firestone for a little over ten years. I requested a one-year leave of absence. I continued with all benefits, including insurance, but without pay. This was not a quick decision; we had been planning this for quite some time. It had been ten years since my last college course, and so much had changed. When I last registered for a college course, you would not be able to find the word "computer" in the course catalog. Now, Memphis State University (MSU) had a Computer Technology Department, but it still did not have an Engineering Department. That was one of the reasons I decided to switch my major from engineering to computer technology. But the main reason was because I sensed computer technology was the career of the future. Looking back now, that would be an understatement.

My biggest problem was the fact that I needed to take a number of computer courses in a short period of time, and every computer course had a lab. I registered for five computer/lab courses my first semester. My advisor told me I would never be able to keep up, taking that many computer courses at the same time. I wanted to tell him that, if I could keep up with my brother building tires, then I would keep up with school. Instead, I said nothing. My first semester was the hardest thing I had ever tackled. I went to classes all morning and to the labs in the afternoon until dark. During the week, I hardly saw Linda and the kids. Speaking of Linda—she took care of everything at the house, including the kids. I did nothing. During my leave of absence, we never went out to eat, since every dollar spent came out of our savings account. If truth be known, that year was probably harder for Linda than it was for me. But she never complained.

The second semester was not as bad, because I had a better feel for the work and had developed a good routine. I took four computer courses and one math course. I will discuss the math course later on. For the summer, I took two courses in session one and two in session two. I ended up with more credit hours than required for the computer technology degree, but it was necessary in order to complete all the required computer courses.

I want to stop to discuss one of my second semester courses for a couple of reasons. First, I want to give you a better understanding of computer programming, and second, I want to point out how this single course made me aware that computer programming was a skillset that seemed to come naturally to me. It requires tons of logic—probably more than even math.

The course was Advanced Fortran, a continuation of Fortran, which I had taken the first semester. Fortran is a computer language that is still in use today, mainly by scientist and physicist for modeling stars, galaxies, and other large-scale models that require extremely high-performance computing. On the first day of class, the professor wrote on the blackboard EZ College and below that a numbered list: valid course, prerequisite checking, corequisite checking, time conflict, hours max, course catalog, schedule, etc. That is a small sample of what I remember from the total list. Our one assignment for the semester was to write a program using Fortran that allowed you to register students in EZ College. You had to code for every item on his list, and once the student's registration was complete, print a schedule that displayed the courses within meeting times on a weekly calendar.

This was far bigger and more complex than the programs I had written during my previous semester. I decided to create an indexed list in a sentence-structured format of all the required conditions my professor had painstakingly written on the blackboard. I used the backside of computer printout paper, since each sheet was perforated, making it easy to fold. When unfolded, my indexed list was twice the length of our living room. Week after week, I would write the code for each of those required conditions. About three weeks prior to the end of the semester, I completed all the code. I figured it would take until the end of the semester to test and resolve all of the issues and bugs.

This was when you still had to punch your lines of code onto IBM computer index cards, arrange the cards in the exact, correct order for execution, and give them to the computer operator in the lab. He would put the cards in a card tray and feed them through the card reader attached to the computer. Once the computer operator fed my stack of hundreds of IBM index cards through the reader, he compiled my program. At this point, I began testing. I tested each item from the list and printed out each test, its results, and each student's class schedule. I did this for each of the five test students.

I hope that what I am about to write does not come across as bragging. There are many, many things I am not good at— if you don't believe that, just ask Linda. She would tell you in a heartbeat. In fact, ask her how many times I have changed a diaper. And how many times she looked at the results, shook her head, and laughed. Looking back, I have written hundreds of programs, and I can truthfully say every one required some degree of debugging, and much more for others. But this EZ College program ran perfectly and gave the proper result for every item on my professor's list. There were no typos, no bad logic, no missing logic, no infinite loops, no nothing. A point of explanation: An infinite loop is when your logic is so bad, the code gets into a loop and goes round, and round, and round. You have to abort the program to stop it. Looking back, maybe it ran perfectly on the first try because of blind luck—or maybe it was another reason, which I will get to later.

I waited until close to the end of the semester to turn in a listing of the program code, details of each test, the test results, and a printout of each test student's class schedule. On the last day of class, the professor handed back our work along with the grade, which was posted on the cover sheet. When he got to me, he said I was the only one in the class who had completed the whole assignment, but that everyone received a passing grade. I planned to omit the grade (since, again, I do not want to come across as bragging). But it was the way he wrote the grade that made me feel proud. The grade was A++, with the ++ circled. One more point: I still have a printout of the program. It has turned yellow, which makes sense, since it is now over forty-eight years old.

Chapter 10

So, I guess you are thinking that after graduation, I left Firestone and got a job in the computer technology field. That's not quite how it worked out. When I notified Firestone that I had graduated, they asked me to come in for a meeting. That was the first time I had been in the plant on first shift since the day I was hired. We had totally depleted our savings, so the plan was to continue to build tires for at least a year. Our plans changed after I was offered a salaried position as a tire engineer. I would work with the other tire engineers for six months and then be given my own line of tires. Considering the pay, my seniority, my vacation time, insurance benefits, and working first shift, we could not turn it down.

For the first couple of weeks, I would tag along with one tire engineer and then another. Most of the time, I would accompany them out to a tire machine in order to have a set of check tires built. I never was required to build check tires as a tire builder, since tire engineers only worked first shift.

The check tires (usually four to six tires) were needed whenever there was an issue with a specific tire, or when a new line of tires was under development. As the tire is being built, the engineer takes measurements of each component to ensure everything falls within the tire specification's tolerance.

After a tire is built, it looks like a rubber drum with both ends missing. For normal production, the builder sets the tire on a conveyer belt, which is directly behind his back. Builders on both sides of the conveyer belt do the same. The tires flow to an inspection area, where they are inspected and sorted by type and size. From there, they are taken to the curing department, which is made up of line, after line, of tire molds. The tires are then cured in their proper mold.

A tire mold is made up of two halves. The bottom half is fixed. The top half opens up from the bottom half. The mold halves are high-quality steel that has been cut with the correct tread design for the specific tire being cured. In the bottom half is a rubber bladder, which has the same diameter as the "rubber drum" tire. The utility man throws the tire into the mold, over the bladder, and sets the switch to close the mold.

As the mold slowly closes, the bladder fills with hot steam, which changes the "rubber drum" shape to the shape of a finished tire. The tire cures in the mold for its specified time, and then the mold slowly opens. The utility man uses a hoist to remove the very hot tire from the mold. Then, the cycle is repeated.

Lest you think the utility man stands and patiently waits for the mold to open, that's not so. He has a whole line of molds for which he is responsible. In other words, I would much rather build a tire than cure it. After curing, the finished tires are inspected, with a few being randomly pulled for endurance test, speed test, puncher test, and tread wear test.

For check tires, the engineer takes them to the curing department and oversees all required testing. One tire is then cut into cross-sections for further analysis.

The builders hated building check tires. They had to back out all of the stock, load in the small rolls of check tire stock, and wait for the mechanic, pipefitter, and electrician to do a complete setup change for the check tires. Once they are built, the stock and machine have to be changed back for the production tire. This usually takes most of the day. Since the builders are down and not building, they only make downtime pay, which costs them money.

It did not take long for the tire engineers to notice how much more cooperative the builders were when I accompanied them. I had worked with some of these builders on third shift. Soon, the tire engineers started sending me out to have their check tires built. At first, there was a lot of kidding by the builders, but there was always mutual respect. Some would even tell me they would build three, if I would build the other three. I would have done that, but was afraid the union reps would have a problem. It is possible I built one, every now and then, to prove to them that I still knew how. After six months, I was assigned my own line of passenger tires.

Everyone knows what a tire looks like, but very few have an understanding of the complexity of a tire's construction and design. A tire is a composition of layers of components, which are applied by the builder around a collapsible steel drum.

The first component is the inner liner, which replaced the need for inner tubes in car tires. The inner liner is a rubber compound that bonds to the inside of the cord body.

Next are the body plies, which are composed of rubber-coated fabric cords. Body plies can be made of polyester, rayon, or nylon. Most passenger tires have two plies, whereas truck tires have four or more, depending on the size and utilization. The body plies extend four or five inches beyond the edge of each side of the drum.

The next step involves setting two beads—one on each side of the drum. A bead is a coil of brass, copper, or bronze-plated, high-tensile steel wires, wrapped in a rubber compound filler. The rubber filler provides stability to the lower sidewall and bead area. The beads hold the tire to the outer edge of a wheel rim. During the bead-setting cycle, the tire machine forces each bead over the extended-ply fabric, tightly up against each side of the drum, and then turns the extended-ply fabric over each bead. The tire's beads, bead filler, and inner liner work together to hold air within the tire walls.

The builder then applies a thin, rubber compound over the edges of the turned-up plies to cover the edges of the cord fabric. Next, the builder applies the belt plies, which are also called tread plies. These are two strong layers of cord, just under the tread area of the tire. They play a role in improving tire mileage, impact resistance, and tire traction. Steel is the most common cord material used in the tread plies.

The final step is applying the tread, the portion of the tire that comes in contact with the road surface. The tread is thicker in the footprint area of the tire and tapers off in thickness as it approaches the edges of the tire. The tread's compound and design have to balance the tread wear, traction, handling, fuel economy, endurance, ride comfort, maximum speed, and other characteristics of the tire.

Once the tread has been applied, the builder collapses the steel drum, removes the tire, and sets it on the belt. A good builder can build one passenger tire about every three to four minutes, depending on the tire specifications.

Designing a quality tire involves the art of compromise. A thinner tread gives higher speed rating, but worse tire wear. A thicker tread gives better tire wear, but a worse speed rating. That is just one example of the many factors involved in the give-and-take of a tire's design. In other words, a tire designed for law enforcement and high-speed emergency use is vastly different than one for a family sedan.

On April 21, 1976, I had been a tire engineer for close to one year. On that date, United Rubber Workers (URW) went on strike, which included the approximately 3,000 union workers at the Memphis Firestone plant, including David. I was on salary and no longer a member of the union. Salaried workers were required to work and were allowed to cross the picket line. This was my first time crossing a picket line, but I will quote from management's notification, "refusal could lead to termination." On the first day of the strike, I arrived at work for my normal first shift, wondering what would we do besides sit around all day. It did not take long to find out; during a very long management meeting, the details slowly emerged.

The plan was to continue to produce a limited number of tires, based on demand. The sales department would give weekly updates on the tire lines and sizes that were most needed. Supervisors, by department, would produce the required components. That all sounded fine until they got to the tire department. The supervisors who started out as tire builders would build the tires. Those who had never built tires would supervise and make sure each builder's machine was supplied with all required stock. The majority had never built a tire. I was the only tire engineer who was previously a tire builder, and it had not been that long ago. All of the tire engineers would do their normal job, except for me. I would build tires.

There would be two twelve-hour shifts seven days a week, with first shift from 7:00 a.m. to 7:00 p.m. and the second from 7:00 p.m. to 7:00 a.m. I quickly did the math and determined I'd be working an eighty-four hour work week. I knew immediately that I would be assigned to second shift, since those tire department supervisors had hundreds of years of seniority, compared to mine.

The first night was a joke—in fact, it took a whole week before everyone started getting their act together. But starting the second week, I finally had everything needed to build a complete tire. Since everyone was salaried, we could not be paid by the tire, so we were given a quota. When I was told my nightly quota, I nearly laughed. I built my quota in four hours, then went up to the lunchroom and read a book until the end of the shift. That was a big mistake—or better said, a stupid mistake. The next night, my quota had been raised by fifty percent. I had a problem: I could not build tires in slow motion like most of the other builders. I tried taking fifteen-minute breaks between each hour of building. They bumped my quota again, but not as much. My salvation was the stock. We were all building different tires and different sizes; therefore, the other departments were having to produce short runs for each tire being built. Quite often, I would end up running out of treads, or body ply, or tread ply, or beads, or whatever, sometime during the shift. Therefore, it was infrequent for me to build for the full twelve hours.

The strike lasted until August 12—that's 114 days. Looking back, I pretty much spent the whole summer doing nothing besides working, sleeping, and eating. Linda did everything that summer, and I mean everything including cutting the yard with our lawn mower. I did not even think about the fact that it included the large hill that ran down one side of our property. Many years later, Linda mentioned cutting the hill that summer. During the strike, I never thought about it. I was too busy whining about having to sleep during the day and then go build tires again at night. After she mentioned the hill, I started questioning her, and what she told me next broke my heart. She would cut half the hill, go sit on the front porch and cry while she rested, then finish cutting the hill. She did this for the whole summer and never said one word to me about it.

Chapter 11

It took a number of months after the strike before everything felt normal. Tire engineers stay plenty busy, but not from labor. After a few more months, I started looking for ways to burn off excess pent-up energy. Looking back, this was the exact time when I could have (and should have) realized Linda could use a little help with the house and the kids. I did all repairs and outdoor work, but it never crossed my mind to give her a hand. Instead, I decided to take up running.

There was a high school track close to our house, and I started there. At first, I would get winded after a few laps. Slowly but surely, I was able to run longer and longer. This took months, not weeks. I was there so often, the high school track coach started giving me pointers. We became good friends, and I guess you could say he took me under his wing.

After a few months, I started thinking about running in one of the weekend road races. I asked the coach what to do to improve my pace and endurance. He said instead of just running long runs on the track, I needed to do my distance training on hilly roads, and at least twice a week run intervals on the track. This would increase both my pace and my endurance.

Interval training is alternating slow jogs with all-out sprints for a number of sets. There was a road near the track that ran north for fifteen to twenty miles to Millington, Tennessee. It had little traffic since most people used U.S. Highway 51. It was also quite hilly, which was perfect. The training runs on the hills were demanding, but the intervals were even more so. I don't remember how long I trained before the first race, the length of the race, or where I finished. Regardless, I was off and running. I would train all week, and then on the weekend, we would head to the next race. Most were 5K or 10K, with a few five and ten-mile races in the mix. Surprisingly, Linda and the kids loved going.

Within that first year, my brother began running with me. Since he still worked third shift, we rarely trained together during the week. On weekends, we would run out on the hills for ten miles, then turn and run back. After one of the races, a guy named Bud Joyner asked if we would be interested in joining Memphis Runner's Track Club (MRTC). Bud had helped start the club. We joined and started inviting guys to our Saturday morning training runs. After a number of weeks, fewer and fewer showed up, until there were none. At one of the races, I told Bud, and added that we were clueless to how we had offended them. He broke out laughing. Finally, he told us what was so funny. He heard a warning going around. I'm not sure I can quote it exactly, but the following is the gist of it: "Don't go on training runs with those Brooks brothers. They are crazy! They run twenty-mile training runs like an actual race. They set a 6:30 pace for a twenty-mile run; ten miles out on hills and ten miles back and then sprint the last quarter of a mile." I didn't see the humor, but at least we had done nothing to offend them. Actually, we tried to maintain a 6:30 pace when the terrain was flat; the hills would slow the pace significantly. The challenge was to get back to the 6:30 pace, once you top each hill.

Chapter 12

Without a doubt, training and racing influenced my life physically, and at times spiritually—with a significant amount being beneficial, and some being either reckless, or downright foolhardy. Over the years, many incidents occurred while I was running and racing that ranged from humorous to hilarious, and from dangerous to life-threatening. I am going to describe a few of those that occurred while we were still living in Memphis. I hope to keep them in some semblance of a chronological order, and once I have completed the list, I will go back and continue my journey.

Linda would put this first one in the category of "hilarious" and describe it as "the day the Brooks brothers got their hats handed to them." On a sunny Saturday morning, David and I were running a training run at Overton Park, a small park in midtown. A road bordered by huge shade trees looped around and through the park. We were about three miles into a five-mile run when we noticed a stocky runner behind us. We soon realized he was closing the gap and that we did not know him. We were running at a six-minute pace, and this unknown runner kept closing. We sped up, but he kept closing. As he passed, he looked over and said, "Morning." As soon as I got home, I told Linda about this guy, who passed us as if we were running in place. She started laughing so hard, but finally said, "I think the Brooks brothers just met their match."

On the following Saturday morning, there was a three-mile

race at Overton Park. This was not a large race—probably between 150 to 200 runners. As we lined up, there stood our unknown runner. After the starting gun was fired, he was running stride-for-stride with John Mohundro, one of the fastest runners in the Memphis area. They ran stride-for-stride for the whole race, with Mohundro pulling away at the very end. As soon as David and I crossed the finish line, we went over to introduce ourselves. He was lighting a cigarette and offered us one. I said, "We don't smoke," but was thinking, "Runners don't smoke." His name was Billy Coats, and he had just moved from Arkansas to Memphis to manage a new Shoney's restaurant in midtown. We became good friends but were never able to keep pace with this stocky, chain-smoking, racing machine.

I actually have the results for this specific race. David would clip the race results from our local newspaper the day after each race. I saved nothing. On my seventieth birthday, Linda gave me a running scrapbook that contained all of the pictures she had taken over the years at the races, along with the race result clippings. She had David make a copy of the clippings and included them in my scrapbook. I loved it. Looking through the scrapbook, and seeing the names and pictures, brings back great memories.

Since I have the results of our first race with Billy Coats, I will use it as an example, and then explain the breakdown.

<u>Overall results:</u>

1st place: John Mohundro 15:21, 2nd place: Billy Coats 15:26,

9th place: Kenneth Brooks 16:51, 11th place: David Brooks 16:56

<u>Results by age category:</u>

Under 25:

1st place: Billy Coats - 15:26, 2nd place: Eric Bolton - 15:28

25 to 35:

1st place: John Sterrett - 16:34, 2nd place: David Brooks - 16:56

36 and over:

1st place: Kenneth Brooks - 16:51, 2nd place: Tom Durham - 17:28

The "overall" results show the order the runners cross the finish line, without considering age. Next is the "age" category. Since this was a small race, there were only three age groups. Larger or longer races have more age categories. A typical example would be: under 20, 20 to 29, 30 to 39, 40 to 49, 50 to 59, and 60 and over.

Notice that Mohundro was not listed in the age categories, although he was the overall winner. Since he won a trophy for 1st overall, he was not eligible for an award in the under 25 group. That is the reason Billy is listed in 1st place for under 25, even though Mohundro was also under 25. In other words, no winner is given two awards for the same race. This same breakdown is used for the women runners; I just used the men's breakdown for my example.

For me, this race confirmed two obvious facts: Mohundro and Coats could run about a minute and thirty seconds a mile faster than the Brooks brothers. And the Brooks brothers ran at nearly the same pace, which made them great training partners, since they could push each other.

Another memorable incident occurred on an afternoon training run on that hilly road toward Millington. I was alone, since it was during the week, and David was probably asleep. There is no telling how many times I had made this same run and never saw a dog, much less a pack of dogs. The houses were few and sat far off the road, since this was mostly farmland. Since this was not on a weekend, it was probably an eight or ten-mile run. I had already made my turn and was headed back toward the car. Just as I passed an old driveway that could barely be seen from the road, because of the heavy overgrowth, I heard growling. As I looked back, there was a pack of dogs coming onto the road. The largest dog was leading the pack, followed by a very young Doberman, and then a group of smaller dogs.

I knew instantly this was serious, and of all places, I was climbing a hill. Even though I began running all-out, they overtook me immediately. Just as the lead dog was about to grab my ankle, I spun around and kicked out soccer-style. Somehow, my left foot landed right under his chin. I heard his teeth slam together while his tongue still hung out of his mouth. He yelped, tucked his tail between his legs, and headed back toward the drive. The other dogs stopped in their tracks. I started running backward up the hill. As I watched, I tried to count, but all of the dogs except the Doberman were jumping around while barking, making that impossible. The Doberman just stood in place, staring at me. As best as I could tell, there were five or six dogs. After a safe distance, I turned and finished my run.

This happened so quickly, I did not think or plan to kick the dog; it was more of an instinctive reaction. I had never kicked an animal before, much less soccer-style. I did feel bad for the dog, but I knew that if they pulled me to the ground, my life would have been in danger. It took a long time before I got up enough nerve to run there alone again. With David, on weekends, it was okay. But after many weeks and not seeing any dogs, I finally got back to normal. I would like to say I never kicked a dog again, but unfortunately, that would not be true. I had another incident with a dog that was actually much worse than this one. I will get to it, in due time.

For the next story, I need to give a little Memphis history on the right-of-way for I-40 and the resulting I-240 loop around the city. The original plan was for I-40 West to run through the heart of Memphis to the Mississippi River Bridge and into Arkansas. But Overton Park and the Memphis Zoo were in the way, which would require the zoo to be moved and part of the park destroyed. The city was all for this, but the citizens were not. Lawsuits and appeals occurred all the way to the Supreme Court. The citizens of Memphis won, and to this day, I-40 West tracks as part of the I-240 North loop around Memphis, through Frayser, where we lived, then intersecting with Highway 51, and looping back toward downtown to the Mississippi River Bridge. I watched this northern loop being built forever, until finally, I saw in the paper that the northern loop was going to open the following week.

For a good while, I had been thinking about getting on the interstate at the Frayser exit and running back to where it intersected with I-40, then turning back and returning to my car. I figured it was about sixteen miles—eight miles out and eight miles back. If I were going to do this, I needed to do it before the opening. On the weekend, I was at the Frayser exit at daybreak. Everything looked so new; it was great. At the I-40 junction, as I was turning around to head back, a Tennessee State Trooper pulled onto the interstate from the offramp. He pulled alongside me, rolled his window down, and said, "Don't you know it is against the law to run on an interstate?" I told him that the interstate was not yet open. He again said the same thing, "Don't you know it is against the law to run on an interstate?" I got his message and asked if I could go back to my car. He nodded, and so I kept running as he started turning around. Then he turned back, pulled up beside me again, and said, "I told you to get off the interstate." I told him that he did not; he had agreed I could go back to my car. I noticed his face was a shade or two redder than when we had started the conversation. He said, "And where is your car?" I told him it was at the Frayser exit. He said nothing, looked at me, shook his head, rolled his window up, turned around, and drove back to the offramp. When I got home, I told Linda exactly what happened. She looked at me, said nothing, and just shook her head. Since that day, I have never had any desire whatsoever to run on an interstate.

There is nothing I remember more vividly than this next running story. As far as I am concerned, it was the day David shoved me off my feet and saved my life. It was the middle of summer, so we were out early on a Saturday morning, running the hills. For this run, we had another runner named Jim with us. I do not remember Jim's last name, but he was from Arkansas, like Billy Coats, and was an elite runner. He let us know when he was in town, and we would plan a long training run. We had already made the turn at the ten-mile mark and were heading back.

On an early Saturday morning, normally there is zero traffic. On this morning, we saw a car heading toward us. There were four guys in the car, and even though they were not in uniform, it was obvious they were sailors heading back to the Millington Naval Base after a night out on the town in Memphis. Right as the car passed, David shoved me suddenly. My first thought was, "Why on earth did he just shove me?" But I immediately understood what had happened. I had seen one of the sailors hanging out of the car, and I realized he must have thrown something at us. David ran over to me and asked, "Why didn't you duck?" I told him I didn't see anything, but I heard it zip past my ear as he shoved me. David said that he saw the guy throw, and he had to shove me to keep the flattened beer can from cutting off my head. We looked and saw that Jim had turned and ran toward the car, shaking his fist as it sped away. We finished our run while complaining about the incident messing up our time. One final point: David has always been very aware of everything that is going on around him, whereas I seem to get so focused on the task at hand, I become oblivious to my surroundings. I still feel blessed to have had my brother beside me that day.

I have to include another specific race, since it was what gave me the inspiration and desire to qualify for, and later run, the Boston Marathon. In the summer of 1981, our local Kellogg manufacturing plant sponsored a 5K and a 10K run. For the event, they brought in Craig Virgin to speak after the completion of the two races. Craig was one of America's top, young, long-distance runners. In April, he came in second to Seko of Japan in the Boston Marathon. His time was 2:10:26, which was exactly one minute slower than Seko. I had watched the end of that Boston Marathon and was so excited to hear that Craig Virgin was coming to Memphis to speak at our race. They were going to run the 5K, then the 10K, and after both races were completed, Craig would pass out the trophies and give a short speech.

About two weeks before the race, I was filling out the entry forms and Linda was watching. She casually asked, "Why are you filling out two entry forms?" I tried to explain that it was because the races were going to be run back-to-back and not at the same time. She stopped me in mid-sentence and said, "So, you want to run both." I probably should have just said, "Yes," but instead I tried to justify my reasoning. Jumping to the end of this conversation, we agreed to disagree.

On the day of the race, there was an abundance of runners and a large crowd. I felt strong throughout the 5K and finished first in the 35 to 39 age group, but then felt tired at the half-way point of the 10K. I had to work to maintain my stride until there was only a mile to the finish line. I steadily picked up my pace during that last mile and finished second in my age group.

Craig gave out the trophies for the 5K first. When he called my name, I went up on the stage. He congratulated me, shook my hand, and handed me the trophy and an autographed 8x10 picture. When he called my name for the 10K, I went up on the stage again. Instead of shaking my hand, Craig said, "So you ran both." I said, "Yes, sir." He shook my hand, handed me the trophy, and said, "Running two races, back-to-back, takes a lot of endurance. Congratulations!" He did not give me a second picture. As I look back, this was the moment when qualifying and running the Boston Marathon became a compelling idea—or maybe "obsession" might be the better word.

This next story will require some background. I don't really recall how it all started, but I slowly became aware that there was something about Linda's skill with a phone that was not logical. And this was with a rotary-dial phone, many years before cell phones. It finally reached a point where the Memphis radio station managers created a new regulation named "The Linda Rule." The rule stated that dial-in contestants who win a prize are ineligible for additional winnings from that station for thirty days. So, why would they do that? I can't explain it, but I know the answer: because of Linda.

Back then, all of the music radio stations were continuously running contests where they would award a prize to the first caller, or third caller, or whatever-number caller. I don't know if they still do that today, but it was prevalent during our last seven years in Memphis. I will give an example. The DJ tells the listeners that the ninth (or whatever number) caller will win two front-row tickets to the upcoming Elvis concert (or a similarly exciting prize). I used this example because Linda actually won a pair of Elvis tickets—and then won another pair the next year. During this time, Linda won money, movie tickets, concert tickets, Thanksgiving turkeys, Christmas hams, and once she won $1,000. To this day, I still do not understand how so many of her calls got through, over the jammed lines, and were answered at just the right time for her to be the winner.

One of the first big prizes she won occurred back when I was on my leave of absence, attending my last semester of courses. To say our savings account was close to being depleted would be an understatement. The radio station was running a month-long contest titled, "Rock the Boat." That was the title for a popular song at the time, so the station used the song title for their contest, with the prize being a Catamaran sailboat. For this contest, whenever the DJ played "Rock the Boat," the first caller who got through would not win but would have their name added to a fishbowl. Linda had her name entered during the first couple of days of the contest, then pretty much forgot about it. About four weeks later, on a Sunday night, a friend called and told Linda she just heard on the radio that Linda was the winner of the "Rock the Boat" contest. That next week, we met with a manager from the radio station at a local mall where the boat had been on display. He told us that if we did not want the boat, they had the name and number of a doctor who saw the boat at the mall and would be interested in buying it. We sold the boat.

This leads into the reason I am including Linda's uncanny winning skills in this section on running. It involves another hot summer and another contest similar to "Rock the Boat"—but this time the prize was a one-week vacation for two in Jamaica. The contest lasted for one month, with the correct caller's names being collected numerous times daily. Again, Linda's name was in the fishbowl within the first couple of days. But this time, she was well aware of the exact time and date of the drawing.

About a month later, on a Friday afternoon, David and I were on the phone discussing the upcoming Saturday morning race—important stuff. I had totally forgotten about the contest. Besides, the odds of her name being drawn out of a bowl with 400 to 500 other names was slim to none—and yet, she had won the boat. For her name to be drawn a second time—the odds would be astronomical. Even so, there was Linda, yelling at me to get off the phone so they could get through when she won. David and I thought she was so funny and continued our conversation. Linda was listening as they drew the winning name; David and I were still talking. They played a complete song and still did not announce the winner. At the end of the song, the DJ said they were having trouble getting through; the line was busy. I am not making this up. In a deep voice, Linda said, "Hang up the phone. I have won, and they can't get through." I hung up the phone, and then it rang immediately. I finally understood: logic and astronomical odds were of no concern to Linda. She was the winner. She told the DJ all about us not having a honeymoon and how this would be our honeymoon vacation. They were recording this conversation and replayed it over, and over, and over, the whole weekend.

A few weeks later, on a Saturday afternoon, Linda and I were on a plane headed to Jamaica. We landed in Montego Bay and boarded a tourist bus that followed the coastline to our resort in Ocho Rios. During the long, winding ride, the bus stopped at a checkpoint where military police with submachine guns searched the bus without any explanation. It made me feel uncomfortable, and Linda was scared, as were others on our bus. Once we arrived at the resort, things were great. The sand was snow white and the ocean was so clear and dark blue. There were no language barriers; all the Jamaicans spoke perfect British English. The food was fabulous, and for coffee drinkers, the Blue Mountain coffee was unbelievable. Linda took lots of pictures. We were having a great time. But by the fourth day, I was complaining to Linda about wanting to run one long training run. She kept reminding me about our bus being searched, and how we had been cautioned to stay within the resort area at check in. They said if we did leave the resort area for shopping or sightseeing, it would be better to go in groups. In my infinite wisdom, I convinced Linda that just one long run along the coastline in the early morning would be okay.

My plan was to run out on the road that led back to Montego Bay for about ten miles, based on my pace, make my turn, then head back. At daybreak, I headed out. For all those years of running, that was probably my most scenic run ever. On one side was mile, after mile, of that beautiful, white, sandy beach, with the clear, blue ocean constantly crashing against the shoreline. On my other side was a thick, green rainforest that stretched for miles. With a slight breeze and the sun slowing rising, I was gliding along to the point I could barely feel my feet hitting the ground.

At about seven miles out, I saw a small store surrounded by a handful of houses that would be better described as shacks. I remember seeing them when we arrived, but I had thought they were fifteen to twenty miles from the resort. I was wrong. As I passed the store, four teenage boys came running out, onto the road. They looked to be between seventeen and twenty-years-old. Soon, they were running beside me and pointing at my feet. They spoke perfect English, but at first, they were not close enough for me to understand what they were saying. As they closed, I realized they were very interested in my running shoes. Where did you get those shoes? Who makes them? What are they called? How much did they cost? Those were just a few of their questions. I answered as best as I could. I told them the shoes were Adidas Marathon 80's, but did not tell them the cost. I may be wrong about this, but at the time, I felt that if it were not for the obvious disparity in my foot size to theirs (size eight-and-a-half compared to their size ten, or larger), I would have been in big trouble. I forgot to mention that all four were barefooted.

They ran with me for about a half-mile, then two slowed and started walking. After another half-mile, the other two started walking. I figured I was two miles to turn-around and about three miles until I was back to where we met. I was not looking forward to retracing my steps and possibly crossing paths with them again. But thank goodness, I did not see another soul until I got back to the resort.

As soon as I got back, I told Linda what happened and that she was right. I was sure she would reply, "I told you so." Instead, she said, "Sometimes you are too stubborn for your own good." In this case, she made a good point.

Chapter 13

These last four fall within a category that Linda and I call "unsolicited miracles." Only the first one actually deals with running, but we considered each one to be a miracle.

I was running the hills alone, since it was a weekday, and David was probably fast asleep. It was a hot, muggy, summer afternoon, without a cloud in the sky. But as I turned to head back to my car, I saw some dark clouds in the distance and soon heard thunder. It had not rained for weeks, and my first thought was, "Great! We need the rain!" But it did not rain. The wind picked up, the clouds moved in, and the thunder slowly grew louder as I closed in on the car. I had two to three miles to go when it started to hail. Since I was shirtless, it did not take long for me to feel the sting from the hail. I cannot say how long it hailed, since in a hailstorm, seconds seem like minutes. I would say three to four minutes, but that would be just a guess. It lasted long enough that there was so much hail on the pavement, I could no longer keep my footing and had to start walking. Most of the hail looked to be about the size of a dime or smaller, but it was still hard to walk on. As I walked, the dime-sized hail became less, as more and more hail was the size of a quarter. At this point, all of the hail was circular, like a marble. But then I began to see scattered chunks of hail that were much larger than a quarter, and were far from round, with jagged edges. It continued like this until I was within sight of my car, and then there was no hail on the pavement. The pavement was not even wet. I could have run to the car, but I no longer had any interest in running. I continued to walk the rest of the way. I did not tell Linda about my close call for a long time. But when I did, we agreed this was an unsolicited miracle. If I had been closer to the car when the hailstorm hit, those chunks of ice would have bashed my brains out.

For this next story, even to this day, I cannot explain what happened, although I do remember it in detail. Linda had a really bad case of tonsilitis, and it was getting worse by the hour. She was in so much pain, she could not sleep. The drug stores were all closed, but her doctor said he would call in a prescription for pain medicine to the hospital pharmacy in midtown, since it was open 24/7. This was great news. I immediately headed for the pharmacy. The streets were pretty much deserted, since it was around 1:00 a.m. I was on a mission and was making every light—until I had to stop for my first red light at an intersection about a block from the old Crosstown Theater.

In order to understand how this happened, I need to give a description of the scene. The streets in the city of Memphis are arranged in a grid pattern, with almost perfectly aligned north-south and east-west streets. The street at this intersection was the exception. It must have been built prior to when the street grid was established. It curved into the intersection from the south, and once through the intersection, made a sharp curve around a very old brick building, which was now a drugstore. There was a parking lot on the side of the drugstore. There was zero traffic and no one in sight, except for two men who were in the process of changing out the drugstore's large trash dumpster.

I eagerly waited on the light. You would think I would have slammed on the gas immediately when the light changed, but I did not. To this day, I still do not understand what happened. I just sat still. I don't know why. I could not, or would not, move my foot. A few seconds later, I saw headlights and then a speeding car headed through the intersection. But instead of following the road, it went flying into the parking lot and crashed into the building, bursting into flames. The two men immediately opened the car door and pulled the driver from the car. I sat for a few seconds, amazed at what just happened before finishing my mission. Once Linda was better, we discussed this for hours. It was not like I heard a voice say, "Be still," or had some thought or feeling to wait. We all know that God can do anything, but at times, the reason why is totally beyond our understanding.

The next miracle I described in *Running with Angels*, and I am going to steal it and include it below. I did enhance the detail somewhat in the book, since it was fiction, but it is probably 90 percent spot-on. I was driving the baby blue and white 1958 Ford Thunderbird.

****

Memphis State

I was late, nearly out of gas, and traveling a bit beyond the speed limit when I spotted an Exxon service station sign. As I pulled off the interstate, it started raining. This was no light shower; it poured. The exit road went down a long hill to an intersection with a traffic light, and on the other side of the intersection, to the right, was my destination: the Exxon station.

Oil residue had built up on the road during the many weeks without rain, and the sudden rain floated the oil to the surface. The hill was long and steep, and I still hadn't slowed enough from my speed on the interstate. The light at the intersection changed to red, and as I touched the brakes, the car's tires climbed onto the oil. The steering wheel went from being a device for navigating to a brace I desperately clung to while the car spun in circles through the intersection. Round and round I hurtled, right through the red light with traffic flying past me in both directions. When I cleared the intersection, the car completed one last spin and continued skidding backwards. I turned around in the seat to see where I was headed. As if the car knew my intentions, it slid off the road into the drive of the Exxon station.

Not only was I going backward, but I was headed toward another vehicle in front of a full-service island. Just as my car attempted to claim its rightful place in front of the pump, the other vehicle pulled away in the opposite direction. I came to rest perfectly aligned with the gas pump, in the exact position held by the car that had just left.

I still had my head turned, looking toward the rear of the car. There, standing beside the pump with the gas nozzle still in his hand, was an elderly gentleman wearing an Exxon ball cap. He stared at me with his mouth open and eyes wide with amazement.

The only thing I could think to say was, "Fill 'er up." We both broke out laughing. As he pumped the gas, I thought, "This is going to cost big bucks." There I was, running on empty and having the tank filled at the full-service pump.

As I attempted to hand the attendant a $20 bill, he said, "Son, this one is on me." "No, sir," I said, "I'll pay for my gas. Why would you want to pay?"

"Son, I am seventy-five years old," he replied. "I'm retired from the railroad, work at the station part-time to stay busy, and I've been a deacon at my church for more than thirty years. In all my years, I've never witnessed a miracle. I not only just witnessed one, but I feel like I was part of it. I watched as you came down that hill too fast. I watched as the light changed to red. I watched as your car spun out of control through the intersection. I saw the two tractor-trailers heading in opposite directions through the intersection with your car in their path. I saw your car align to its narrowest position as the two rigs passed on each side. With just one extra coat of paint, your car would've been too wide to avoid contact. Not only did it align to its narrowest position, it seemed to pause as the two rigs flew by, then it continued spinning.

"I'm here to say someone was looking out for you today. Someone is watching over you for a reason. I want to pay for this gas so that I can feel a part of it. I can't wait to get home to tell my wife."

****

This last one was not only an unsolicited miracle, but at the time, was beyond my comprehension. It took many years before I came to terms with what happened. It took place during the time I was writing *Running with Angels*. As I wrote the book, I used my training runs to develop the storyline, and this worked exceptionally well, month after month, until I reached the end. Wrapping up the story became more than a challenge; it seemed impossible. One training run, after another, resulted in absolutely nothing. This was worse than "hitting the wall" during a marathon. I admit that, after three weeks, I was very discouraged, but I had no thought of giving up.

The following Monday, I left work, fully intending to run my eight-mile loop. When I got home, Linda was nowhere to be seen, but there was a small pamphlet (approximately thirty pages) lying on our bed. It was titled, ***Hopegivers Christian Orphanages of India*** by Bishop M. A. Thomas. Instead of running, I picked it up and began reading. After only a few pages, I realized this was my answer – orphanages. I was no stranger to them, but what Bishop Thomas was accomplishing with his orphan ministry was mind-boggling.

In 1967, Bishop Thomas founded Hopegivers International, whose mission was to rescue and house abandoned orphans. Hopegivers not only rescued these orphans, but also educated, cared for, and trained them to become missionaries. The ministry has trained over 30,000 missionaries, who have help start more than 70 orphanages, 100 Bible colleges, and 25,000 churches across India. Bishop Thomas passed away in 2010. He was a humble man who had a heart for God. His accomplishments were amazing, and yet most of the world does not even know his name.

As I finished the last page, Linda walked in with an arm-full of groceries. My first words were, "Where did this come from?" Before giving her reply, I need to give some details on Linda's job at the time. She was the front desk receptionist for a cardiology healthcare clinic in our town in Tennessee.

She said, "Well, it was kind of strange. This nice man came

up to the front desk. I asked if he had an appointment. He said yes, and then said he had something he was supposed to give me. Then, he turned around and went out the front door. After a few minutes, he came back into the office carrying that little book and he handed it to me. As soon as I completed the check in, a nurse took him back to see the doctor. He signed in as Bishop M. A. Thomas. When I got home, I tossed it on the bed."

At the time, I did not even try to make sense of how this happened—but God just delivered the inspiration I'd been seeking through Linda's chance encounter at work. The Christian Orphanages of India became an integral part of the book's ending.

These running adventures (or misadventures) are a small sample of what David and I experienced during those years we were able to run together. I excluded the marathons; when I get further along in my journey, I will loop back and devote a segment to them. Preparing for and running marathons is very different than getting ready for the shorter races. Therefore, I want to consider and discuss them separately.

Chapter 14

I want to get back to my journey and highlight some of the events that impacted us during those last years in Memphis. We continued to attend Bellevue Baptist Church, and I had begun reading my Bible regularly.

If you remember, I mentioned having another confrontation with a dog. I am about to give you the details. But first, I want to reaffirm that I don't dislike animals; things just happen, and sometimes, it is beyond your control. It was in the middle of the summer on a Saturday afternoon. I was on the side of the house cutting "the hill," and Linda was sitting on the front porch with our dog, Frosty stretched out beside her. Suddenly, I heard Linda screaming over the sound of the mower. I let go of the mower and ran toward the front yard. I could now clearly hear Linda screaming, "Kenneth, he is killing Frosty!" It was as loud as I have ever heard her voice. She was screaming it, over and over.

Right at the curb, in our front yard, was a very large Doberman that had Frosty by the neck. This dog had to weigh over eighty pounds, and the top of his back was at least two feet from the ground. I ran up and started kicking the dog, over and over, as hard as I could. I was wearing tennis shoes, and to say the least, it did not faze him. In fact, it was as if I was not even there.

He flipped Frosty over on the curb and had hold of the underside of his throat. I could hear Frosty gasping for air. Then, a car pulled up right beside us. A man got out of the car holding a tire iron. He said his dog had gotten loose, and he was looking for him when he heard my wife yelling. They had only had the dog for a couple of weeks. Holding out the tire iron, he said, "I can't do it." By now, I could tell Frosty was hardly breathing and had quit squirming. I took the tire iron and looked down at the dog; it had such a small head. I thought, "Lord help me!" Then I hit the dog, dead center on the top of his head. The dog's front legs buckled, but he did not let go.

Frosty was now limp, and the dog still had a death grip around his throat. I hit him dead center again. This time he let go and fell over on his side. As I watched him fall, I could see his skull. That is all I will say about his head. I was sure I had killed him, and with Frosty still not moving, I thought he had killed Frosty. I was wrong on both counts. Linda was now trying to pick Frosty up, and he started moving. Then, the Doberman staggered to his feet. I was amazed, and whispered, "Thank you Lord."

As I handed the owner his tire iron, I told him that I would take care of my dog, and he could take care of his. As he drove away, I examined Frosty's neck. He was bleeding on the underside, where some teeth had penetrated the skin, but it was not that bad. Still, I took Frosty to the vet. He said we were fortunate Frosty had thick, shaggy hair. Without it, the Doberman could have easily broken Frosty's neck or choked him to death. I was so thankful Frosty was a very shaggy sheep dog.

Once I was back home, Linda explained how the dog came walking up to our driveway, and Frosty ran out to play with him. Frosty thought every person or animal he met was his very best friend. The dog immediately grabbed him by the throat, and you know the rest.

The next day, my left foot was totally black-and-blue, from the ankle to the tip of my toes. Later in the day, a neighbor who lived across the street came over to talk to me about what happened. He was a policeman, and since he worked the third shift, he was asleep when he heard Linda screaming. He came out on his porch and saw me holding the tire iron. He said I jumped straight up in the air—at least a foot—as I swung the tire iron, and then did the exact same thing again. He, too, was amazed that the first blow did not kill the dog, much less the second.

The owner of the dog lived one street over and had recently rented the house. For the first couple of weeks, when I drove past the house, I would see the dog sitting on the front porch with a huge, white bandage on his head. It seemed like he was in a daze and looked pitiful. But the next time I drove by, they had moved.

I really felt bad about what happened and kept questioning whether there may have been a better way. This had a sobering impact on me for a long time.

Later in the fall, we had another event happen that was scarier and more dramatic than the Doberman episode. David and his family came over for pizza. We were all in the house, except for Mark, and David's son, Tony. They were outside, playing with their toy cars in the driveway next door. It was sloped, like our hill, whereas our driveway was flat. They were rolling their toy cars down the slope. Tony came running into our house yelling that Mark had been run over by a motorcycle and was dead. Before you panic like we did, Mark was unconscious, but not dead. We all rushed outside. He was still lying on his back on the driveway, but was now conscious. Linda told us not to move him and ran back into the house to call 911. While we waited on the ambulance, I talked to the boy who was riding the motorcycle. He was very scared, and upset, and kept saying he was sorry. He said he lived a few streets over and that his parents gave him the motorcycle for his sixteenth birthday. This was his first time to ride it, and as he was making the corner, he lost control and veered up into the driveway.

Tony added that they were bent down, rolling their cars, and when they raised up, he saw the motorcycle. The headlight hit Mark in the head, knocking him up into the air, and he landed with the back of his head hitting the pavement.

As Tony was talking, we could hear the siren wailing. They allowed Linda to ride in the ambulance, and I followed in our car. Everyone else stayed behind. The ER took him immediately to have an X-ray. After about thirty minutes, a doctor came out and told us there was no radiologist currently at the hospital to read it. We could take him home, and they would let us know if there was a problem.

This was a mistake; at the time we did not know enough to question that decision. Right after we got home, someone from the hospital called and told Linda they had sent the X-rays to another hospital, and we needed to come back—but to the other hospital. When we arrived, a doctor was waiting to talk to us. Mark had a concussion and two separate skull fractures; one on the front, where the headlight struck, and the other on the back, where his head hit the pavement. Linda had to leave the room to keep Mark from seeing her cry.

We stayed at the hospital overnight so they could monitor him 24/7 to make sure he did not go into a coma and to check for swelling of the brain. If your prayer life ever needs some motivation, this will do the trick. We walked and prayed, sat and prayed, and cried and prayed. There was no coma and no swelling. The doctor told us that Mark's injury was significant enough to cause swelling and possibly a coma. He then said we were very lucky. I wanted to say, "Luck had nothing to do with it." We took him home the next day.

The boy's father came over and told us he would pay for all the medical expenses. I told him my Firestone insurance would cover everything in full, and we were okay. As he was leaving, he turned and said his son told him to sell the motorcycle, and that he would never ride on one again. I said nothing. It would have been easy to be bitter, but I was so thankful to God that Mark was okay, I really had no room for bitterness.

Chapter 15

Looking back, I could say this next event was the beginning of the end, but at the time it seemed the opposite. In the fall of 1980, Firestone announced the closing of their oldest tire plant, which was located near their home office in Akron, Ohio. All the plant's tire production was being moved to their other plants. The Memphis plant would receive a few new passenger tire lines, a few new truck tire lines, and a special line of tires that had never been built outside of the Akron plant.

I had been a tire engineer now for a number of years, and felt very comfortable with my line of tires, but was not prepared for what happened next. I knew we would be taking in new tire lines, but did not know about a special one—until I was asked to attend a meeting the next morning. At the meeting, as I looked around the room, I observed that I was the only tire engineer present. I also did not recognize a small group of people in the room, who were all in business suits, including ties. It was obvious these guys were from our home office in Akron.

I will try to make this as brief as possible, but still give enough detail so you will, at the least, understand how significant it was to my journey. The Memphis plant had been chosen to build two special LXX Mach 1 airplane tires. I would keep my current tire lines and would be assigned this special airplane tire line, as well. The new passenger and truck tire lines would be assigned to our other tire engineers. We had to have the airplane tires in production within six months, since they only had a six-month inventory.

After the meeting, my department manager introduced me to William Woodall, who was the Akron Head Airplane Tire Engineer. For the first month, he would be making trips from Akron to Memphis to train me and help me create a timeline for qualifying. He looked like Walter in a business suit. But unlike Walter, I was never comfortable calling him by his first name. I always called him Mr. Woodall, even though he kept telling me to call him William. My first question of many was: Why are these airplane tires so special? I followed that with: What are the sizes? The following is his reply, as best as I can remember.

The LXX Mach 1 airplane tires were specially designed for jet landings and takeoffs on both paved and unpaved runways. Depending on the need, these unique cantilever tires were tailored to accept efficient braking for short runways, or to use their unmatched deflection abilities to operate at the very low air pressures needed for unpaved runways. Since many Third World countries require the speed of a jet aircraft, but could not afford the costly reinforced long runways that otherwise are needed, the LXX Mach 1 tire design provided the solution to this problem. Many Boeing 737 jet aircraft take off and land on unpaved airstrips around the world on Firestone's LXX Mach 1 airplane tires.

The nose tire was 24.5x8.5-12 LXX M1-210 (N - 8 for 12) and the main landing gear tire was 40x14.0-21 LXX M1-210 (N -16 for 26). I will give the meaning for the main tire, and the nose tire will follow the same scheme. The main landing gear tire diameter is 40 inches. The width is 14 inches. The size of the wheel rim, to which the tire will be fitted, is 21 inches. The name of the tire is LXX-M1. The tire's speed rating is 210 mph, and the tire has sixteen nylon body plies that have a 26-body ply rating.

After those statements, my first thought was, "Why me?"

During that first month, Mr. Woodall spent more time in

Memphis than in Akron. We developed two timelines: a worst-case scenario of six months, and a best-case of four months. It was impossible to foresee the exact number of check tire builds, or tire failures incurred in getting both sizes qualified—not even considering the tire must measure within specified limits before it could even be tested. Plus, we had to consider the fact that the tolerances for airplane tires were much tighter than those for passenger or truck tires.

During those first couple of weeks, my builder was in Akron for training. The union allowed us to hand-pick the builder from a group with the most seniority, which was a rare happening on their part. After a set of check tires had been built and cured, I would have two of the six tires cut into sections, and would spend hours making measurements, analyzing, and recording the results. Then, I discussed all the results with Mr. Woodall. Amazingly, he would ask my opinion on each and every specification change that we had under consideration.

The first and second set of check tires for both sizes failed to measure within the limits, which means they could not even be tested. Mr. Woodall said that if the third set did not measure within tolerance, we might have to have the molds recut, which would delay us many weeks. For us, the saying, "The third time is a charm," was true. Both sizes measured in tolerance on our third set of check tires. It was now a matter of getting each size through the testing requirements, which were much more stringent than for non-airplane tires.

Somehow, we got both sizes totally qualified within four months. In between building the check tires, our builder was training other builders. Four months after that first meeting, the Memphis plant was building airplane tires for the first time. I am not sure which I looked forward to more: the end of the 114-day strike, or the airplane tires going into production.

In August of 1982, the airplane tires had been in production for nearly one year. All the tire engineers were gathered for our Monday morning departmental meeting. The plant manager was in attendance, which was unusual—in fact, I could not recall him ever attending our weekly department meeting. As he got up to speak, we were whispering to each other something to the effect of, "Do you know what's going on?" None of us had a clue. I will try to give a short version of what he said, since he talked, and talked, and talked.

He told us there was going to be an important announcement this morning, and he wanted to discuss it with us first, since it would immediately impact the tire engineers. We still had no clue.

The Memphis plant was going to be totally shut down by the end of the year. All the tire lines would be phased out, as they were qualified at our other plants. Once our tire lines were qualified, we would no longer be needed. If we agreed to assist those tire engineers who were qualifying our tire lines— either by phone or plant visits—then we would be retained until the plant was shut down. You should not need to guess; we all agreed to assist the other plants.

After the meeting was over and the plant manager had left, I asked my department manager what plant was getting the airplane tires. He told me it had not been decided. During the next four months, I made one trip to our plant in Des Moines, Iowa, and one to our plant in Oklahoma City to give them a jump-start on qualifying my tire lines. After that, I took a few of their calls, but that was about the extent of it.

One other important event occurred during that time, but I do not remember exactly when. I think it was during the first month after we learned of the plant closing. Mr. Woodall called and told me he was in the process of retiring, but they called him in to assist with the LXX Mach 1 negotiations. Firestone was selling the LXX Mach 1 technology, patents, tire specs, tire molds, and all related LXX Mach 1 equipment to the Dunlap Aircraft Tire Company of Birmingham, England. Their representatives had been in Akron for a week and had just completed the agreement for the sale.

He said the reason for the call was they were interested in

interviewing me for a tire engineer position. Mr. Woodall had told them about me being the tire engineer at the Memphis plant who worked with him to qualify the LXX Mach 1 tires. He then added that they planned to produce the LXX Mach 1 in a tire plant in Spain.

This was an important issue, and instead of giving it some thought and consideration—much less discussing it with Linda—I instantly said, "There is no way I would make my family move to Spain." Mr. Woodall said he absolutely understood. Looking back, it is obvious I should not have responded with such a knee-jerk reaction on such a consequential decision. No matter the final outcome, I should have involved Linda; we could have discussed, prayed, and come to an agreement before responding.

Unlike the strike, the time flew for the next few months, and before I knew it, over 3,000 Firestone employees at the Memphis plant no longer had a job. A couple of things happened during those last few months that opened my eyes to Firestone's reason and method for downsizing. It was no coincidence that the Akron plant was their oldest plant, and the Memphis plant was their second oldest. With the old buildings and outdated equipment, it was their obvious choice. But for me, it became apparent there was another factor: their oldest workforce. First, I was offered a cash buyout for my pension, along with everyone else. I not only immediately turned it down but warned everyone I knew not to take it. Second, I found out, while talking to one of the tire engineers at the Des Moines plant, that they had received a notification prohibiting the hiring of laid-off employees for a period of twelve months from their termination date. So, I assumed, if less than twelve months, the employee would retain their seniority, if greater, they would lose it. Looking back, I now see it was a business decision and all about the bottom line—but at the time it seemed cold and unfair.

Chapter 16

I sent out a number of resumes around the Memphis area for computer technology positions, but once the plant was closed, I expanded my search across the country. It soon became apparent that we needed a backup plan. We switched positions; Linda took a job as a bookkeeper, and I became the homemaker (or maybe "home destroyer" would be the more appropriate term). At first it was a disaster. I could do nothing right—and this was coming from the kids, not Linda. She actually felt sorry for me. I did not know how to do laundry, cook, and even making the bed "properly" was a challenge. Linda did admit that I was really good at cleaning and "detailing" the house. After many months, even the kids said I was doing a much better job. Looking back, I had no appreciation for all the work and responsibility managing a household entailed, until it was my turn.

After being unemployed for five months, GMI Engineering & Management Institute in Flint, Michigan, called and asked if I could come to Flint for an interview. I had sent GMI an application and resume, based on an academic computing position they posted in a higher education newsletter that featured job postings from colleges and institutions across the nation. This was an answered prayer, after no response to my many other resumes.

The interview seemed to go well—even though I was nervous since this was my first interview ever. They were much more interested in my time at Firestone as a tire engineer than in my lack of computer experience. As we talked, and as I found out more about GMI, I begin to see the close ties the school had with manufacturing corporations.

Since 1926, GMI was owned by General Motors and was named General Motors Institute. They were currently in the process of separating from General Motors (GM) to become a private institute—although GM would still be heavily involved in their co-op program. They were one of the few colleges in the country whose enrollment was totally co-op. Work and school were mixed in twelve-week rotations, dividing the student body into A-section and B-section. At any given time, when A-section was in school, B-section was at work. After twelve weeks, the two sections would rotate. This resulted in students moving four times a year and a 48-week school/work year. GM used the school to train engineers and managers for its manufacturing operations worldwide. GM would still be sponsoring a large number of students, but GMI was rapidly adding additional corporations for sponsorships.

One week later, they asked me to return for a second interview. This one was very different. In fact, looking back, it was more like a meeting than an interview. I will try to give the short version.

Two days after my interview, the Administrative System Manager for their Student System expressed his desire to return to teaching. He was tenured and therefore was "above the law" (or a more acceptable phrase would be, "could not be fired"). GMI was in the middle of installing a new Student System that was purchased from a higher education software company named Information Associates (IA). The functional and technical users had been in training for more than six months and were within a month of go-live. The Administrative Manager was previously a GMI professor and had taught computer courses to GMI students for many years. He took over managing their old Student System when the previous manager retired. So, now there were two openings: one in academic computing, and the other in administrative computing. That is the reason Babu and I were both brought in for the interview/meeting. This was the first time we had met, and neither had a clue what was going on. We were formally introduced and then given an explanation. Babu and I were the final two applicants for the original opening, so with this new opening, they decided to bring us both back to figure it out. The end result was that we were both hired—I for the administrative system, and Babu for the academic. We always wondered which one of us would have been hired, if there had been no second opening, but it did not matter. We were both elated.

Babu was a nickname; his full name was Babusankah Rangathan. He had left India six months prior and was staying with his nephew in Chicago while job hunting. I don't want to wander too far from my journey, but Babu was the humblest, kindest, smartest person I have ever known. It was as if the Lord's hand was directly involved in us being hired together. During that first year at GMI, whenever I ran into something technically challenging, I would ask Babu his thoughts. He would explain it at a level I could understand, and I would write the code. When a professor came to Babu, whining about a problem with a program, he would tell me exactly what they said, and I would reword their simplistic statements and explain them at a higher level that Babu could understand. In other words, we were a match made in Heaven.

Here's an example that will give you an idea of how really gifted Babu was. During our third year at GMI, Babu handed me a neat stack of typewritten pages and asked if I would proof them. He was always asking me to "proof" something. What he was really asking was for me to straighten out his written English. He could speak English very well (of course, with an accent). But when writing in English, he would get the words mostly right, but they would be out of place within the sentence. The title on the first page was "Programming Artificial Intelligence into Computer Systems." I had to read the paper, over and over, just to grasp the concept. Once I finally got the wording straightened out, he submitted the paper, and it was later published in a technical journal. This was in the 1980's, when 99 percent of the US population had never heard the term, "Artificial Intelligence." Babu and I developed a close friendship that lasted for many years after we both left GMI.

Right after the interview, someone told me about a house for rent in Flushing, which is a small town located right outside of Flint. It belonged to a professor who had accepted a position at the University of Arkansas. On my way to the airport, I stopped and checked it out. As soon as I got back home, I told Linda about the job and the house. She was much more interested in the house than the job, and began asking all kinds of questions about the house. I was ready for this and told her it was twice as large as ours. We rented the house. They wanted me to start July 1, which was in three weeks. We did not have time to even consider selling our house, so we rented it out to a couple who were friends with some members in our church. GMI covered the moving expenses, including the packing. The moving van was supposed to arrive in Flushing the day we arrived; it did not. They told us they were behind, and it would arrive in five days. We slept on the floor those first five nights. After we finally had everything unpacked, Linda realized her jewelry box was missing. She had packed all her jewelry, including her wedding ring, thinking it would be safe. After checking through everything again, Linda was missing her jewelry box, some of her nicer shoes, and a few hats.

After we contacted the moving company, their insurance called and asked Linda many questions, including a description of what happened the day of the packing. The packer had brought her sixteen-year-old daughter, who would help with the packing and then disappear for a while. Linda finally asked the girl's mother about it. She said her daughter was not feeling well and kept going to their car to rest. They interviewed the mother and daughter separately, and although neither would admit anything, their stories did not match. We ended up getting a small settlement, since the diamond ring was the only thing of real value. Linda felt terrible about putting her wedding ring in the jewelry box, and a replacement ring would not be the same, since it would not be her actual wedding ring. In fact, she insisted we not buy another diamond ring. I finally talked her into getting a simple gold band to wear on her ring finger.

Chapter 17

The first few days at GMI were so hectic, with go-live just a matter of weeks away. At first, I was overwhelmed. I sat in on both the technical and functional training for the new system until go-live, and then took the training manuals home for the next three months. Babu was of no help; he had his plate full dealing with all those pampered, illogical professors.

The Student System created by IA was written in COBOL, which is still used by most business, finance, and administrative systems today; in fact, COBOL is an acronym for "common business oriented language." Since it is a business language, the technology department did not offer it as an elective, much less as a required course. The fact that COBOL was such an easy language to learn was my salvation. It consists of English-like structural components, such as verbs, clauses, and sentences. Therefore, writing programs in COBOL was much easier than in Fortran.

My first big issue was when the functional users discovered this new system did not support numeric grading. I had never heard of a college using numeric grading (0 to 100); I thought all schools used letter grades (A to F) or (A+, A, A- to F). But I soon found out GMI had been using numeric grading for the last eighty years and did not plan on changing anytime soon. Unfortunately, they did not realize this was an issue during all their months of training, prior to my arrival. I contacted IA, and they admitted their system did not support numeric grading, since they thought all colleges used some form of letter grading. So, it was now my problem.

I began searching all the programs in the Student System to find which ones contained code that dealt with the grade process. Then, I searched through all the data files to find all the locations where the grade data was stored. I had to do many other searches, which I won't describe, because it would be too technical. The bottom line was the grade processing rippled throughout the system. But the code changes did not look that difficult; in fact, they looked pretty straightforward. There was only one issue that was going to be a problem. I called IA and asked for their student tech expert. Jason Moyer got on the line. The reason I am introducing you to Jason is because he became one of my best friends. To this day, we still exchange Christmas cards. I gave him an overview of the problem and brought him up-to-date on my research. Then I told him the one issue that led to my call. The grade fields in the data files could only accommodate two digits, since the letters grades' maximum length was two digits (A+, A-, B+, B-, etc.). For my numeric grading, the two-digit field would handle 0 to 99, but not the 100. I needed a grade field of three digits length instead of two.

GMI had already moved the grade data from their old system to the new system before I was hired. When I realized this was an issue, I looked at the migrated history data, and sure enough, I found 00 grades. Can you imagine what the zero grade would do to that student's GPA? Instead of telling me how I should proceed, Jason asked what I thought should be done.

I told him that we needed to find a new location in the data file that could hold up to three digits. Then, I would need to modify the grade migration program to point to the new grade field and rerun it. That would fix the old grade data. Finally, I would need to modify every program in the new system that processes grades to point to my new three-digit grade field instead of IA's two-digit field. Jason said, "You got it." It took me two weeks to make the changes, test, and then move them from our test to our production system.

The reason I have gone into so much detail on this grade issue is the impact it had on my career and my future, which I will get to shortly. Plus, there is an interesting point I want to make about the similarity between the fix for my grade problem and the issues the industry faced with Y2K, when the date went from 1999 to 2000. I had existing two-digit grade fields that needed to be expanded to three-digits. For Y2K, everyone worldwide, including myself, had two-digit year fields that needed to be expanded to four-digits. Without four digits, when the century (and millennium!) changed, the program would think it was 1900 instead of 2000. As you should be able to see from what I described above, this was a pretty simple fix; it was just a matter of finding all the places that needed to be changed. It was the same in 1999, when we were hunting down that feisty Y2K bug. I told Linda at the time that they were making a mountain out of a molehill, and it was really not necessary to build a bomb shelter or buy survival food and equipment.

It was now in late October, and I was no longer having to spend every spare minute on work-related issues. For those first three months at GMI, training runs were few and far between. We had our first snow in early November, and it was like nothing I had witnessed: eight inches of snow, and Thanksgiving was still weeks away. When we tried to let Frosty out for the first time, he looked back at us like we were crazy, but finally relented. I bought a snow shovel and was shoveling the snow from our driveway, when my next-door neighbor came over and said, "It didn't take you long to figure out which end was for holding and which was for shoveling." I just smiled. He said I was welcome to borrow his snow blower any time. I told him thanks; the exercise would be good for me.

We drove to Memphis for Thanksgiving and hit a snowstorm on the way that was so bad, they had to close the interstate. We spent the night at a motel but were able to continue the next morning. I spent the next three days whining to David about Michigan's winters. Once back in Michigan, it snowed off-and-on for five months. That first winter, training runs were rare. Linda and I never got used to the snow and the cold, sunless days the whole time we lived there. The kids loved it—from ice skating to snowmobiling.

During the first week in the new year, on a late Friday afternoon, Linda answered the phone. I remember it well; it was now one year since the Firestone plant closed. Linda handed me the phone and said it was the Des Moines plant manager. You probably already know why he called, but I will quickly go over it. He had a tire engineer position open up three months ago, but held it until he could call and offer me the position. He went over all the benefits and advantages the newer Des Moines plant had, compared to the old Memphis plant. He finished by offering a substantial raise over what I was making in Memphis. I thanked him and asked if he would call back on Monday; I wanted to talk it over with my wife.

My starting salary at GMI was about twenty percent less than my salary at Firestone; therefore, this would be a considerable raise. I loved my job at GMI; everyday was a new adventure, kind of like starting a new crossword puzzle, each and every morning. But we both agreed Michigan winters were awful, and although Des Moines would not be as nice weather-wise as Memphis, it had to be better than Michigan. We went back-and-forth and finally realized this was such an important decision, we needed to pray about it. We would not discuss it again until Monday before the call.

On Monday morning, I got up knowing for certain how we should respond. Before I could bring it up, Linda told me she was sure how we should reply. We were in agreement: We turned it down. Both of us felt it would be like taking a step backward, and it was not in the direction the Lord was leading us. Speaking of my journey, we did not attend church the whole time we lived in Michigan. Looking back, I cannot explain or justify the fact that we did not even look for a church—though I did continue reading my Bible.

Our renters had signed a one-year lease, and when the year was completed, David called and said he had bad news. He had gone to check on our house before we agreed to sign for another year. The bad news was they had pretty much destroyed the inside. The carpets were sticky when you walked on them; the walls were covered with colored crayon markings, all the way up to the reach of their two toddlers—and I could go on, but I think you get the picture. The place was a total mess. I replaced all the carpet and had to primer the walls before repainting in order to keep the crayon markings from bleeding through. I had to make repairs in every room in the house, with the kitchen and bathrooms needing the most work. I was thankful Linda and the kids stayed in Michigan; she would have cried if she had seen it. It took most of the week, and once I finished, we put it up for sale. While I was still on the road, headed back to Michigan, our realtor called and told Linda he had sold the house to the first couple who viewed it.

Now into my second year at GMI, I was able to get back into training and I began running in local races. My plan was to run the Detroit Marathon in the fall. I actually ran my final five marathons while I was at GMI but will exclude them for now. Since they had such a constant influence on my journey, I plan to devote an entire segment to marathons. Babu went with us to every race; we pretty much did everything together. We taught Babu how to play tennis, and although we thought we were decent at ping-pong, he ended up teaching us how to play. When we were in Jamaica, Linda came in second in a ping-pong tournament at our resort—but after the first time playing against Babu, we realized we were mere amateurs. With his help and training, we steadily improved, but were never in his league. In tennis, Babu improved to the point we could hold our own in doubles matches against a lot of the GMI professors.

Two events occurred in the Fall that are worth noting. On September 19, 1985, Firestone announced they were shutting down all passenger and truck tire production at their Des Moines plant by the end of the year—though they would continue producing tractor tires and tires for other farm equipment. This had a profound impact on both of us. Without praying and then listening, we could have made a terrible decision. Our faith grew stronger, and it strengthened our resolve to involve the Holy Spirit in all aspects of our lives.

This second one is trivial, compared to the one above, but at the time, it seemed like an answered prayer. I was complaining about how much I hated running on those snowy streets, when one of my co-workers mentioned the indoor track at the University of Michigan Recreation Center (UOMRC) in downtown Flint. After work, I went by to check it out. They had a one-tenth mile, banked, oval track above their basketball courts. I joined on the spot. I would be hard-pressed to estimate the number of miles I ran on that track during our winter months in Michigan.

I was at GMI for three-and-a-half years, and although the work was challenging at times, I learned a great deal and became very skilled at writing COBOL programs. GMI was an elite school that produced some of the top graduates in the nation. Based on their co-op work/school curriculum, they were uniquely qualified to immediately step into management and engineering positions—not only in the states, but world wide.

I have two more events to cover that occurred during our last year in Michigan. Both impacted my journey and our future. The first dealt with my modifications to IA's grade processing, and the second involves our move back to Tennessee. Again, I will try to give the short version.

IA was in the process of selling their Student Information System (SIS) to a technical institution in Georgia, when their sales team was asked, "Does your Student System support numeric grading?" Well, we know the answer to that question, but their sales team did not. Jason Moyer quickly entered the picture, and this naturally led to me becoming involved. I had all the grading modifications and documentation saved in a file, since I had to reapply them each time IA sent out a new version. I downloaded the file to Jason, and he installed it in their client's version of SIS. A few weeks later, Jason called and told me they were about to start working on a major release of SIS that would include many enhancements. It would be renamed Student Information System Plus (SIS+), and he wanted to let me know they were going to include my grade modifications in it. This was good news; I would no longer have to reinstall the grade changes, since they would be in IA's base version. One other thing happened that I later became aware of: IA gave GMI a year of free SIS maintenance for the grade modifications.

We had been living in Michigan for approximately three-and-a-half years, and for the most part had settled in for the long haul (except for maybe the winters). I am afraid this will not be the short version; it was too important, and had such a tremendous impact on not just my journey, but on my whole family. I received a call from IA, and it was not Jason. The person on the line introduced himself as John Robinson. I had seen his name on IA release documents and kind of knew he was part of management. He told me there was an IA position coming open that, for IA and myself, would be a "match made in Heaven." Well, that is not actually what he said, but it was how I took it.

IA had just signed a multi-million-dollar contract with the state of Tennessee for IA's Student (SIS), Finance, and Human Resource administrative systems. The contract was for the twenty state colleges governed by the Tennessee Board of Regents (TBR). Of those twenty, six were four-year institutions, and fourteen were two-year. This was, by far, IA's largest group of colleges under one contract. IA was in the process of setting up a Satellite Maintenance Office (SMO) at TBR in Nashville, where they would have three on-site IA employees working full-time. They had already hired one person, who would be responsible for both Finance and HR. The Student System (SIS) was so large, it dwarfed Finance and HR combined. SIS was made up of Admissions, Records, Business, and Financial Aid. They had hired a second person to be responsible for the Financial Aid component. I would be responsible for the Admissions, Student Records, and Business components.

I had already told Mr. Robinson that I was very interested in the offer, but would need to discuss it with my wife, which he fully understood. But as we were ending our conversation, he mentioned one other small item. The two already hired would start working at TBR on January 1. They wanted me to work for six months at their home office in Rochester, N.Y., then I would be assigned as part of the SMO at TBR in Nashville.

As soon as I hung up the phone, I called Jason. I quickly got his side of the story. Yes, he was aware IA was going to contact me with the job offer. He sat in on meetings where the SIS+ release deadline of July 1 was discussed, as well as the SIS position at the TBR SMO. My name came up during both discussions, since management was aware of who I was because of my grade modification. But Jason knew a critical piece of information that those at the meeting did not know: I was from Tennessee and would be very interested in returning. He was surprised John Robinson was the one who called, and I immediately asked him why. Once he told me he was the Founder, Owner, and CEO of IA, I understood his surprise. He finished our call saying John Robinson was a hands-on guy. I soon learned how true that was.

It probably does not even need to be mentioned that Linda and I were both elated with the thought of moving back to Tennessee. Nashville was not Memphis, but it was a lot closer than Flint. It did not require a lot of thought or prayer; we accepted the offer. From this point until the move, we did not have a minute to spare. There was so much to be done and so many decisions to be made in such a short timeframe. But it all worked out, and the move went far smoother than our move to Michigan.

GMI understood our leaving, and after using SIS for three-and-a-half years, both our technical staff and functional users had plenty of experience with the system. Our biggest concern was Babu. We had become close friends from the beginning, and now it was like he was a part of our family. Babu well knew how much we missed Tennessee and was thrilled for us. Then he told us he had been planning a trip back to India to visit his family but had been putting it off. I then realized that he had not gone home since we met, whereas once a year we would make a trip to Memphis and/or Texas. A week before our move, we took Babu to the airport for his flight to India.

Although our move went smoothly, working out the details was challenging. We rented an apartment in Murfreesboro, which is about thirty miles southeast of Nashville. Once Linda and the kids were settled in, I headed to Rochester.

Chapter 18

Once in Rochester, I had no problem finding the IA office, thanks to Jason's directions. I do not remember a lot about that first day, except it was like a whirlwind. At the time, there were about 100 employees working there. I think Jason introduced me to about half of them before taking me to Mr. Robinson's office.

As I already mentioned, Jason had told me Mr. Robinson was a hands-on guy. Well, it did not take long for me to confirm that for myself. I had planned on staying in a motel for the first few days, until I could find a place to rent. But after Jason introduced us, Mr. Robinson said he found a place he wanted me to check out. He then proceeded to take me to "see if I liked it." It was in a nice area of downtown that contained large, restored, older homes. It was one of a few that had been recently converted from a single-dwelling residence to one that contained several apartments. The apartment was super nice, with one bedroom, a bath, a kitchen, and a small entry room, and it was totally furnished with old, expensive furniture. I told him it was perfect. He said he had put down a deposit, and since I liked it, would give them a check for the six months. During the hiring process, IA said they would pay the rent on an apartment while I worked in Rochester. They also said they would purchase tickets for me to fly home every other weekend.

There were six full-time people assigned to the SIS+ enhancement project, including Jason and me. There were two more who had other responsibilities but would help us when they had spare time. In order to try to meet the deadline, the team had been working six days a week. They had me scheduled to fly out every other Thursday night and return Sunday night. That meant I would work eleven days during each two-week period, and the rest of the team would work twelve. I felt that was unfair and said I would work seven the first week, then five the week I went home. I did this for six months and made eleven trips home, before driving the last one.

After about a month, a call was transferred to my cubicle from the front desk. Babu was back in Michigan and had important news. First, he had accepted a position with Bell Labs in Chicago, which was where his cousin worked. And, by the way, he was now a married man. We knew he had applied for a job with Bell Labs right before his trip, but nothing about any marriage plans. His new wife was going to meet him in Chicago once her visa was approved. We agreed to keep in touch, and as soon as I hung up the phone, I called Linda to give her the news.

During those six months, I really missed my family, but my team developed a close relationship. The closer we got to the deadline, the longer we stayed each night. We were bound and determined to finish all the enhancements by the deadline. During our last month, we would sometimes work until midnight. I worked on some Admission and Business modifications, but mainly on those for Student Records.

We would take the technical specs that had been written for the modification, study it, write the code, install it in our test system, test, and then have another member of the team retest. If any issues occurred, we would make the corrections and start the test process again. Once okayed, we moved it into the SIS+ release system where the functional staff would do additional testing—mainly to ensure it contained all the new functionally, as requested. A week before our scheduled release date, we completed the enhancements, and I spent my last week in Rochester helping review our writing team's functional documentation for each enhancement.

During that last week, Mr. Robinson met with our team, thanked us individually, and gave each of us a bottle of wine from his vineyard. He then announced that we would be receiving a substantial bonus for our dedication and hard work. He said since our success was based on a team effort, each team member would receive the same amount; the bonus would not be based on seniority. That was good news for me; I had no seniority. On my last day in Rochester, Mr. Robinson came to my cubical and told me how important the Tennessee SMO was to the future success of IA, and how thankful he was to have me as part of the SMO team.

I have one more point to make about Rochester. I am sure you remember my opinion about Michigan winters (and snowstorms, in particular). After spending one winter in Rochester, I realized Michigan snowstorms were not as bad as I thought. Rochester is thirty-four miles from Lake Ontario. Being from the south, I had never heard the term "lake effect." Lake effect is when a cold air mass moves across long expanses of warmer lake water, like Lake Ontario. This causes large amounts of moisture to be pulled into the cold atmosphere, which results in heavy snowfall within fifty miles of the water. Buffalo, Syracuse, and Rochester compete each year for the most snowfall in the nation, with yearly totals ranging from seventy to 120 inches. Looking back, I think Rochester had as many snowplows as taxi cabs.

Chapter 19

On my last day in Rochester, I worked until 4:00 p.m. and spent about thirty minutes telling everyone goodbye. My plan was to spend one last night in my apartment, then get up very early and head for home. But as I drove back to my apartment, I realized that I would never be able to sleep; I was too excited. Therefore, I turned toward the interstate and was on my way. From Rochester to Murfreesboro is a little over 800 miles. I drove through the night, only stopping for gas. I did not get sleepy throughout the night. It was either the excitement, or the fact that I had worked at night for ten years.

For that first week at home, everything felt awkward. Everyone had their own routine, including the dog and cat, and I was at best out-of-step, and at worst in the way. After that week, I begin feeling like a part of the family again, thank goodness. Linda and I had already discussed buying a house but decided to buy a lot instead and have the house built. After a few weeks, we selected a one-acre lot in Hanes Haven subdivision in Murfreesboro. We looked at numerous floor plans before deciding to design our own. I drew up the blueprint, showed it to a builder, and after a lot of discussion, came to an agreement on the price. We took out a construction loan, which was converted into a fifteen-year mortgage once the house was completed. The construction started in the Fall, and we moved into our new home in the Spring of 1988.

After my six months in Rochester, I eagerly returned to my

running routine, with one major difference: I no longer had the desire to run races, long or short. I still loved the training runs—especially the longer runs on the weekends. After those many months without running, I realized what I missed the most: It was that point in time, during a long run, when you can barely feel your feet hitting the ground. But my running schedule was erratic, with very few long runs, until we moved into our new home. Dealing with the day-to-day issues of the construction was time consuming. Once we moved in, I was able to keep a more consistent schedule. I did change my Saturday morning long run from twenty to eighteen miles. I could leave my house and run east, then north, then west, and then south, in a nine-mile rectangle, arriving where I started. I would make two loops on Saturday, and one loop a couple of times during the week.

For that first year in our new home, we spent most of our time settling in. I was in charge of landscaping the grassless yard, and Linda arranged the interior, decorating everything in sight.

We had not attended a church since leaving Memphis and had pretty much run out of excuses. It was another year before we decided to visit a small Baptist church near our home. We attended regularly, although we never officially joined. It took us over a year before we understood why. First, the church was not growing, although there were weekly visitors. But the main problem was we witnessed so much constant bickering and tension between members of the congregation.

Linda and I decided to look for another church and to keep looking until we found one that felt more like family. We began to visit different churches in and around Murfreesboro, mostly Baptist. And this, too, was erratic; we would go to a church for two or three weeks, discuss, and move on to another. I am not implying there was something wrong with every church; looking back, it probably was more on us than the church. Lord knows, you will never find a perfect church, and if you did, you could not join without messing it up. This went on for an extended period, and at times we became disillusioned and would take a break from our search.

This cycle continued until the fall of 1991, when an acquaintance told Linda about her husband's upcoming concert at World Outreach Church (WOC) in Murfreesboro. He had a Christian band that traveled throughout the mid-south, performing mainly in churches. Surprisingly, Linda and I decided to attend. As soon as we walked into WOC, people introduced themselves to us, and when we were seated, people from the row in front and the row behind were introducing themselves. The concert was great, but it was the congregation that made the night special. As we walked to our car, I looked over at Linda, saw tears in her eyes, and knew immediately they were tears of joy. Linda looked back and said, "We have found our church." The next Sunday, we attended WOC's morning service and have attended regularly for over 30 years. After our first service, we agreed that we had also found our pastor. Many years later, we took my mother to WOC for the first time, and as we were leaving, she said, "Son, your church is filled with the Spirit." In her special way, she pretty much summed up what we felt during our first visit to WOC.

Chapter 20

S ince I ran my last marathon prior to moving to Murfreesboro, this is a good point to go back and highlight the impact training for and running marathons had on my life and journey. Twenty years ago, if you asked how many marathons I had run, I would have immediately said fifteen and would have felt totally comfortable in saying that total. But over the years, I have come to the conclusion this was misleading and untrue. I did physically run and time fifteen 26.2-mile runs, which is the distance of a marathon. Eleven of those runs were with a large group of runners, waiting for the starting gun to be fired and then taking off. For the other four, I was alone on a quarter-mile track, waiting for daybreak, then starting my stopwatch and taking off. I will cover these "other four" first, then tell you about the remainder in a more chronological order.

Before we get started, I want to explain what the term "hitting the wall" means. It is a condition of sudden fatigue and loss of energy in the runner, which is caused by the depletion of glycogen (carbohydrates) at some point during the marathon—usually occurring around the twenty to twenty -two mile mark. Up until this point, the runner's energy is coming from both glycogen and fat; thereafter from body fat only. I describe it like a car running on high-octane gasoline (90-120 octane) then suddenly switching over to kerosene (15 octane). This is the point where all but seasoned marathon runners will begin walking. The more trained the runner, the more likely he will be able to run through the wall and, to some extent, maintain his pace.

Of all our yearly trips to Texas to visit Linda's relatives, there are three trips, in particular, that I want to point out. I no longer remember the dates or even the years, but I have no problem recalling the occasions. In my infinite wisdom, I thought running a "training run" marathon would help my body adapt to the rigors of getting through the wall. Therefore, on three different trips to Texas, without mentioning this to Linda, my brother, or anyone else for that matter, I drove to the local Garland High School track before daybreak. I set out water and waited until it was light enough to see. I started my stopwatch and took off around the quarter -mile track and continued for 105 laps. That accounts for three of my four "training run" marathons.

Two years before I finally qualified to run Boston, I took a one-day vacation on the third Monday in April (which by no coincidence was the same day as the Boston Marathon). I got up before daybreak, drove past the Frayser High School track to the turnaround for our many twenty-mile training runs. I set out water at the turnaround, drove back to the track, and then waited until it was light enough to see. I started my stopwatch and took off around the quarter-mile track and continued for 25 laps, headed out to the turnaround, and then ran back. I do not remember my times for these four "training runs," but I do know the run on those hills was far more difficult than the other three. It was years later before I confessed these four "training runs" to Linda, and cannot remember if I ever told David.

I will list the remaining eleven marathons and will describe and give some detail about many of them. Every marathon had its own unique set of challenges and problems. I think it was these challenges that motivated me to keep training for them. Besides the physical challenges of pace and endurance, the mental challenges are every bit as important.

You will never finish the race strong, if you cannot mentally handle the extreme discomfort from the wall to the finish line. You have to develop a mental toughness that prevents you from even considering letting up. I cannot describe the deep satisfaction you feel as you finish, knowing you held nothing back and gave everything you had. For marathons, I never felt I was running against the other runners; I was running against myself. This was unlike shorter races, where I felt I was competing against the runners in my age group.

There is one more challenge you have absolutely no control over that has as much of an impact on your overall time as any of those above: the weather. As I describe some of these marathons below, this will become very apparent.

The Jackson Marathon in September, 1978

The Memphis Express Marathon in February, 1979

The Jackson Marathon in September, 1979

The Memphis Express Marathon in December, 1980

The Memphis Express Marathon in December, 1981

The Dallas White Rock Marathon in December, 1982

The Detroit Marathon in October, 1983

The Dallas White Rock Marathon in December, 1983

The Boston Marathon in April, 1984

The Memphis Express Marathon in December, 1984

The Detroit Marathon in October, 1985

I ran my very first marathon in Jackson, Tennessee, in September of 1978. This was before David started running. Linda, the kids, and I drove to Jackson, which is about eighty miles from Memphis, on a Friday afternoon. The race started Saturday morning in downtown Jackson, looped out into the suburbs, and finished back at the starting point. I will not go into detail, but there are two events during the race that I want to point out. The first was when I hit the wall; I do not remember the mile marker, but I well remember hitting the wall. Although it is hard to describe, the best I can say is things went from difficult to really, really difficult. It becomes a simultaneous battle between mental and physical strength, where you have to constantly force yourself to stay focused and maintain your pace, even though your extreme fatigue is telling you to slow down.

I continued and held to my pace, but at the 23-mile marker I encountered a totally different problem. As I came back into the downtown area, I was nearing a major intersection, along with a handful of other runners. No traffic was allowed on the route, but cars at intersections were being allowed to cross when there were large gaps between the runners. Since this was a major intersection, there was a policeman on foot, motioning to the cars when to hold back and when they could scoot across. The policeman was motioning to the driver of a Volkswagen bug to continue holding back as the runner in front of me cleared. I was just entering the intersection, but the driver attempted to lunge across in front of me and we met in the middle. He was coming from my left side. When I saw we were about to collide, I extended my left arm, placed my hand on the hood, and leaped over the front of his car without breaking stride. I glanced back and saw the policeman dragging the man from his car. I kept running. I must have had an adrenaline rush from the close call, because I picked up my pace during those last three miles. I had started the race hoping to finish under three-and-a-half hours. My time was three hours and twenty-seven minutes, which was my slowest marathon. One last point—I did not realize until after I crossed the finish line that I had sprung my left wrist. It was very sore for about a week.

You would think after running the first marathon, they would get somewhat easier. They don't. The second was the Memphis Express Marathon on February 25, 1979, and because of the time of year, it presented a whole new set of challenges. It was not only cold, it was bitter cold, with gusty winds, light snow, and sleet throughout. After I got through the wall, I realized I had no feeling in either of my arms, from my elbows to my fingertips. As I crossed the finish line, Linda ran out and wrapped my shoulders in a blanket. I did not know it at the time, but Nita took pictures as Linda was draping me with the blanket. To this very day, I cannot look at those pictures without seeing the pain in my eyes, and if I stare at the pictures very long, I can feel and remember that pain.

The third was in Jackson on the second Saturday in September of that same year, 1979. But this time my mother, Nita, and David were with us. Instead of starting and finishing in downtown, the race started and finished at Union University's main campus, which was about seven miles from downtown. David was now running, but not long enough to attempt a marathon. He wanted to run the last five miles with me. So, our plan was for him to be at the 21-mile marker, and we would run together to the finish line. I will say again, every marathon has its own set of problems and challenges, including this one. It was so hot and humid during the race, I actually believe the saying, "you could have fried an egg on the pavement." Both the temperature and humidity reached the nineties. At every water station I would grab two cups, drinking one while pouring the other on my head. By the tenth mile, runners were dropping out of the race and waiting to be picked up.

This is the only marathon I ever ran where I cannot recall the details vividly. I know I went through the wall but could not describe it. By the time David joined me, I was having trouble remembering the mile marker numbers. But I do remember crossing the finish line. They had tables with food for the runners set up right beyond the finish line. Everyone was telling me that I needed to eat to get my strength back. All I wanted was water, but I filled a tray with food and then passed out. Nita caught me before I hit the ground. I was only out a minute or so, but an ambulance took me to the ER in Jackson, with Linda following in our car.

The ER was full of runners, but as soon as they rolled me in the door, a nurse was waiting with an IV. Everywhere I looked, runners were getting IVs for dehydration. The nurse said I weighed 128 pounds, which was six pounds lighter than my normal weight. We were there for about an hour, then

Linda drove us back to the campus, where everyone was waiting.

Either Nita or David (I cannot remember which one) was holding a large trophy. I had come in second in my age group. I figured everyone else in my age group must have dropped out of the race. I found out the overall lead runner quit with one mile to go. And some time later, we learned that Jackson was going to change their marathon date from September to late October because of the heat. To say the least, this was not the best race for me to have invited my mother; she never attended another marathon (or any other race, for that matter).

The fourth was the Memphis Express Marathon on the first Saturday in December, 1980. There are two reasons I am giving detail on this one: It was David's first marathon, and it was my first with the weather not being a factor. My time was three hours and two minutes, and David's time was three hours and ten minutes, which was a really good time for his first marathon.

The fifth was, again, the Memphis Express Marathon on the first Saturday in December, 1981. In this one, the weather was perfect for the whole race, causing both of us to run our individual fastest marathon. I finished tenth overall, with a time of two hours and fifty-four minutes, and David finished eighteenth overall with a time of three hours. I do not remember the number of runners for these Memphis marathons, but it was probably somewhere between 400 to 500. In 2002, St. Jude became the sponsor, and the numbers increased yearly by the thousands.

The seventh was the Detroit Marathon on the third Sunday in October of 1983. This was about four months after we moved to Michigan. I will give a little more detail on this one; it was somewhat different than all the others.

We drove to Detroit on Saturday and spent the night in a hotel in downtown. On Sunday morning at 5:00 a.m., I stood in line as one bus after the next loaded up with runners. We were taken to a park in Windsor, Ontario, where we waited for the 8:00 a.m. start time. Linda and the kids stayed at the hotel until around 10:00 a.m., checked out, and drove to the finish line.

The park was about three miles from the Detroit-Windsor Tunnel. It is a one-mile underwater highway tunnel that connects Detroit and Windsor, and is recognized as the world's only underwater international border crossing for automotives. In this "once a year" special case, it is reserved for runners only. As we were nearing the tunnel, I saw men in what looked to be police uniforms standing on each side of the street. Every so often, one would lunge out into the stream of runners and tackle a runner, dragging him to the curb. You probably already figured out what was happening, but at the time I was clueless. A runner was tackled right in front of me, and as I dodged to keep from tripping over them, I saw the issue. The runner did not have a Detroit Marathon runner's tag number on his shirt.

The weather was good, and I finished with a time of three hours and seven seconds. The qualifying time for the Boston Marathon from 1980 to 1986 was 2 hours, 50 minutes for the 19-39 age group. For the 40-49 age group, it was 3 hours, 10 minutes. Since I was thirty-eight when I ran the 2 hour, 54 minute marathon in Memphis, it was four minutes too slow to qualify for Boston. For Detroit, I was now forty, so I finally qualified.

The ninth was the Boston Marathon on the third Monday in 1984. This is the race I had set my sights on since that day in the summer of 1981, when I met Craig Virgin. That's why I will provide more background and detail for this particular race.

After we returned from our trip to Dallas in December of 1983, I started making my training plans for running Boston in April. I had done most of my training for the Dallas marathon on the one-tenth mile indoor track at the UOMRC. Since the next three months would be even colder, with even more snowstorms, I decided to do all my training at the rec-center. I probably averaged about fifty miles a week on the indoor track. I varied the miles for each run, with my long Saturday morning run being the exception. Every Saturday morning at the 7:00 a.m. opening, I would run twenty miles, starting out at a 6:20 pace for the first few miles, then trying to maintain 6:30 to ten miles, 6:40 to fifteen miles, and then get back to 6:30 during the last five. I doubt I ever averaged 6:30 for the whole run, but that was always my goal. Since I was at the track so often, you would think that I knew everyone in the building. I actually only knew the people who worked the front desk. But as the weeks went by, I would have a runner show up during my Saturday run who would track right behind me for a number of laps. Some would follow right behind me for a mile, and others for up to five miles—but they would drop off before I completed the run. Therefore, I never met any of them.

It was two weeks before the Boston Marathon, and I had just finished what would be my last twenty-mile (two hundred laps) Saturday run. A young guy in his late twenties in a business suit introduced himself as a sportswriter for the Flint Journal. He said he was a member of the rec-center, and some guys at the front desk told him about a runner who had been training for Boston on their indoor track. He wanted to interview me for a story about my training for Boston. Looking back, I did not really give it much thought and agreed. He asked if he could take my picture, and I agreed again. He took out his camera and just stood there. I waited, and waited, and waited some more, to the point it felt like we were in a Mexican standoff. But I did not know why. Finally, he asked if I needed to freshen up before we took the picture. I went to "freshen up" and saw the problem. I looked like a salt lick, with long, white streaks from dried salt all over my face.

A week after the interview, one-fourth of the Flint Journal sport's page was used for the picture and the article titled "UM-Flint's indoor track makes dream come true for Brooks." It gets worse. Even though he took notes all through the interview, very little of what he wrote matched my answers to his questions. It was as if he had this "southern hillbilly" theme; a barefooted bumpkin from Tennessee, who had never seen snow until moving to Michigan, was doing all of his training for Boston on the UOMRC's indoor track. He said I ran ten miles every day of the week except Saturday, when I ran twenty miles. I said that I ran twenty miles on Saturday and varied my miles Monday through Friday. He said my best previous time was two hours and fifty-two minutes. I told him two hours and fifty-four minutes. He said I weighed 130 pounds; I said I weighed 134 pounds, and it goes on and on. He did get my Detroit qualifying time for Boston of three hours and seven seconds correct. And he did get Linda, Mark, and Mandy's names correct. Either he was not very good at listening, or my Southern accent was more than he could handle. When I got to work the next day, everyone at GMI took the time to kid me relentlessly. Even Babu mentioned it, but much more politely than everyone else.

I landed in Boston at noon the day before the race and took a cab to the Hampton Inn. The taxi driver could not understand a word I said, and I could not understand him either, although we were both speaking English. So, it was another Mexican standoff, except this time I came prepared. I showed him a copy of the name and address of the motel, and he nodded. When I tried to check in, they could not find my reservation. I showed them the same copy I had shown the taxi driver. He had dropped me at the wrong Hampton Inn; my reservation was at the hotel three to four miles away. I had just paid a small fortune for the taxi and was not going to pay twice. I walked to the hotel, carrying my backpack.

The next morning, I waited my turn as over 6,000 runners boarded the buses for the 26-mile trip to the starting line at a high school in Hopkinton, Massachusetts. During our ride, it started raining. The school's gym was the only building open at the school, and it was packed with runners. It was 39 degrees and was now raining in sheets. If someone before that day asked if I would pay two dollars for a 36-gallon garbage bag, I would have said, "Are you nuts?" I gladly paid, as did every runner around me. I sat in the rain in my garbage bag for hours, waiting on the noon start.

When the start gun sounded, it was still raining, but not nearly as hard. The rain was cold, but I quickly warmed up. It had rained so hard, there was water standing in the street in spots where it came up over the tops of our running shoes. But the rain was not the problem; it was the wind. We ran the whole 26.2 miles straight into a relentless headwind that was constantly pushing against my chest. After the first few miles, the rain turned into a steady, cold drizzle.

As bad as the conditions were, I felt strong for the whole race. Near the seventeen-mile marker, I started up the first of three small hills and could see runners walking up ahead. At the twenty-mile marker, I saw Heartbreak Hill straight ahead; there were now runners walking as far as I could see. I had held my pace through the three small hills, continued to hold it up the half-mile incline of Heartbreak Hill, and for those last six miles to the finish line. My time was three hours, fifteen minutes, which is my second worst time for a marathon. I normally would have been very disappointed with the time, but I was not. I was elated. For the first time ever, I had finished a marathon without hitting the wall.

After Boston, I ran two more marathons: Memphis in December of 1984, and Detroit in October of 1985, which would be my last. I had come to realize that continuously running strong from the start, to the middle, through the wall, and on to the finish line was what was worthwhile and lasting. It wasn't about your overall time, which was so dependent on conditions you had no control over. This is when I decided I had run enough races. I hung up my racing shoes and only ran training runs after that—many, many training runs, with possibly one exception.

Chapter 21

At this point, I need to give an overview of the Tennessee Board of Regents (TBR) and our Satellite Maintenance Operation (SMO), since for the next twenty-eight years, they had such a tremendous impact on my journey. I will describe TBR as it was organized during my time there, not as it is currently. TBR is one of two public university systems in the state of Tennessee, with the other being the University of Tennessee system. The TBR system consists of twenty institutions (six universities and fourteen two-year community colleges) and twenty-seven technology centers, with a combined annual enrollment of over 200,000 students, making it one of the nation's largest systems of public higher education.

The Tennessee SMO was staffed by four IA employees and four TBR employees who were responsible for maintaining IA's Finance, HR, and Student System for the six universities and fourteen community colleges. The following is a listing of these universities and community colleges:

Universities –

Austin Peay State University (APSU)

East Tennessee State University (ETU)

Memphis State University (MSU), which changed its name to the University of Memphis (UOM) in 1994

Middle Tennessee State University (MTSU)

Tennessee State University (TSU)

Tennessee Technological University (TTU)

Community Colleges -

Chattanooga State Community College (CSTCC)

Cleveland State Community College (CSCC)

Columbia State Community College (COSCC)

Dyersburg State Community College (DSCC)

Jackson State Community College (JSCC)

Motlow State Community College (MSCC)

Nashville State Community College (NSCC)

Northeast State Community College (NESCC)

Roane State Community College (RSCC)

Shelby State Community College (SSCC)

State Technical Institute at Memphis (STIM) — Note: SSCC and STIM merged in 2000 to form Southwest Tennessee Community College (STCC)

Volunteer State Community College (VSCC)

Walter State Community College (WSCC)

Although hired early in the process, I was the last member of the SMO team to show up for work. Just like at GMI, those first weeks at TBR were another whirlwind. I initially had no idea the number of institutions that were governed by TBR. When I found out it was twenty, I immediately realized why John Robinson had stressed how important the TBR SMO was to the future success of IA. This one account had to be at least five times bigger than IA's next largest. Now looking back, it is apparent the Holy Spirit had a hand in each decision that led me from Firestone to GMI, from GMI to IA, and from IA to the TBR SMO. There is no way I would have been prepared for this assignment, if not for the three-and-a-half years at GMI and those six months in Rochester. At GMI, I learned IA's Student System from the outside in, and in Rochester I learned it from the inside out. At GMI, the functionally for the users was the driving force; at Rochester, the system's technical capability was what mattered.

For those many years at TBR, I worked with and supported a significant number of state employees, both at TBR and the twenty TBR institutions. There are two who had the most impact on my journey and time at TBR: Elijah (Lige) Hall, the Director of Computer Services at TBR, and Raja Kodali, his supervisor. Whereas Jason Moyer was my lifeline to IA, these two were my lifeline to TBR.

During my first four months, I spent a good portion of my time assisting the institutions with the installation of the SIS+ release. This went smoothly, since the TBR SMO had yet to make any institutional modifications to the system. During all these installs, I realized a large portion of the enhancements made to SIS while I was in Rochester were the result of TBR requests made during the contract negotiations between TBR and IA. Now, any future TBR enhancements would be done by the SMO and would be applied to TBR's version of the Student System, not IA's version. At this point, I could not have fathomed the size and scope of the enhancements that I would make to TBR's Student System over the years.

I need to pause and give a brief job description of my responsibilities as IA's TBR SMO Student Records Technical Specialist. First, I responded to all emails and calls dealing with functional and technical questions, or issues with the Admissions, Records, and Billing components of the Student System. Thank goodness this was long before cell phones and text messaging. So, who and where did these questions and issues come from? The short answer would be everyone and everywhere. Mainly, the functional questions and issues came from the Admission Director, Registrar, and Bursar at each of the twenty institutions. The many technical questions and issues came from each institution's System Tech and Student Tech.

Secondly, I was the lead on all TBR modifications and enhancements to the Admissions, Records, and Business components of the Student System. This brings me to my first enhancement at TBR, and looking back, it fell right in line with my journey. The grade field enhancement at GMI led to my opportunity to work in Rochester those six months and then be assigned to the TBR SMO. Now, the first major enhancement at TBR also dealt with grade processing. I would be hard-pressed to estimate the number of modifications I made to TBR's Student System. But I will give some detail on three: this first one, since it was the first; another that was the most difficult and complex; and finally, one that was so large, it took more than six months to complete and another three months to test and release. In this chapter, I will only discuss the first two—we'll get to the last one in a later chapter.

TBR had a Student Records Committee whose sixty members were the Admission Director, Registrar, and Bursar from each institution. They met four times a year at TBR. I was requested to attend their upcoming meeting, and to keep me from having to sit through their agenda, the first topic was a student records modification to IA's Student System. I will attempt to give a short summary of this request, and the reason it was critical for the TBR institutions.

The TBR admissions guidelines allowed students who did not meet the minimum requirements for admission, based on high school GPA and/or aptitude test scores (ACT/SAT), to have additional testing for placement into their Remedial/Developmental (R/D) program. This program offered less-than-college-level instruction to fill in knowledge and increase the skill level of students deemed unready for college -level coursework. The credit hours for these courses did not count toward the hours required for graduation and their earned degrees. The coursework fell in three areas of study: Math, English, and Study Skills. Based on their scores from this additional testing, the student could be placed by study area in remedial, developmental, or college-level coursework.

IA's Student System had the capability of maintaining two sets of GPAs: an institutional GPA, and an overall GPA. The institutional GPA was based on college-level credit taken at the institution, and the overall GPA included both the college-level institution credit and all transfer credit. The request was to add a combined GPA. This combined GPA would include the college-level institution credit, plus the remedial and developmental credit.

I would need to make modifications for this request in the exact same areas of the Student System where I made the grading change at GMI. This eliminated all the study and research, which was about half the work. The size and scope of these changes would far exceed the other, but it would be applied to the same files, the same online screens, and the same batch and online COBOL programs. I would be adding the following new data elements: combined attempted hours, combined earned hours, combined quality hours, combined quality points, and combined GPA. This would require additional space in the student record file; therefore, I decided to call Jason. We discussed and agreed that I would add my own TBR Student Record's file. Creating a TBR data file accomplished two important objectives: It gave us a secure and safe place to store all future TBR added data elements, and it reduced the time and effort required to install IA's Student System releases.

I guess it would be appropriate for me to explain why they needed the combined GPA. College GPAs are used for graduating with honors, class rank, participating in sports, scholarships, financial aid Pell Grants, student classification, and possibly a few other purposes. The issue was student classification: freshman, sophomore, junior, and senior. I will use an example to the extreme to make my point: After the additional testing, a student is placed in remedial English, Math, and Study Skills (for a total of nine credit hours), which would be followed by developmental English, Math, and Study Skills (for a total of nine credit hours). Therefore, during the student's first year of college, those eighteen credit hours would not be included in the student's institutional GPA. He could pass all his first year's courses and start his second year still classified as a freshman with no credit hours and a zero GPA. If I were a school administrator, I would have a hard time explaining this to the parent, thus the need for the combined GPA.

I need to make a couple of additional points. All students admitted to GMI were ranked in the top five percent of their high school graduating class; therefore, I had never heard the expression "less-than-college-level coursework." The TBR data file became invaluable over the years. We even allocated an area in the file where the TBR institutions could store their own institutional data elements.

Those first few years at the SMO were hectic at times, since there was so much to learn and so many people who depended on my help to resolve many of their day-to-day issues and problems. And that does not take into account the SIS Committee, which continually approved modification requests for the Student System. Most were small and took little time or effort—like adding a new data element to our TBR student record file. But then, when I seemed least prepared for a major modification, they would request my presence in one of their quarterly meetings.

There was one particular modification that turned out to be very difficult, since the code change was confined to one specific and challenging spot. The problem was the needed change was right in the middle of very complex code that performed the student's tuition-calc assessment, and it was only needed for the six four-year universities. The issue dealt with students who took a mixture of undergrad and grad courses in the same semester. TBR had two separate rates per hour for grad and undergrad courses, with the grad being greater, and each having a different twelve-hour max. IA's tuition-calc processed these two sets of courses separately, with the total undergrad hours being capped against the undergrad max, and the total grad hours being capped against the grad hours max. TBR's request was for the undergrad and grad hours to be combined into one total, which would be capped by the grad max.

Here is an example of the issue: In a term, a student takes three undergrad courses for a total of nine hours, and two grad courses for a total of six hours. IA's tuition-calc process would compare the nine undergrad hours to the undergrad twelve-hour max, and charge for all nine hours, since it was less than the max. It would do the same for the six grad hours, comparing them against the grad max, and causing the student to be charged for all fifteen hours. With the modification request, the combined fifteen hours would be compared to the twelve-hour grad max only, causing the student to be charged for twelve instead of fifteen hours. The bursars at the universities were having to make manual adjustments to the tuition-calc assessment to refund this overcharge.

I discussed the issue with Jason before working on the request, and we agreed this would be a very complicated modification. He doubted any other university in the country was combining two different rates against one twelve-hour max; therefore, I was on my own, since IA would not need to put this change into their base code. After I finished the changes and did some limited testing, I installed the modification in the test systems at TTU and MTSU. Both bursars would test different combinations and let me know what worked and what did not, then I would make changes and reinstall. We continued this process until they finally could no longer break it.

I cannot recall how much time was spent on this modification, but if I had to guess, it was at least two months. One additional point: The code change could be (and was) released to all twenty institutions, even though the circumstance required to activate the extra processing (whether the course was grad/undergrad) would never be present at the two-year colleges since they had no graduate-level courses.

Chapter 22

W ithout a doubt, a person is truly blessed if they look forward to going to work each day. So, for all those years at TBR, I felt blessed. I actually told Linda once that I love my job so much, I would work for nothing, if I could afford it. In saying that, there is one thing from day one that I dreaded: the twenty-four-mile drive from Murfreesboro to the TBR office in Nashville. It was not the distance; it was the slow, stop-and-go morning and afternoon traffic. It took close to an hour to get to work on a good day; when there was rain or a wreck on the interstate, it would take at least an hour-and-a-half. If the interstate had to be shut down, then just forget it. I just hated the wasted time waiting in traffic. We started each day at 8:00 a.m. central time, but the TBR institutions in east Tennessee started an hour earlier, since they were on eastern time. I had worked at TBR for about three years before finally getting the nerve to bring up the idea of starting at 7:00 a.m. instead of 8:00 a.m. I discussed it with Raja first, and he did not have a problem, but said Lige would be the one who would have to be convinced. It took a week before I mustered up the courage to ask Lige, and amazingly he gave his okay.

That first week was great; I left home at different times to pinpoint which was best, and found that if I left my house before 6:00 a.m., the interstate had zero traffic. This put me at work by 6:30 a.m., but took the least driving time. That is when I first got the idea of taking my Bible to work. I could read it for at least 30 minutes every morning and start working at 7:00 a.m. At first, I kept it hidden in my desk, but co-workers would come in early at times, while I was still reading. So, I decided to just keep it on the top of my desk. I did this until I retired, and not one person ever objected, even though this was a state office. If you tried to do this now, you would probably be fired, arrested, or both.

This is a good point to introduce what Linda referred to as our "yearly free vacation." Once a year, IA hosted a three-and-a-half-day user's conference for all IA clients worldwide. The conference would be scheduled in a different city each year, and the city needed to have the hotel capacity and a convention center large enough for the event. A couple of months before each conference, IA would send out a notification about the upcoming event. Those who wanted to attend the conference were required to do at least two presentations. So, each year I would send a write-up on my presentations and it would be approved. Then, as Linda put it, we would prepare for our "annual vacation." Our only cost was for her airline ticket; my meal allowance more-than-covered both of us. Over the years, we attended conferences in Atlanta, Orlando, New Orleans, Dallas, San Antonio, Philadelphia, Nashville, Salt Lake City, Phoenix, Las Vegas, Rio, San Diego, San Francisco, Seattle, and Hawaii, visiting some of the cities multiple times.

I cannot recall after which conference this occurred, but it was either the third or fourth we attended. I received a call from the IA Manager for our Eastern Region. He asked what I thought about a business trip to San Juan, Puerto Rico, and then explained how a group of tech users from the University of Puerto Rico had attended one of my sessions at the conference. Their school had been live on IA's Finance, HR, and Student System for over a year, and they had yet to install any IA upgrade releases. After the conference, they called the Eastern Region office to inquire about scheduling these installs by an IA tech. During the time he was talking, I was thinking, "What does this have to do with me?" Then he said, "They want me to send you."

I knew Puerto Rico was somewhere in the Caribbean

Islands and that they spoke Spanish, but that was about it. After explaining the many reasons this was not a good fit (I was too busy, I could not speak Spanish, I only worked with the Student System, and whatever else came to mind), he explained how this was our first client in the Caribbean and its importance to our future expansion in that area.

I landed in San Juan on a Monday morning at about 10:00 a.m. and was greeted by a man holding a sign. Instead of taking me to my hotel, we went straight to their San Juan campus. My return flight was scheduled for Thursday afternoon. I met with their computer staff in a short meeting, and we went over the game plan. In the meeting I learned they were two full releases behind for Student and one each for Finance and HR. We had planned for three installs, not four; therefore, I decided to work longer hours the first couple of days to make sure I would not have to reschedule my flight home. But this was not my only surprise. My computer had a Spanish keyboard. The letters on the keys were in Spanish, and to make matters worse, the location of their letters did not line up with an English keyboard. I asked for an English keyboard but was told they had none. I used sticky notes to cut twenty-six very small labels the size of a key, wrote an English letter on each, and stuck each one on top of the key they indicated. Typing was a pain that first day, since I had to look at the keyboard for each letter as I typed, but it slowly improved. By the next day, I was much faster. Since they had not made a single modification to any system, the installs went smoothly. I still worked until 7:00 p.m. each night, then one of their staff would drop me off at my hotel and pick me up the next morning. By Wednesday, I had completed all the installs and only had to delete some obsolete files that morning. I spent the rest of my last day attempting to show and explain how easy it was to install a release when there were no local modifications. Undoubtedly, the training was insufficient; for the next two years I repeated the trip with pretty much the same results. There was one significant difference: I hand-carried an English keyboard there and back.

The next year, I received my annual call from our Eastern Regional Manager, but this time it was months earlier than normal. I had already planned on telling him they needed to learn how to make these installs themselves—especially since they continued to use IA's base version without any institutional changes. But before I could speak, he explained that the call was not about making my annual trip. They were negotiating with IA for on-site support year-round, kind of like a one-man SMO. This time I knew exactly where he was headed and interrupted to say there was no way I would leave the Tennessee SMO to work in Puerto Rico. He said he had told them exactly what I just said, and that there was a tech guy in our Eastern Region who would be very interested in the position. Even so, they wanted me to bring my wife for a visit, and if they could not convince me to change my mind, they would interview the other tech guy. I reluctantly agreed, and Linda was delighted for another vacation trip. The trip was wonderful, and everyone we met was so friendly and gracious. As we said our goodbyes, I told them how much we enjoyed being on their beautiful island, but Tennessee was our home. They understood.

There were a couple of events that occurred during our stay that set Linda back on her heels a bit. We were staying at a luxury hotel in San Juan that was next to a beautiful beach that reminded me of the beaches in Jamaica. On our first afternoon, we decided to go for a walk, and then go down to the beach and take pictures of the palm trees and ocean. It was a hot, humid, sunny day, and within thirty minutes both of us were dying of thirst. There was a service station directly across the street that had a drink machine outside by the door. Traffic was heavy in both directions, so I told Linda I would run over and get us a drink. I sprinted between the cars, and as I was taking the second bottle from the machine, I heard Linda yelling, "Kennnnth! Kennnnth! Kennnnth!" This was a yell, not a scream, like the dog attack. A car had stopped beside Linda and was now pulling out into traffic. Linda was as pale as a ghost and was talking so fast I could barely understand her. The driver did not consider the possibility that this pretty lady was patiently waiting for her husband to return with a Coke, but thought she was standing there for an entirely different reason. Therefore, he scared her first, and then she scared him when she started yelling my name.

Late that afternoon, their computer center director and his wife picked us up at the hotel and took us into downtown San Juan. This was my first time to go into town; for my previous visits, I only went to my hotel, their campus, and the airport. They were taking us to an exclusive restaurant that featured Flamenco dancers.

As we drove, Linda and I noticed new car dealerships that were surrounded by eight-foot, chain-link fences with coiled, barbed wire at the top. All the storefronts in downtown had metal bars crisscrossing the windows. We said nothing, but this was something we had never seen before.

The food was great and the dancers were stunning, but while we were dining it started raining. We stood under the awning that covered the restaurant's entrance and discussed our strategy for retrieving the car. They wanted Linda and I to wait under the awning while they got the car, but I thought only the men should go. They said this was the wet season, and they were very used to these pop-up showers. I was too; I ran in rain all the time. Finally, we compromised and left Linda waiting under the awning. Well, I guess I had not learned my lesson about leaving Linda alone. When we pulled up, she was talking to a well-dressed lady who, for lack of a better word, looked elegant. As she got into the car, I asked about the lady. Linda replied, "I think she is the restaurant manager. She was telling me how bad the rain is for her business." The computer manager's wife turned to us and whispered, "That lady is a lady of the evening, not a restaurant manager." Linda said "Oh, I was wondering how she could think the rain was hurting her business, with the place being packed with customers."

Except for those two minor incidents, the trip was truly a wonderful vacation. During those few days, they took us on sightseeing trips outside the city. My favorite was touring a rain forest; I have never seen so many beautiful and different types of flowers, trees, and plants. For us, it was a great place to visit, but not to live; Tennessee was home.

Chapter 23

After working at TBR for nearly five years, I received a call from someone at IA who I never expected to call me: John Robinson. I had not spoken to him since my last day in Rochester. I had seen him a few times, at a distance, during some of our user conferences when he would be the keynote speaker. When I answered the phone, he asked how I was doing and said he had been hearing great reports about the success of our SMO. He then said there were a couple of things he wanted to say, "in confidence." If you think that got my attention, you would be right. What in the world would John Robinson need to discuss with me in confidence? I was not looking forward to this conversation. I was thinking, "This is not good." He said that in a few days there was going to be an announcement that IA had been sold to Dun & Bradstreet, and that his last official act as owner of IA was to give me a raise. I told him I had already received my yearly raise last month. He said this was not a yearly raise; it was a personal raise from him to me, and that its purpose was to make me aware of how much he appreciated my attitude and work ethic over the years. I was at a loss for words but attempted to thank him. A few days later, I acted as surprised as everyone else when it was announced that IA had been sold to Dun & Bradstreet. This was no ordinary raise; I will just say it was far greater than anything I could have imagined. I only told Linda, and now, more than twenty-five years later, this is my first time to mention it.

The raise meant the world to us and had a lasting impact on our finances over the years. But that is not the reason for its significance in my journey. It took me awhile before I started understanding why John Robinson took the time and effort to make this unexpected, thoughtful gesture of kindness and encouragement. This was not just about money; he did this to express his appreciation for my effort and the amount was to show how much he valued me as an employee. Letting someone know they are valued is the key. This made me want to treat my friends, co-workers, and family this way, and over the years, I have strived to let those around me know how much I value them.

The Dun & Bradstreet ownership was so short-lived, I did not even know where their home office was located. In less than a year we were sold again to a company named System and Computer Technology (SCT), whose home office was in Malvern, Pennsylvania, near Philadelphia. SCT was a much better fit, since their client base was exclusively higher education, just like IA. But there was one big drawback: whereas IA had hundreds of clients running SIS+, SCT had even more clients running their Student System, which was called Banner. Now we had one company that owned two competing products. It would be many years before this had an impact on my journey, but by then it was significant to the point of affecting the timing of my retirement.

Through the rest of the 1990's, my job was pretty routine. I still did a number of TBR enhancements and state-mandated modifications that required many new TBR data elements, which were easily added to our TBR Student Record file. Linda and I regularly went to our yearly user's conference. With the year 2000 approaching, and the whole country in a Y2K panic, we installed and tested the changes to SIS+ to handle the two-digit to four-digit year issue. In the spring of 2000, Shelby State Community College and State Tech in Memphis merged to form Southwest Tennessee Community College. I had to write a number of COBOL conversion programs in order to merge the two schools' data files into one merged set of files. This required a few trips to Memphis, which allowed me to visit my relatives.

There is nothing work-related that I accomplished over my entire life that compares to this next project I am about to tell you about. It surpassed every other project in terms of the time it took to develop, the satisfaction it gave me, and the way it benefitted so many people. At the beginning of the 2000 fall semester, Lige told Raja and me that he wanted to meet with us the following morning, which was not unusual. But this meeting lasted into the afternoon, and when it ended, we both knew this was no ordinary assignment. In reality, this was more than an assignment; we were being asked to develop a totally new system that would be the online gateway between the nineteen TBR state institutions and a new, state-purchased, online course delivery system called Desire2Learn (D2L). D2L is an integrated learning platform designed to create a location where the students and instructors can interact within online courses.

My biggest challenge is to give you a thorough understanding of this project without being too technical or—Heaven forbid—boring. If the American author Herman Melville can write pages upon pages about the process of butchering whales in such grisly detail in his 1851 masterpiece, *Moby Dick*, then hopefully you can bear with me and steer your way through this section without any mishaps. I will attempt to be as brief as possible, while still giving enough detail so you finish with an understanding of the size, scope, and importance this project had on the TBR institutions, their many students, and my journey.

The TBR had just approved the funding for the development of a Regents Online Degree Program (RODP) and for the software development to support it. At this point, I need to introduce one more member of the RODP development team. Robbie Melton was assigned as the Academic Director for RODP, giving us a team of four: Robbie, Lige, Raja, and myself. Raja would still be supervising, and I would still be supporting student records. When we found out the planned go-live was for the 2001 fall semester, we both thought, "When pigs fly."

The week after our first RODP team meeting, we started developing an academic and a gateway system timeline, with phases containing specific tasks, dates, and deadlines. Robbie's first task was to create a RODP academic committee, containing one academic coordinator from each TBR institution. This committee would be responsible for developing numerous online student support resources, like an online bookstore, a 24/7 help desk, tutoring, test proctoring, and disability services. Those were all important, but their completion for go-live was not critical, since they could be phased in during a semester. The item that was critical was the online courses—not only for the academic RODP committee, but also for our online gateway system.

In order to explain the importance of online courses to our timelines, I need to give a simple definition of "course catalog" and "course term file." A "course catalog" contains all the courses (online and campus) that an institution can offer. A "course term file" contains the specific courses being offered in a given term (spring, summer, or fall). Robbie and the academic RODP committee immediately began developing a list of the campus courses that would be offered online for our go-live term. Once the committee had the list, the courses were divided up, with each institution receiving their "fair share." All nineteen institutions then started developing an online class model of coursework from the traditional version of their assigned courses. The online model had to be flexible, self-paced, and support online lectures, which could be live or pre-recorded. This was a huge undertaking, but with nineteen institutions participating, and Robbie getting help for those who fell behind, they were getting it done.

While Robbie was able to hit the ground running, we had a lot of research to do before even considering creating our functional and technical specs. During the first few weeks, we met with Lige daily, trying to figure out how to get started. We even checked with a number of colleges across the South to pick their brains, but to no avail. Some were in different stages of creating online programs, but our situation was far more complex than their one institution with one campus, or one institution with multi-campuses. No one was dealing with more than one institution; we were navigating nineteen. We had to solve this problem before attempting to write the first line of code.

After much brainstorming, we figured out how to handle this multi-institution issue. For state reporting, each institution already had a state-assigned, two-numeric-digit institution code. It was only being used for reporting and was not contained in any data in their student data files. We decided to make use of this existing code in two places. We added a new two-digit field called Home Campus in the TBR student file, and a new two-digit field called Course Inst in the course term file.

For the Home Campus field, we gave all nineteen institutions a simple COBOL program that inserted their institution code into the Home Campus field for every one of their students. As an example, I will use MTSU (institution code – 24) and JSCC (institution code – 15). Every student registered at MTSU had 24 loaded into their new Home Campus field, and every student registered at JSCC had 15 loaded into their new Home Campus field. Course Inst was different; only the newly developed RODP online courses would have the institution code inserted.

As each RODP online course was completed, Robbie's team would send out a notification to the institutions to add the RODP course to their 2001 fall course term file. In that notification, all institutions would be instructed to insert the institution code for the institution that developed and would teach the course. As an example, if MTSU developed the course and one of their professors would teach it, then all nineteen institutions (including MTSU) would insert 24 in the Course Inst field in their course term file. As I get further into this story, it will become clearer how critical these two new fields were in our ability to successfully process these RODP online courses.

We decided to divide the work into three areas: institution, middle, and D2L processing. I would be responsible for institution processing, Raja and I would work together on the middle, and Raja would be responsible for D2L. I will give detail on institution processing, and touch base on middle and D2L processing. I am only going to describe how this ended up and spare the details of what it took to get there. For institution processing, two COBOL programs were required: one for extracting the RODP course registrations from the institution's data files, and one for inserting the D2L RODP grades back into the institution's data files.

The RODP registration processing program had to be designed to run in two different modes: Add Mode and Change Mode. The institutions would run in Add Mode up until the first day of the term, and then switch to Change Mode. They would run in Change Mode until the end of the add/drop period, which lasted about three weeks. Dropped courses prior to the first day of the term were removed from the student's record; thereafter they stayed in the student's record, but their status changed from E (enroll) to D (drop).

When running in Add Mode, the program pulled every RODP online course in the term that had a numeric value in the new Course Inst field, loaded them into an output file, and copied the file to the TBR server. This would be run five nights a week, Sunday night through Thursday night. For the middle processing, we developed a program that merged these nineteen enrollment files into one large file. A second program would do error checking on the data in the merged file and would create an enrollment report for Robbie, which allowed her to daily monitor the enrollments.

For error checking, each enrollment was compared to our TBR master list of RODP online courses being offered for the term. If the enrollment was not on our list, it was rejected and written to an error report, which was used to notify the school for correction. The enrollment report was critical to our whole operation. Robbie used it to determine when to add additional sections of a course. As a course's enrollment was approaching the class size limit, Robbie and her staff would contact the school that developed and was teaching the course. They would okay the new section if they had a professor who could teach it. If the course could not be covered, Robbie would send out a notification to the schools to close the course, which immediately stopped any additional registrations.

Once the error and enrollment reports were given to Robbie, we deleted the merged enrollment file. This continued daily, right up until the first day of the term. At this point, we notified all the institutions to switch from Add Mode to Change Mode, and the merged enrollment file from that last Add Mode run was uploaded to D2L, using the procedures Raja developed. For Change Mode processing, only those RODP online courses that were either added or dropped since the institution's previous run of the program were selected to be sent to D2L. The added course enrollments were loaded into D2L, and the dropped were removed from D2L each morning, Monday thru Friday.

For grade processing, the professors posted the grades in D2L, and once all grades had been posted, D2L created a large grade file, containing the nineteen institution's student's grades. Raja's procedures moved the file down to our TBR server.

Raja and I developed one last program that read the D2L grade file, then, based on the Home Campus code for each student/grade record, it created nineteen grade files, with each containing the student/grade records for a specific Home Campus. We moved the nineteen grade files to the institution's servers and notified the schools. They loaded the RODP course grades into SIS+ using my ROPD grade processing program. Our biggest problem with grade processing each term was getting the last few tenured professors to post their grades by the deadline.

Chapter 24

Raja and I finished our part with time to spare, and Robbie's team was closing in on finishing their list of RODP online courses that would be available for our first term. We had loaded our SIS+ modifications into the test systems at MTSU and TTU. They were in the middle of testing and had only found a few glitches that were easily corrected. Looking back, we were feeling pretty good about ourselves over how much had been accomplished in such a short period of time: Then the bottom dropped out.

We received a phone call that I have no problem remembering, to this day. MTSU's Bursar called me, and when I answered, TTU's Bursar was on the line, too. They had been testing the tuition-calc assessment against the RODP online courses and found a very serious problem. My immediate thought was, "How can there be a problem with tuition-calc when we had not made any changes to the program?" But after they explained, I realized it was so serious that our go-live was in jeopardy.

SIS+ tuition-calc had the ability to process grad and undergrad courses independently, using different tuition assessment codes. This allowed the bursar to charge one rate for the undergrad and a higher rate for the grad courses. It also had the ability to process campus and online courses independently again, using different tuition-assessment codes. But it did not have the ability to take it to the next level and use different tuition assessment codes for specific RODP online courses. We were probably the only client in the country that needed this additional functionally. Who else but TBR would have courses in their course term file that did not belong to them? The revenue from those courses belonged to the institution that developed and taught the course, which was not necessarily the institution where the student was enrolled. My bursars emphatically explained the reason this was so critical, and it had everything to do with money. If I were speaking now, I would say, "Listen closely," but since I am writing, I will say, "Read closely."

SIS+ could charge and collect tuition for undergrad campus courses and undergrad online courses separately. It could also charge and collect tuition for grad campus courses and grad online courses separately. What it could not do was charge and collect tuition separately for RODP online courses being offered by nineteen different institutions. To say this was a game breaker would be an understatement. The institution's business administrators would not settle for anything less than all the revenue they were due. We would be collecting the RODP online tuition revenue in one large bucket that held all the RODP online tuition revenue; whereas we needed to collect it in nineteen smaller buckets— one bucket for each institution.

As soon as I got off the phone, I told Raja we needed to have a team meeting. During the meeting, we all agreed this had to be fixed quickly; if not, go-live would have to be pushed to the spring term. I felt terrible after all that work by Robbie's coordinators, the registrars, the bursars, and our RODP team of four. There was one good thing that gave me hope: We were still a month from go-live. I felt it was my fault for not realizing the revenue collection could be an issue. For the next few days, I focused on this around the clock, dreamed about it, prayed about it, and whined to Linda about it. Looking back, I cannot say whether it was a combination of the four or just the praying, but when I got up that third morning, it came to me so clear, and the answer dealt with FedEx. In fact, later on I called it, "The RODP Online Tuition Assessment FedEx Model."

Fred Smith, the Founder of FedEx, came up with the

revolutionary method of delivering packages overnight by utilizing a package sorting hub based in Memphis. Since both of us were born and raised in Memphis, I was well-versed on his method. Now my challenge was to explain it.

Once I understood what was needed, I realized half the work had already been done. The Course Inst field that we added to the course term file for identifying RODP online course registrations could also be used, not only to identify the online course to tuition-calc, but to also identify which institution was teaching the course. This would be a tremendous help, and I was already very familiar with the tuition-calc code, based on my modification for capping tuition charges for undergrad/grad combinations. As soon as I got to the office, I started working on the code in the tuition-calc program.

When Raja arrived, he asked what I was working on so frantically. I gave him the short version, then added, "I am going to have this fixed by lunch." Looking back, I know that sounds over-confident, but in my mind, I could see exactly how the code needed to be altered to make this work without creating any problems or issues.

I installed the modification in the test systems at MTSU and TTU, and then gave their Bursars the instructions for setting up the rate table in order to utilize this new functionally. MTSU, TTU, and the four other universities needed one RODP grad entry in their rate table for each of the six universities, and nineteen RODP undergrad entries (one for each TBR institution), for a total of twenty-five. The thirteen two-year colleges only needed nineteen undergrad entries (one for each TBR institution), since their students were not allowed to take the grad courses.

MTSU and TTU spent a full week testing every combination "known to man" (or those they could come up with). After all that testing with no issues, we sent the modification out to the rest of the schools. I asked my two Bursars if they would help the others with the setup and handle any questions, since they were now experts.

I am not going to attempt to explain the details of this change (although I would like to), because it would get too technical. So instead, I will try to explain the results, using FedEx as a model. FedEx uses their planes to fly packages to the hub in Memphis, sorts the packages based on destination, and loads them back on the plane assigned to fly to that specific city. This is exactly how the RODP online course revenue needed to be handled, except instead of planes and packages, we used spreadsheets and wire transfers.

At the end of the course add/drop period, all nineteen institutions had their RODP tuition revenue, along with the revenue belonging to the other eighteen institutions. Each institution created a RODP income revenue spreadsheet, which had this revenue broken down and totaled by institution, based on their Course Inst codes. Each institution forwarded their spreadsheet and all RODP revenue (including their own) to the TBR business office. The business office merged all nineteen spreadsheets, sorted the merged file by Course Inst codes, and totaled by Course Inst code. Then, the business office deducted a TBR RODP operating expense (around 5% to 8%) from each institution's revenue total. Finally, each institution received their exact amount of RODP revenue, based on the number of the online courses taught by their professors. This was much harder to explain than I imagined, and if you had trouble following, so did Linda.

A couple of weeks after the 2001 fall term, we had a RODP term wrap-up meeting. We spent the first part of the meeting bragging on how well everything went, and how well it was received by the schools and the students. Robbie had projected between 3,000 to 4,000 student registrations; we had over 8,000. Robbie's biggest problem was the number of courses that had to be closed, for lack of trained instructors—especially nursing courses. She promised to make this a priority for the upcoming spring term, along with having the institutions continue to develop more online courses.

Looking back, Raja and I were just proud that everything worked so well and had been so well received. At the time, none of us really understood the size, scope, and impact RODP would have on the thousands of students across the state of Tennessee. It took many years of watching it grow and prosper before it began to sink in.

Since explaining RODP was quite the challenge, and surely just as challenging for the reader to understand, I am going to try to impart a final bit of humor on this topic. One of my two sessions at the 2003 SCT's users conference in San Diego was titled, "RODP Online Tuition Assessment: The FedEx Model." I was scheduled to do a session on the first day, and the "FedEx Model" session on the third day. When I finished my first day and got back to our room, Linda told me someone from the conference had called about my Friday session. So many people had signed up for the session, they were moving it to their largest conference room, which would seat 500. Compared to all my previous sessions, this would be the largest, by far. I arrived early and watched as the room filled with bursars and business officers. I was a little nervous at first, but I knew my topic inside out, and once I got started, it was clear sailing. At the end of the session, so many schools wanted a business card, I ran out.

Linda had gone to all my user conferences but had never attended a session. Over the years, she had developed friendships with other spouses, and while we were at the conference all day, they would find plenty to do, from shopping to sightseeing—but not this time. Linda told me she wanted to know what all the fuss was about and had come in as I was starting. She sat in the back of the room and stayed until the end. I was impressed, but what she said next is the reason I am including this part. There was a man in a business suit sitting next to her. After about thirty minutes, he leaned over and said, "I don't know about you, but this is going over my head." Linda replied, "Me too, but I am not supposed to understand. I am his wife." He stayed for the whole session, but never said another word.

In February of 2004, we were notified that SunGard, Inc. was purchasing SCT for $590 million, and our name was being changed to SunGard SCT, Inc. This did not seem any different than the previous times our ownership changed, just another name change. But little did we know, this was the beginning of the end for SIS+. It was in 2005 when we started hearing rumors that SunGard was making plans to give all their SIS+ clients incentives and discounts to migrate from SIS+ to Banner. In order for you to understand their reasoning, I need to give a brief description of these two Student Systems. I would say SIS+ was the more mature product, but others, including SunGard, would say it was aged and past its prime. SIS+ was based on an older technology and was written in COBOL, a 3GL (Third Generation Language), whereas Banner was based on a newer technology that utilized Oracle's relational database management system and uses both 3GL and 4GL languages.

In the Spring of 2006, TBR and SunGard reached an agreement on a contract to migrate the nineteen TBR institutions to Banner. The contract included migration programs to move the SIS student data from SIS+ into Banner and included moving my TBR student records modifications into Banner—but there was plenty it did not include. Immediately, meetings were scheduled, and committees were formed, with the first order of business being a timeline for the migration process. At first, developing the timeline was a nightmare, but once the committee realized migrating all the institutions together would be impossible, a plan began to take shape. The decision was to migrate three universities and seven community colleges the first year, and the other three universities and six community colleges the second year. The next major decision was scheduling the functional and technical training for group one and the TBR SMO.

At this point, I began to realize the sheer magnitude of all the projects that I would be leading or be a part of for the next two years. Although SCT had included twenty of my TBR modifications to SIS+ in the contract, they would only be providing technical staff to duplicate them in Banner. I would be actively involved in each and every one—from writing the functional and technical specs, to doing the testing to ensure each worked and contained all the required functionally. SCT was providing the migration programs to move the SIS+ data into Banner, but I would be the one assisting data migration for ten institutions the first year and nine the next year. Plus, I would need to write my own migration program to migrate the data from our TBR student records file. And finally, I would still be supporting the day-to-day processing of RODP, along with continuing to be the technical support for any institutional issues with our "old worn out" SIS+.

Looking back, I can truthfully say that the two-and-a-half-year period to my retirement reminds me of those last two-and-a-half miles to the finish line in a marathon. I had never worked on so many tasks at the same time in my life; I lived and breathed migration. Linda would say, "Your body is here, but your mind is still at work." The first group was the most challenging by far, but all ten went live on Banner by the deadline.

At this point, Raja announced his retirement. He was going to retire and then work part-time as a consultant for RODP. He had talked to me about doing the same, but I think he knew I was bound and determined to get all nineteen live on Banner by the deadline. Migrating the second group was much easier. All my TBR modifications were now in Banner, including the two programs for RODP course and grade processing and the Course Inst modification to tuition-calc. But now, Raja (part-time Raja) and I were having to handle RODP course and grade processing from both SIS+ and Banner. This created new challenges, but we worked through them. The last nine schools went live by their deadline. I could finally breathe a sigh of relief.

During those last few months before my retirement, Linda and I spent quite a bit of time discussing the idea of my working for TBR part-time as a consultant for RODP. Raja and Robbie had presented their case and were "waiting patiently" for my decision. Linda was not against it; she just did not want the work consuming my life like those last two years. I had no argument for that.

Finally, I met with Robbie, and we had a long conversation. She asked if I understood how valuable our RODP program, especially the Master of Science in Nursing degree program was to the state of Tennessee. I knew it was growing every year, based on the number of new nursing courses being added to our course term file, but beyond that, not so much. Prior to RODP, Tennessee had a critical shortage of nurses across the state, especially in rural areas. As our nursing program expanded, hundreds of RODP nursing graduates began filling positions in hospitals and doctor offices statewide. To make her case, she showed me some of the feedback they received each year from former graduates. It was very impressive; I had no idea the number of lives that were being changed by RODP. Finally, I told Robbie how much I loved working with RODP, but I did not want to put work before my family like I had done for the past two years. At that point, we had a meeting of minds and worked it out. Raja and I would work from home but go to the office for a couple of hours each Monday morning. We would sign one-year contracts, with the first contract being for thirteen months, so it would end on January 1 each year. We would be paid as if we were working half-time, but our hours would be totally flexible, based on getting the job done. Robbie was pleased, Raja was pleased, and after explaining it to Linda and getting her approval, I was pleased.

There was one other point Robbie brought up during our meeting that concerned an event in May of 2008. At the time, I was aware it happened, but was so focused on migration that I never slowed down to recognize its significance. The IMS Global Learning Consortium (IMSGLC) announced the results of their world's annual competition of high impact use of technology to support and enhance learning. The Learning Impact Awards recognize the use of technology to improve learning across all educational or training organizations in all regions of the world. It brings transformative digital learning tools that work together to ease the learning experience for educators and learners, while saving institutions time and money in implementation. The finalists were evaluated according to eight criteria of impact, like improving access to learning, improving affordability of learning, and improving the quality of learning. There were four winning levels: Platinum, Gold, Silver, and Bronze, with three winners chosen at each level. The following are the three winners chosen for the top Platinum level:

Tennessee Board of Regents Online Campus Collaborative – USA

Online Learning Environment at University of Wollongong – Australia

Learn eXact at Volkswagen Group Italia – Italy

Before our discussion, I knew we had won an award, but I had no idea it was against worldwide competition, or that it brought so much recognition to TBR and RODP. To this day, it is hard for me to believe our little team of four developed an online learning system that has been so successful and has achieved such worldwide acclaim.

A couple of weeks before my retirement date, the nineteen TBR institutions held a TBR users conference at MTSU to celebrate their successful move to Banner, with around 400 users from our nineteen institutions gathered in Murfreesboro at MTSU. They used the occasion to throw me one big retirement party, and then the following week, TBR had a second retirement party at our office. I was really uncomfortable with all the attention, but felt so honored to have so many coworkers wishing me the best.

September 30, 2008, was my last day working as part of the TBR SMO. The SMO offices were on the 3rd floor; RODP offices were on the 6th floor. I cannot estimate the number of times each Monday morning I would get off the elevator on the 3rd floor, then have to turn around and get back on the elevator in order to get to the 6th floor. Although Raja and I thought we would work for RODP two to three years at the most, it did not happen. We ended up signing seven one-year contracts, and then finally a six-month contract. This means I fully retired on July 1, 2015, at the age of seventy-three.

I need to explain why it took so long to retire, and I will try to give the short version. Our RODP middle processing was developed and ran on the same outdated mainframe computer that was used by all our institutions for SIS+. Once all were live on Banner, which ran on more powerful IBM computers, everyone got rid of their old mainframes including TBR, except for TTU. They agreed to maintain theirs for our ROPD middle processing, since our processing would not operate on the newer IBMs. This meant TTU's system tech guys had to keep this outdated computer up-and-running for two people: Raja and me. Plus, TBR had to pay yearly maintenance and licensing fees for it. This meant RODP not only needed to replace us, but to replace our RODP middle processing code with something more compatible with Banner and D2L. For the first couple of years, there was little urgency to get this done. By the third year, they realized Raja and I did not intend to work forever, so they added two technical staff assigned to write the programming required to replace our COBOL code. This did not go well, and after a couple of years, they signed a contract with a small computer tech company in Florida to adapt their software package to support the RODP middle processing. After a lot of work, we did parallel testing for the 2015 spring term, and at the end of that term, we officially retired.

I need to make a few points about our working part-time for those seven-and-a-half years. We worked from home, except for Monday mornings. We also worked in the office the week when we processed the ROPD course feed to D2L, and the week we fed the RODP grades back to the institutions. Our daily RODP processing took far less time, since we had a mainframe computer, with all its resources and power fully dedicated to executing our programs. The first time I ran a program on TTU's machine, it finished so fast I thought it had aborted. After checking the log and seeing it had completed successfully, I realized our processing was now going to take one-tenth the time as before, when we were competing with so many other users. In other words, working for RODP did not take up much of my time each day. Compared to those two years migrating to Banner, it felt like I was hardly working.

Chapter 25

I cannot recall exactly when this occurred but can say for sure my age was between fifty and fifty-four. I was still doing my regular training runs, one nine-mile loop twice a week, and two loops on Saturday mornings. Mandy got the bright idea that I should run in one more race, and my question was, "Why?" She said she was too young to really remember the races I ran and would like to go to one now that she was older—and besides, there was a 10K race at MTSU and some of her friends were going. I got the picture and agreed to run one last race. I am aware of previously stating that I hung up my racing shoes and quit running races, but with one exception. Well, this is that exception. The race started at MTSU's campus, looped around Murfreesboro's streets and back to MTSU, with one lap around their track to the finish line. There were far more runners and spectators than I imagined, and unlike other races, I knew no one other than my family. I finished second in the fifty to fifty-four age group, which was a surprise since I had not run a race in many years. Looking back, I think I agreed a little too easily, and it was probably because I wanted to see how it felt. If that was the case, it was okay but gave me no desire to continue racing. I can now truthfully say that was my last race.

There are a couple of more running incidents that happened on training runs prior to the 10K race. Prior to moving to Murfreesboro, all my training runs were outside the city limits with little to no traffic. But my nine-mile loop was within Murfreesboro's city limits with plenty of traffic. Therefore, I had to pay more attention, especially when crossing intersections. At times, a driver would pull alongside, roll their window down, and ask for directions. I was about two miles from my house when a car with two teenage boys—one driving and the other in the front passenger seat—slowed for directions. The one on the passenger side was holding a large drink as he leaned out the window to ask for directions. Instead, he threw the liquid in my face, and both laughed as they sped away. Now you would think that would have made me mad, but it did not. It did startle me, but since it was a very hot day, it was refreshing. Linda found no humor in it at all, and it actually upset her.

The second event occurred fairly close to the drink incident, and it was very hot that day, also. I was running along, minding my own business, when I saw a few quarters on the edge of the street and then dimes, nickels, pennies, and more quarters. I normally never slowed down, ran in place, or stopped—except to avoid being run over by a car. But in this case, I had to make an exception; I could not leave all that change just lying on the side of the road. My problem was my running shorts had no pockets. I began picking up the nickels, dimes, and quarters, but soon both hands were full, and there was more change stretched out on the street. I tossed the nickels, but soon both hands were again full, with still more quarters in front of me. I tossed all the dimes and continued to pick up only quarters. When both hands were full again, I saw no more quarters; it was a miracle. I ran the last two miles with both hands full. I excitedly showed Linda my new-found treasure and laid them out on the table. And if I remember correctly, Linda was much more amused than excited.

One more event occurred during this time that brought back memories when it happened. It was kind of like me running that last farewell race, except it was Linda's turn this time. She had pretty much retired from radio contests, but for whatever reason, she entered one for Billy Joel / Elton John concert tickets. After I came home from work, she asked if I would like to go to a Billy Joel / Elton John concert. Before I could answer, she said her name was in a drawing to win them. I immediately thought, "Why a drawing? They normally give the tickets to the correct caller, not put your name in for a drawing." I know you are thinking this is impossible, but not me. I had long ago figured out that, when it comes to Linda, you can throw out logic, probability, odds, and chance. So, I said, "When are we going?" And she replied, "Oh, I haven't won yet." When they called to confirm she had won, I found out why it required a drawing. I assumed the concert was in Nashville, but it was at the Georgia Dome in Atlanta. The radio station drew three entries, with Linda being one of the three. So, on a Saturday afternoon, Linda and I, along with two couples and one of the DJs from the radio station, took off on a Learjet for Atlanta. A limo was waiting to take us to an Italian restaurant in downtown, and then to the Georgia Dome. The concert was great but lasted over two-and-a-half hours. On our way back to the plane, the limo driver took us through a McDonalds drive-thru, since everyone was starving after the long concert. It was a long, tiring day and around 2:00 a.m., we crawled into bed. Looking back, it was a whirlwind of a day that left lasting memories.

If I were to try to list those choices that had the most influence on Linda and my life, joining WOC would have to be at the top of the list. Linda says it was a match made in Heaven. Looking back and following our journey, it still is amazing to trace all the decisions Linda and I made that resulted in our family ending up in Murfreesboro and then WOC. Remember, we did not visit WOC because it was next on our list; we went to see a concert, so this was no "leap of faith." That is not even considering the fact WOC is an Inter-denominational church, not Baptist. When we joined WOC, the church had a congregation of 300 to 400 members. The building looked like a small airplane hangar, but instead of a small plane, it contained approximately 450 metal folding chairs, which leads into our first church fundraiser. In order to replace those hard, metal chairs with ones that would be more comfortable, each member was asked to pay for their chair and a chair for a future church member. Linda and I gladly donated enough for four. After sitting in our new chairs, Linda said it was the best donation we ever made.

During those early years at WOC, I joined the usher team, mainly ushering at our Sunday night service, but would help during the Sunday morning service when needed. Linda joined children's ministry and worked with preschool children. Together, we joined a weekly Bible study small group, and over the years, we attended many small groups. When a small group grows to the point of needing to be renamed "large group," it had to split into two small groups. With WOC's rapid growth, new small groups were popping up regularly. Our pastor's father started a Tuesday night men's Bible class at a time when Linda and I were not currently in a small group. With Linda's blessings, I joined during the second or third class and attended every class thereafter for a number of years. This class not only increased my desire to better understand the Bible, but it also left me with many fond memories of our meetings and discussions.

After attending the men's Bible class, I think it was in 1994 that Linda and I taught a fourth grade Sunday school class together. The next year, we moved up to teach fifth grade, in order to stay with our group. I would teach the lesson, and then Linda would handle Bible games and activities. I had never taught kids before but thought that I was doing okay—until Linda confided about the number of times someone in the class would ask when Mr. Brooks was going to quit talking so they could play their games. That took a little wind out of my sails, but I don't think that was the reason I went back to ushering, and it is not the reason I am including it in my journey. A number of years ago, I was picking up bulletins left scattered in our sanctuary after the service when a young man approached and said, "Mr. Brooks, you will not remember me, but I was in your fourth and fifth grade Sunday school classes." I did not know him; he was about six -foot-eight, weighed at least 250 pounds, and was built like Grizzly Adams without the beard. When he told me his name,

I remembered it from our class. His family had moved away years ago, but they were back, visiting relatives. It was what he said next that struck me and resonated. He said, "Do you remember the Bible verse magnet you and Mrs. Brooks gave to the class?" I nodded. He then said, "I still keep mine on my refrigerator." I barely remembered, and yet it had that much importance to him. I cannot, to this day, explain why that left me feeling humbled; but when Linda and I discussed it later, we both were amazed at the impact such a simple gift could have on a child.

Chapter 26

This next incident is the first of a sequence of events that occurred over a six-year period, with each having an impact on my journey. They seemed to happen one after the other; therefore, I will do my best to keep them in some sort of order. The first was in the spring of 1996, and it happened on the second loop of a Saturday morning eighteen-mile run. I was about two miles from our house when, without any warning, I felt a sharp, hot pain behind my right knee. At first, I could barely walk, but after a few steps, I was managing. Then, I saw a teenage girl running from her house toward me. She saw me when I stopped running and started limping, and she wanted to drive me home. At the time, I did not want her to have some stranger in her car, so I told her no; I just needed to stretch it out. After about a half-mile, I regretted my reply. Two miles is long and slow when you are dragging one leg.

The doctor said it was a complex tear (multi-tears) of the meniscus versus a simple tear (one tear). Many simple tears can heal without surgery; complex cannot. Complex tears are usually in thin, worn cartilage and will not grow back together. Therefore, they must be surgically trimmed away. I had the surgery two weeks later, then spent three months doing physical therapy and rehab before being given the okay to start back running. Of course, I asked the doctor why it happened. He said I had worn the cartilage in the knee so thin, it put too much strain on the meniscus and was a wreck waiting to happen. Plus, he said I should think about cutting way back on my running, which he had already told me during rehab. I did think about it, but my knee felt so good that I was soon running my regular loops. Looking back, I can see that after that first surgery I was running on borrowed time. But at the time, I was just grateful that I could run again, and everything felt normal.

This next event will require some background in order for you to understand its significance and importance. The first time we heard the word "Hoedown" mentioned was in the fall of our first year at WOC. Of course, we had to ask, "What is that?" We immediately discovered everyone in the church, from the toddlers to the senior citizens, were experts on this subject. As an alternative to trick-or-treating on Halloween, WOC offered an annual celebration for the kids called Hoedown. For the event, WOC rented a large tent for pre school kids and another for elementary school kids. They rented pre school and elementary school games for inside the tents, and all kinds of outdoor games and inflatables. In addition, there were two snack stations, four drink stations, four cotton candy stations, four popcorn stations, a cupcake walk for small kids, a cakewalk for school-aged kids, face painting, cookie decorating, a petting zoo, pony rides, two mechanical bull rides, and more candy than you can imagine. Each game, inflatable, and station required two to six volunteers. The cookie decorating, petting zoo, and pony rides required even more volunteers, and thirty to forty volunteers were needed for parking. One final point: Everything was free.

In 1998, the person who managed the job assignments for the Hoedown volunteers was transferred to France. I was offered and accepted the position, not realizing it would become permanent. Starting on the second weekend in September, a signup card would be handed out with our church bulletin. The card contained the time and date of three setups, a first and second shift for the event, and a takedown shift for the day after the event. It normally took four to five weeks of cards to get enough volunteers. That first year, I had to create the 1998 spreadsheet. After that, I could copy the spreadsheet to the next year (for example, 1998 copied to 1999). Then I would delete all the volunteers, remove the games and inflatables from last year that were not rented for the current year, and finally add all the new games and inflatables. This was much easier than starting from scratch.

I would assign each volunteer a slot in the spreadsheet, based on the selections and preferences they indicated on their card. My biggest problem was the cards that were unreadable, even though in large letters it said, "Please Print Legibly," or something to that effect. I would give those cards to Linda, and she would call the church office and give me the corrections. There was also a spot on the card for the volunteer to make a comment concerning their assignments. Thank goodness most did not make use of this feature, since it created extra work on my part. It was useful for those who had a specific request like cannot work in direct sun, cannot work near animals, cannot lift heavy objects, senior citizen, bad back, and many more. But I also had comments like, "I want to work with my best friend, Johnny." That was a challenge, unless the two cards were attached in the stack. I would set the card to one side, finish entering all the cards from that weekend, then search for the friend's name in the spreadsheet. Most of the time, I would find it and assign them together.

And finally, there were those comments that were from funny to hilarious. A good example dealt with the four cotton candy stations. First, I need to explain how these machines work. The volunteer holds a cone down into the machine as it is spinning the cotton candy, which wraps around the cone. They must do this quickly, one after another, since there were usually lines waiting for their cotton candy fix. The problem was there was no way to work near a cotton candy machine without getting the sticky, sugary, cotton candy in your hair, nose, ears, and pretty much all over your entire body. So, each and every year, the most common comment I received dealt with cotton candy. There were two types of comments: "Anything but cotton candy" and "Cotton candy, cotton candy, please, please." I would set the cards aside into those two groups and enter them once I completed all the no-comment cards. My last point about cotton candy is this: The "Anything but cotton candy" cards were all adults, and the "Cotton candy, cotton candy, please, please" were all high school kids.

Each year, I saved the final version of the spreadsheet that was used to print the assignments for the WOC volunteers. That means I have Hoedown 1998 to Hoedown 2019—that's twenty-one years of spreadsheets on my computer. Over those twenty-one years, each event would be somewhat larger than the year before, with more games and inflatables, more volunteers, larger crowds, and every so often we had to increase the size of the two rented tents. In order to show the size and growth of the Hoedown, the following will be the numbers for 1998 and then for the most recent. For 1998, there were approximately 500 volunteers assigned to work the Hoedown event, and another 200 volunteers for the setup and takedown, for a total of 700 volunteers. I have no saved estimate for the number of people who attended but would guess between 3,000 to 5,000. For the most recent, there were approximately 1,200 volunteers for the Hoedown event, and another 500 volunteers for the setup and takedown, for a total of 1,700. Again, I cannot give an exact number of attendees, but based on the number of cars parked on our campus, there were well over 20,000 at the Hoedown.

There are two reasons I have given so much detail. One is about the kids, and the other is about their parents. When our grandson was a toddler, we started taking him to the Hoedown and continued taking him until he was old enough to go with friends. By then, we were so hooked, we continued to go just to see the joy on the faces of so many kids. Each year, being able to witness our church campus overflowing with children having that much fun made all the hard work worthwhile. And I am not speaking only for myself, but also for our pastor, our church staff, and each person who volunteered.

For the second reason, during all those years, I was also ushering. As an usher, I met visitors and new church members on a weekly basis, and in my greeting, I would always ask how they heard about our church. Many times, the answer would include the word "Hoedown." There were even some visitors and new members who said it was their first time to step on a church campus; this was said, not just to me, but to other church members and church staff. I am sure there must be others who attended Hoedown, then ended up joining one of the many other churches in our area.

The next event began on December 17, 1998, when Nita called to let us know she had to check Mom into the hospital. Lately, she had been having trouble with shortness of breath, but had gotten worse and was now in the hospital on a ventilator to stabilize her breathing. That weekend we drove to Memphis, and it was heartbreaking seeing her hooked to those tubes. She was in the hospital for 114 days, and at times they thought she would not make it. Nita would let me know when the doctor said her condition was critical. I would drive to Memphis, sit with her a few hours, and then drive back home, always thinking that might be my last time to see her. But after all those months, she started improving and was finally taken off the ventilator. Linda and I drove to Memphis the weekend she was released from the hospital. During the drive, Linda mentioned having Mom stay with us for a while, since Nita had been practically living at the hospital all these months. I thought it was a great idea, and when we got to Memphis, everyone agreed, including Mom.

When we got back home, we put her in our bedroom on the first floor, and we moved to one of the upstairs bedrooms. For the first few months she had to have oxygen, and this was long before the small tanks in backpacks; hers was a big tank in a roll-around cart. We got her to walk around the house twice a day, pushing the cart, and she slowly got stronger until the oxygen was no longer needed. She went to WOC with us each week and joined a senior small group Bible study. The teacher and his wife, who lived near us, would take her to and from their Bible study class. On Saturday mornings, Linda would drop her off at our Senior Citizens Center where they would have different activities for two hours. One day when I was picking her up, she said, "Son, you will never guess what we did today." Before I could speak, she said, "Line dancing." Now, I knew that was a country music dance, but for the life of me, I could not picture my mother participating.

In January of 2000, we took Mom back to Memphis to live with her youngest sister, and she immediately went back to her little Pentecostal church. Mandy was expecting our first grandchild in April, and Linda was eagerly planning for his arrival. Prior to knowing about this blessed event, Linda and I had signed up for WOC's annual Israel tour in June. When Linda realized there was a conflict between our trip and his arrival, she cancelled. I volunteered to cancel also, but it did not take much arm twisting to convince me to go alone. Linda was already in the middle of making our house baby-ready, since she would be the one taking care of our grandson while Mandy worked. On April 10, 2000, our only grandchild, Brooks Reed, was born. And in June, I joined a group of approximately thirty-five WOC members for the trip to Israel.

At this point, I must reflect on the impact touring Israel not only had on me, but will have on each and every person who considers themselves to be a Christ-follower, regardless of where they are in their journey. Listening is good, reading is good, but seeing is like that last piece of a puzzle that gives you the full image. We visited all the normal Christian tour sites: Bethlehem, Capernaum, Caesarea, Haifa, Sea of Galilee, Jordan River, Dead Sea, Jericho, Masada, Mount of Beatitudes, Mount of Olives, Garden of Gethsemane, Wailing Wall, the Holocaust Memorial & Museum, and more. Each and every place was special and left lasting memories, but there were three things that were so unforgettable, they now seem etched in my mind and heart.

The first occurred at the beginning of our tour as we were on the bus descending into a valley. With the rapidly-falling elevation, I could see for miles down into the valley. On the left side of the road, as far out as my eyes could see, was a square (or maybe rectangle) patch of bright red. We kept descending, and I kept staring until I could see it was actually a mixture of green and red. Finally, I could make out a two to three-acre field of tomatoes. There were so many ripe tomatoes on each plant that, from a distance, the field looked solid red. Workers were picking the tomatoes, putting them into boxes, and loading the boxes into trucks that were backed up to the edge of the field.

Now, the question is, "Why was this such an unforgettable sight?" Well, first let me tell you that I have planted a small area with tomatoes for many years and still plant them to this day. Therefore, I can appreciate what is required to grow tomatoes. As we drove past that field, it made me connect something from the Old Testament with what I was seeing right before my eyes. All through the Old Testament, the Promised Land is described as "the land flowing with milk and honey." That field, with its drip irrigation and incredibly fertile soil, displayed the fruition of this Old Testament promise to the Jewish people.

The next was during our visit to the Mount of Olives in Jerusalem. We were in the yard of the Church of All Nations, next to the Garden of Gethsemane, admiring the ancient olive trees. There were eight magnificent olive trees with their gnarled, twisted, time-worn trunks that made me feel like I had just stepped back into the very time of Jesus, in the very place Christ prayed the day before His crucifixion. Whether these trees were 1,000 years old or dated back to the time of Jesus was irrelevant; this was the exact spot. If I have ever felt like I was standing on hallowed ground, it was then and there.

Another memorable moment took place on our last full day of the tour in Jerusalem, which was a free day with no scheduled tours. Five of us decided to take a cab to see the Skull of Golgotha. It was not part of the tour, and since this was considered to be the place of Jesus's crucifixion, we decided it would be appropriate to make it the end of our journey. After a short drive, the driver let us out on a street lined by buildings on both sides. As we were paying the fare (and at the same time scouting the terrain), the driver chuckled and said, "I get this same reaction, every time I drop tourists here." I found little humor in his attempt at wit, but he finally pointed at an opening between two apartments and told us to go to the opening and look toward the top of the hill. As I scanned the hillside, the rock formation that resembles a human skull stood out like a sore thumb. In fact, it looked as much like a skull as the four massive sculptures on Mount Rushmore look like our four presidents. It was easy to see why this place was used for crucifixions; without all the houses it could be seen from miles away. To think that 2,000 years later I was viewing the exact spot mentioned in all four gospels was amazing—the perfect ending for our tour.

In the fall of that year, I went to the men's retreat at Fall Creek Falls. Then in December, I had the fatty tumor removed from my neck and a bad reaction to the medicine. In January, I started writing *Running with Angels*. At that point, I changed my running schedule from two loops on Saturday and one loop twice a week, to one loop four times a week. After about three months with this schedule of running and writing, I began to feel a slight pain in my right knee. But I was making so much progress, I ignored it and kept running. By the time I finished writing the book, the pain had gone from a dull ache to a sharp bite each time my right foot hit the ground.

At this point, I told Linda my knee was bothering me a little, and she immediately called to schedule an appointment with my doctor. He was no longer in our area, so we researched and selected a doctor in Nashville. After checking my knee, the doctor said there was a spot in the joint that was bone-on-bone, with no cartilage. He gave me two choices: knee replacement, or a new procedure where he would transfer some of the thicker cartilage from a spot in the joint around to where it was bone-on-bone. He also said my running days were over, either way, and since I was so light, the cartilage transfer could possibly buy five years before needing a knee replacement. That was not a choice I had to ponder; move all the cartilage you want.

The surgery was successful, the pain was gone, and during my follow-up I could see how pleased he was with the results. As I was leaving, he cautioned me for the umpteenth time, no running or walking for exercise, and that I should remember foot strike was my knee's enemy. None of this caught me by surprise; I knew during those last few months I was putting off the inevitable, but I was bound and determined to finish what I started.

At that point, I began working on self-publishing the book. I discovered publishing is more than printing. It includes editing, proofreading, cover design, and formatting (font size, word count, page numbering, line spacing, paragraph breaks, etc.). In other words, formatting is taking the manuscript format and converting it into a book format. This took at least six months, since I was learning as I went.

Chapter 27

In the Fall of 2001, Nita called to let me know she had selected a nursing home for Mom. She had been looking for a couple months and finally found one with an opening that was close and appeared to be suitable. Mom was living with her youngest sister, but her health had reached the point she needed a lot of care and continued to struggle through breathing issues. Once she settled in, we went for a visit. Visiting a nursing home, especially for the first time, is not a pleasant experience. Over the years, I learned the importance of visiting with an uplifting and positive attitude. Everywhere you look there are people in need of a few kind words. Mom was one of the exceptions; she found joy, no matter the circumstances, including living in a nursing home. Her room was small, but there was a window by her bed, a phone, a small television, plus an oxygen machine for when it was needed. Mom never was much of a TV watcher. Instead, she was an avid reader, and amazingly, she could still read without glasses. Since she stayed with Linda and me, I was well aware of her reading favorites: her Bible, the daily local paper, *Guidepost, Reader's Digest*, and novels about pioneer women. Nita made sure she was well-stocked with reading material.

Once Mom went to the nursing home, we made it a point to go to Memphis every Thanksgiving, Christmas, and Mother's Day. We would always go straight to see her, spend a few hours, and then stay with Nita. For a number of years, we were able to check her out for a few hours on those holidays, but after a couple of breathing scares requiring medical assistance, we stopped.

Mom was there for thirteen years, and looking back, I can truthfully say if it were not for Nita, she probably would not have lasted five. I cannot speak for all nursing homes but can for this particular one. I do not think it was one of the worst or the best, but probably just typical. A person's quality of care in a nursing home is directly proportional to the amount of attention they receive from outside, meaning family members, relatives, church members, friends, etc. Unfortunately, there are many in nursing homes who either never have visitors, or they are few and far between. It did not take Nita long to figure this out, and it did not take the director, staff, doctors, nurses, and aides long to discover how interested Nita was in mother's care. She would show up on different days, at different times, two to three times a week. She was on a first name basis with everyone, from the director to the nurse's aides. At times, when mother would need hospital care—whether from flu, a virus, or anything that affected her breathing—Nita was always there to make sure it happened.

Mom passed away in her sleep in the early morning hours on November 29, 2014, at the age of ninety-three. We had traveled to Memphis the Wednesday before, heading straight to the nursing home. As usual, I greeted her with, "How are you, Mom?" She said, "Son, I'm tired. I'm real tired." Usually, her response was, "Oh, I'm doing okay," or something along those lines. I noticed the difference, but at the time did not pursue it. We stayed a few hours, talking, laughing, and (of course) taking pictures. When she began to get drowsy (which was not unusual), we said our goodbyes. We went back home the next day, after a Thanksgiving meal with Nita's family and many other relatives. Nita called early Saturday morning and gave us the bad news. They were all planning to go visit her that morning, so we were the last to see her.

It was like all funerals, solemn and sad. But there is no doubt Mother's long life was a blessing to her children, family, and everyone who knew her. I loved the way she could get to the heart of any issue with a few simple words that immediately brought clarity and resonated, long after the conversation. Like the time when I asked her how she knew where I was, and she replied that she did not know—God did, and she only knew which direction to turn. Or after her first visit to WOC when she said, "Son, your church is full of the Spirit." I guess one of the things I miss the most is Mom calling me "son."

Chapter 28

During 2001, WOC announced a fundraising campaign called "Operation Promised Land" for the construction of two new sanctuaries called New Harvest and All Nations. In order to meet our campaign goal, members were asked to make a three-year commitment pledge. Once we reached our target, WOC held a weekend celebration. At the end of each service, members were given a small hardwood tree, which was to represent the growth of our church. In reality, our small hardwood tree resembled a small three-foot stick—no limbs, no root, and no sign of life. But because Linda was overjoyed with our new WOC tree, I put the stick in our garage instead of throwing it away. In the fall, Linda asked if it was now time to plant our tree, which I had totally forgotten about. Although it took a little time, I realized two things: this was very important to her, and she was dead serious. With my shovel and the "tree" in hand, we circled the house as she decided the perfect spot for planting it, which was on the northeast corner of the house by our bedroom. As I was digging the hole, Linda came back out, looked at the hole, and said, "That is too close to the house. This is going to be a huge tree." So, I doubled the distance to about twenty-eight feet and planted it, knowing full-well this was wasted effort.

Sometime in the spring, as I was cutting the yard, I passed Linda's tree and noticed small, greenish bumps scattered along the top half. By the time I made my loop and was approaching it again, I convinced myself I was wrong; it must have been the way the sunlight was reflecting. But I was not wrong. I stopped the tractor and examined it closely. This was no stick; it was a tree, and it was definitely alive. When I rushed in and told Linda, I was thinking of how excited and surprised she would be. She was very excited, but not surprised.

Our WOC "stick" is now a twenty-year-old black walnut tree, over forty-feet tall, perfectly shaped, with limbs extending out to within five feet of our house. In the fall, hundreds of walnuts cover the ground, yet I have never picked up any of them. This one tree provides food for every squirrel in Hanes Haven. Each year, from November until Christmas, Linda and I watch them come into the yard, pick up their walnut and scamper off. One last point—I know what you are thinking: "Why did you doubt Linda's belief in her WOC tree?" Well, I really wanted to believe, because of her track record, but just could not wrap my head around this one. At the time, in my mind, it just seemed impossible.

In the fall of 2006, I begin to feel a slight pain in my right knee, especially when I went up and down stairs. This lined up with my doctor's timeline of around five years before I would need knee replacement. I had not attempted to run since my knee surgery—in fact, I had not exercised at all. During that time, every person who knew me would end up asking either, "Do you regret running so much?" or "Do you miss running?" My answer to the first question would be, "No, I would not change a thing." For the second, I would say something like, "Yes, but I have accepted it." But what I was actually thinking was, "Yes, more than you would ever know or understand."

Another fundraising campaign at WOC took place in the summer of 2007 called "Invest In Forever," and our church broke ground for a new 2,800-seat sanctuary called Three Crosses. Since our last expansion, I had been the lead usher for the 5:00 p.m. Saturday service in All Nations Sanctuary. Once Three Crosses opened, I just moved to the new sanctuary for the same day and time. We now had four sanctuaries: our original 450-seat sanctuary, now named

Genesis, our 950-seat sanctuary named All Nations, our 450-seat sanctuary named New Harvest, and our new 2,800-seat sanctuary named Three Crosses.

New Harvest was not your normal sanctuary; instead of pews or rows of chairs, it was filled with tables and chairs and two very large screens. Church members could and did sit around the tables and drink coffee during the service. Prior to Three Crosses, our pastor would preach in All Nations and the sermon would be shown on the screens in New Harvest. Once the new sanctuary opened, the live sermon moved to Three Crosses, and New Harvest still got the livestream. Two large screens were added to All Nations, and it was used for weekday events and as overflow for Easter and any special weekend services. We had services on Saturday nights at 5:00 p.m. and 7:00 p.m. and on Sundays at 8:30 a.m., 10:30 a.m., and 6:00 p.m. Our pastor preached at all five services every weekend, which was truly amazing to me.

My knee pain ever-so-slowly grew worse, but a new complication arose. People began asking me a three-word question, which I literally grew to dread. I remember the first time was on a Saturday night while I was ushering in Three Crosses, after I had gone up and down the tiered seating a few times. A church member asked, "Are you limping?" I know I answered, but do not recall my response. After that first inquiry, gradually but steadily, the question kept recurring, but always as a matter of concern and sympathy. Concern is okay, sympathy is not. Linda finally told me to stop complaining about the question and make an appointment with the doctor. We discussed this "doctor issue" for months, but my work was so demanding at the time, I would not even consider seeing a doctor. I was determined to hold out until my retirement date in the fall of 2008. When I was within weeks of the date, I saw the doctor, and it did not go well. He said I definitely needed knee replacement; in fact, I had about the worst-looking knee he had ever seen, and he could not understand how I was walking on it. As he discussed scheduling the surgery, I asked if the knee replacement would take care of the limp. He said not necessarily; my leg was torqued from the knee down. In other words, I was bow-legged on one side. So, in all likelihood, I would still have the limp, but no longer the pain. This was not what I wanted to hear; I would rather keep the pain and get rid of the limp. I declined the surgery.

As a point of humor concerning the limp, I will share another learning moment with my mother. During those years when we were still checking her out of the nursing home for Thanksgiving, and I had accepted the fact that I did actually have a "slight" limp, the following occurred every year. With Nita's house full of relatives, sometime after our meal, Mom would blurt out, "Son, are you limping?" Now, the first time this happened, everyone was polite, and I brushed it off with something like, "Maybe a little." But the next year when she said, "Son, are you limping?" everyone in the room broke out laughing, including myself. Thereafter, I actually looked forward to her question and the room's response.

Chapter 29

At this point, there are a number of important points I want to reiterate. During those years leading up to my retirement, my work steadily required more and more of my time and energy and was gradually wearing me down. Not exercising since my second knee surgery did not help matters. A few years after I stopped running in 2001, I began to notice I seemed to have less and less stamina. All my life I had been very active, even before taking up running. While I was working and running, I would be tired after a long day, but that next morning, I would wake up totally reenergized. Now, at the end of each day I would feel very tired, and the next morning I still felt weary. I knew the cause, and I did not like it. Exercise improves both stamina and endurance; without it, no stamina, no endurance. So, about four years before my retirement, I started formulating plans on how to reverse this lack of exercise once I retired. We all slow down as we get older, but I intended to do whatever was necessary to combat it.

Then, around two years from my retirement, while reading Ecclesiastes, a light came on. I suddenly realized the obvious. I not only needed to improve physically, but also spiritually. Plus, I knew who was my perfect role model for finishing strong spiritually. In Part 2, I will talk about this in depth. This is when I reached the decision that improving physically was good, but improving spiritually was even better. In order to enjoy my senior years, I needed to improve both physically and spiritually. At that time, I had no desire or interest in writing another book; the thought never crossed my mind back then. But if my mother could spend her last thirteen years in a nursing home and never once lose her joy, no matter the circumstances, then I would use her as my role model for improving spiritually. And as far as improving physically, if I had the willpower and mental discipline to train and run marathons, there was no reason I could not apply it toward some other form of exercise.

As I walk through my progress, my intent is to show what can be accomplished if you make it a priority and put forth the effort. My hope is that the details do not come across as bragging. I just want to inspire those who are approaching their senior years to consider some form of exercise of their choice for (slowly) becoming more physically fit. Each person must find what works for them, considering their current condition and health, and should consult with their doctor before developing any exercise plan. One thing I know for sure: If you just sit in a rocking chair once you retire, that will soon be all you can do.

The week after my October 1, 2008, retirement, I took a tour of our local gym in Murfreesboro. I had been planning this for quite a while, but waited until my work no longer consumed my life. I now had the free time to do what I wanted, and not what I felt was an obligation. This was the first time I had ever stepped foot in a "fitness center," since running was all I knew. One of their staff quickly corrected my use of the word "gym" to "fitness center," as we started the tour. It did not work; after over twelve years, I still call it a gym. I spent about an hour going from one area to the next, as he gave his sales pitch and answered my many questions. I noticed a few guys with clip boards working with some of the members as they exercised. These were private trainers who members could hire for individual training. Once we were done, I told him I would come back the next day to meet with the manager, and I would be sure to let the manager know who took me on the tour. After discussing with Linda, I went back the next day, joined, and then asked about speaking to a private trainer. He began by explaining all the benefits of using a trainer, and how he would develop a tailored training program for me that we would adjust each month as I made progress. I explained I just wanted a trainer for one month so I could become familiar with the gym and equipment. We agreed on two, one-hour sessions a week, for the next four weeks.

That first month was a new experience for me, since my belief and knowledge about exercise was in direct conflict with what I was being shown and was witnessing. But the month of training was invaluable because I learned a great deal, including the difference between a dumbbell and a barbell. Not only was I learning from my trainer, but I would closely watch those around me who were working out. It was on my third visit that my trainer finally broke down and asked about my limp. I gave him the short version, and once he understood, we discussed what machines and exercises to avoid. He was very knowledgeable and was really invaluable in getting me comfortable with this new training regimen. This does not mean I agreed with the trainer's primary goals of reducing body fat and increasing muscle mass. My primary goal was to increase my stamina and endurance, like I used to do from long-distance training runs. Unfortunately, running was a thing of the past, but I was determined to develop a training plan at the gym that would give the same results.

I ever-so-slowly begin to develop my routine. Since Raja and I would go to the office for a couple of hours each Monday morning, I decided to go to the gym five days a week, Tuesday through Saturday.

We did our RODP processing very early each morning. The daily loading of the RODP course changes (adds/drops) into D2L put a load on D2L and would slow down response time for the online students. So, what time of the day would you think the fewest students would be logged into D2L? You are correct, 4:30 a.m. As soon as I finished the RODP processing, I would head to the gym, which opened by 5:00 a.m. On Saturday, I would go when they opened at 7:00 a.m. I followed that exact schedule for the next seven-and-a-half years, until fully retiring in 2015.

For those first six months, I experimented with my training routine using some exercises based on my work with the trainer, and some based on what I had observed. I will save you from all my various trials, errors, and adjustments, and just give the hard-earned results.

For aerobic, I selected the Arc Trainer, which is similar to an Elliptical; both are stationary cardio machines that are ideal for increasing endurance and stamina, and for building lower-body strength. But for me, the Arc Trainer gave a better workout and was significantly easier on my knee. In fact, I felt no pain in the joint while using the machine. One section of the gym had a group of lower-body weight machines, which I avoided, and another section had a group of upper-body weight machines. After experimenting with different combinations of the upper-body machines, I selected twelve that each worked different combinations of muscle groups. In the weight-lifting area, I came up with a set of exercises that used both barbells and dumbbells. For these, I utilized the weight bench in order to avoid any exercise that put weight on my knee. And my fourth and final area was for core exercising. Core exercises are those that focus on stabilizing and strengthening the muscles in your pelvis, lower back, hips, and abdomen. I tried a number of core exercises and finally settled on three: abs crunch bench, push-ups, and planks. I chose these three because each not only strengthen your core, but also increase your endurance, stamina, and mental discipline. A plank is an isometric core strengthening exercise that involves maintaining a position similar to a push -up for an extended period of time.

Those eight years without exercising were not helpful to my training startup, but looking back, I think all the years of running did speed up the process. When I reached the point where I felt my endurance level was back on track would be hard to determine, but by the end of my first year at the gym, my training was working smoothly and efficiently. I was back in a groove. After that first year, I settled into the following routine, which I maintained until my full retirement in 2015.

On Monday's RODP processing, I did not exercise. Instead, I would go to the office for a couple of hours. On Tuesday through Friday, I would do RODP processing and then head to the gym.

- Tuesday: one hour Arc Trainer, thirty minutes upper-body machines, thirty minutes core

- Wednesday: one hour Arc Trainer, thirty minutes weight bench, thirty minutes core

- Thursday: one hour Arc Trainer, thirty minutes upper-body machines, thirty minutes core

- Friday: thirty minutes upper-body machines, thirty minutes weight bench, thirty minutes core

- Saturday: three hours Arc Trainer, starting at 7:00 a.m.

For each of the above thirty-minute sessions, I would do different combinations of exercises in order to work out different muscle groups. That way I would never work the same muscle group two days in a row. I would do three sets of twelve reps or three sets of fifteen reps, depending on the difficulty of each exercise. Sets are how many reps you do in a row between short periods of rest. Reps are the number of repetitions of the exercise. For example, three sets of twelve reps would be thirty-six total reps with a short rest between each set of twelve.

On the Arc Trainer, I set the resistance level to sixty percent for the one-hour sessions. For the Saturday three-hour session, I set it to sixty percent for the first hour, fifty percent for the second hour, and forty percent for the last hour. These settings seemed to work best for controlling my fatigue level during that last hour. If you are asking yourself why I did the Arc Trainer for three hours, so was Linda and about everyone else I knew. Well, I tried to design all my workouts to increase my stamina and endurance, but that third hour would also test my willpower and mental discipline. It was not quite the same as that final leg of a marathon, but it definitely required you to finish strong.

There was one other exercise that would really test my willpower and mental discipline: the plank. Normally I would do a set of three planks: a six-minute plank, a five-minute plank, and finally a four-minute plank. But occasionally I would do one ten-minute plank, with the last two minutes pretty much matching the discomfort level of those last two miles in a marathon. That is the reason it was only occasionally.

During those first seven years at the gym, I continued to have a slight pain in my knee, but it was limited to when my foot made contact as I walked. As long as I was not walking, there was zero pain in the knee joint. Since the Arc Trainer does not require foot strike, it caused no pain. It is hard for me to pinpoint when this first started, because it was so gradual, it took a while before I realized it was happening. Some months before my full retirement, I began to notice the pain in my knee when walking was less; it was still there with each step, but to a lesser degree. I immediately concluded that since the pain was less, the limp was less. That seemed perfectly logical to me. I asked Linda if she noticed my limp had gotten better. She had me walk back and forth across the room. "Nope, looks exactly the same." Okay, I know that was wishful thinking, but there is good news. A couple of weeks before my retirement date, when I got out of bed one morning, I instantly realized there was no pain whatsoever as I walked across the room. To this day, I have no knee pain. I still have the limp, and after a long day, my leg grows weary.

One more detail about the knee, and I promise to not mention it again. It was at least a year later when Linda and I were at her doctor's office. About ten years earlier, Linda had back surgery to fuse two lower vertebrae. It was successful in eliminating her lower back pain, but at times over the years she would overdo and cause her back to ache. If it persisted, she would go back to have it checked and usually ended up having an injection, which always worked wonders. That is the reason we were there. After the exam, her doctor scheduled the injection. As we were about to leave, he asked about "my limp." I gave him the short version but did tell him I no longer had any pain in the knee. This got his interest, and he wanted to examine the knee. I agreed, thinking he would make an appointment. That was not the case; he did a full exam of the knee, and then wanted the longer version. When I got to the part about the gym, he was very interested in the amount of time each week I spent using the Arc Trainer. He then showed Linda and me the x-rays and told us why he thought the pain had slowly gone away. Even though the joint was bone-on-bone, amazingly, all those hours on the Arc Trainer had slowly worn the joint perfectly smooth, thus eliminating the pain. That was good news, but he agreed with my other doctors: My lower leg was bowed.

Since June 30, 2015, was on a Tuesday, Raja and I went to the office that morning instead of our normal Monday. This was our last official day to work for RODP, but instead of retirement parties, we said our goodbyes and made sure the tech guys had our phone numbers. I had a few calls during the first couple of months, but soon we were no longer needed, thank goodness. I started working part-time at sixteen and continued working until I was seventy-three. I never planned or intended to work that long, but I have no regrets.

On the following Monday, I made two changes to my training schedule: I reduced my Saturday Arc Trainer session from three hours to two hours, and I moved my Friday training to Monday, making Friday a rest day, like Sunday. These changes were the direct result of some discussions with Linda, as I was approaching that June 30th date. Her argument was that if it had been seven years since I joined the gym, then my body was also seven years older. Her point was that three hours on the Arc Trainer was totally excessive, ridiculous at best, and stupid at worst. I admit to paraphrasing her point, but without changing the meaning or her opinion.

It took more than thirty years, but in 2014, Linda finally agreed to a matter we should have resolved many, many years earlier. I have debated whether to include this in my journey or bite the bullet and embrace it. I even asked Linda to get her opinion. She could not believe I would be considering not including something that meant the world to her. Therefore, I now must include it and in much detail. But first, I need to explain why the hesitation.

Remember in Texas, when I spent my hard-earned money on a beautiful baby blue and white (used) 1958 Thunderbird? I was aware it was wasteful, but now blame it on my youth. Before I start, I want to stress this was nothing like that, and hope once I explain, you will agree. For years, I tried to convince Linda we should replace her stolen wedding ring, to no avail. She always said we had too many other expenses—and besides, it would not be her real wedding ring. But over the years, the "other expenses" argument fell to the wayside. She did wear inexpensive rings on her ring finger, but I always felt guilty for not being more forceful and giving in. As we approached our fiftieth wedding anniversary, it had been over thirty years since the ring was stolen. I finally realized the real reason I wanted Linda to have a quality wedding ring, and it was all because of John Robinson. Remember when John Robinson gave me that special "personal" raise? It was not the extra income that made it so special; it was the idea that he valued me and my work ethic that much. Since then, I have always tried to show my friends and family how much I value them. And now I wanted to show Linda how much I value her; therefore, I decided this was the year. For many years, we had added money to our emergency fund and never had an emergency. Since earning interest from a savings account seemed to be a thing of the past, I was able to convince Linda we could use a portion of our emergency fund to pay for the ring.

Knowing absolutely nothing about diamond wedding rings was a problem, but I fully intended to learn. Therefore, a few months before our anniversary, I began researching books about diamonds. I selected, *How to Buy a Diamond*, by Fred Culler. It took a number of weeks to read, since I was taking a lot of notes. But once finished, I realized buying a quality diamond ring was far more complex than I ever imagined.

Although I still was far from an expert, I felt confident that I would make a good choice, with a lot of effort, my notes, and the book.

I wanted Linda to select the wedding ring, and I would select the center stone. I researched jewelry stores in our area, and selected one in Franklin, which is about twenty-five miles from Murfreesboro. The store was founded in 1929 and is the largest privately-owned jeweler in the country. She looked at ring after ring, and then suddenly, as the sales-rep handed her the next ring, she said, "This is the one." The ring had a cluster of small diamonds, which circled the spot for the center stone. Of course, the price was at the very top of our quoted price range. The sales-rep explained the cluster of diamonds were not diamond chips, but were small high-quality round diamonds, cut precisely like larger diamonds, which is the reason for their sparkle. After discussing the price, which was now less than the original quote, I gave him a choice. If they would reduce the price another ten percent, we were ready to pay in full, or we would visit some additional jewelry stores before deciding on the ring. He left us to confer with management. As Linda was explaining how this was the one, I told her we were definitely going to buy it, but maybe not today. She breathed a sigh of relief. After an appropriate amount of time, he returned and confirmed management had accepted our offer.

Now the real work began. I will omit the details of the weeks of researching and comparing center stones and just give the final results. I purchased the center stone from an online diamond retailer in New York, took it and the ring to our jewelry store in Franklin, and paid them to mount it. The jeweler who did the mounting was impressed with the quality of the diamond but was even more impressed with the price. He said my price was thirty percent lower than the best price his store could offer for a similar diamond. I made Linda wait patiently for our anniversary before allowing her to see the finished product. When I gave her the ring, the look on her face made all that effort worthwhile.

Chapter 30

My journey has reached the point where I made the decision to write this book. If you can recall in the introduction chapter, I said that on our son's fifty-first birthday, January 23, 2020, something happened that shook me to my very core. Two weeks before his birthday, Mark developed a bad sinus infection. He worked with it for a week, but when the medication was ineffective, he called his doctor and was prescribed a different medicine. The following week he stayed home, laid around, and rested, as his doctor recommended. We were calling each day to check to see how he was doing, but he was improving so slowly it became obvious we would have to postpone the birthday celebration. Linda had recently had knee replacement surgery and was still recovering; therefore, our plan was to wait until he felt better and celebrate at our house with a take-out meal.

On his birthday, Mark called around 5:30 p.m., and Linda answered the phone. She quickly turned to me and said, "Mark cannot get up off the coach. He said his heart is racing." She called 911 as I headed to his townhouse, which was less than three miles away. While I waited for the security gate to open, I heard the sirens. By the time I parked, they were pulling in, right behind me. When they checked his heart rate, it was around 150 BPM. I tried to follow the ambulance, but it was raining in sheets, and they were driving so fast, I quickly fell behind. When I got to ER, they took me straight to Mark's room. I called Linda and told her everything I knew up until that point, which was little. Mandy was headed to our house from her job in Nashville but was stuck in rainy afternoon traffic.

The nurse gave Mark an injection to lower his heart rate, but after an hour it was still around 150 BPM. She gave him a second, stronger injection with the same results. While this was happening, the ER doctor was asking Mark numerous questions like was he having shortness of breath, lightheadedness, chest pain, coughing up blood, etc. Mark's answer to all these questions was, "No." Finally, the doctor said he was going to schedule a battery of tests to find out what was causing this elevated heart rate. These tests could take most of the night.

He left the room but returned in a matter of minutes and said he had changed his mind. He wanted to take chest x-rays first before starting the tests. Almost immediately, two male attendants were rolling Mark out of the room with our ER doctor following in close pursuit. Within ten to fifteen minutes, the ER doctor came bursting into the room and said Mark had a massive blood clot in his lung, right up against his heart. He needed emergency surgery as quickly as possible. The vascular surgeon and his team had already been called and were rushing to get to the hospital, since time was critical. I think it was now around 10:00 p.m.

There was so much bad news coming so fast, I was barely able to take it all in. They had taken Mark to a room in ICU to start preparing him for the surgery. Our ER nurse told me that she would take me up to ICU to see Mark as soon as they finished the prep work, and that all the ER nurses were praying for him. Then she told me why they decided to do the chest x-ray before starting the battery of tests. She was outside our room discussing Mark's high heart rate with another nurse when our ER doctor left the room. He stopped and listened as the other nurse was explaining how years ago, she had a patient like Mark who did not have any symptoms except for the high heart rate, and it turned out to be caused by a blood clot in his lungs. Therefore, our doctor immediately scheduled the chest x-rays.

I decided this was as good a time as any to call Linda, although I dreaded telling her. Mandy answered the phone. She said Mom was very worried and nervous, but we should tell her the truth. I agreed.

I do not remember how long I waited until the nurse took me to ICU, but it seemed like hours. When I got to his room, Mark explained what the ER doctor had told him about the surgery. He could not be sedated because his heart rate was so high, but he would be numbed so he would not feel anything. I told Mark I wanted to pray for him, and as I was finishing, the vascular surgeon came into the room and summarized what was happening: Mark had a pulmonary embolism, a life-threatening blockage in the lungs that required emergency surgery. Mark would be awake during the procedure but should feel no discomfort. The surgeon would numb the groin area, make a small incision, guide a catheter (thin flexible tube) into the artery in the lungs to a position next to the clot, and then use syringes to break up and remove the clot. At this point, Mark said, "Doctor I think I am a little nervous." I immediately thought, "Forget nervous! 'Terrified' would be the better term!" As I looked at Mark, in my mind I saw him as a little boy lying on the pavement in his mother's arms waiting on the ambulance. I thought this might be the last time I'd see him alive: It broke my heart.

Our surgeon offered to take me to a private ICU waiting room. As we walked, he said Mark's blood clot was huge and was resting right up against the heart, making it much more difficult to break up and extract. The more they were able to remove, the less clot-buster medicine would be required after the surgery. If that was not bad enough, he said the clot-buster medicine was so strong, it caused death for some patients. For me, the only good thing about our conversation was that Linda was not present to hear it. When we got to the waiting room, he said that after the surgery he would come talk to me right away. Finally, he said, "I am going to do everything possible to save your son's life."

I called Mandy, told her what the doctor said, but skipped the part about the clot-buster medicine. Mandy was coming to be with me as soon as she got Linda calmed down. I sat down and started praying but was so nervous I could not sit still. So, I started pacing the room while praying. I prayed specifically for the Lord to guide the doctor's hands so all of the blood clot would be removed. As I walked and prayed, I kept hearing a light clinking noise; I finally realized it was my teeth chattering. Mandy got there around 1:30 a.m., and that made the waiting so much easier because I had someone to talk to. It was 4:30 a.m. when I saw the surgeon coming down the hall. I waited until he was near the door and could wait no longer. I left Mandy and met him in the hallway. Together, we went back into the waiting room as he told us he removed all the blood clot, and Mark would not need clot-buster medicine. He was going to be fine. That was the greatest news I had ever heard. As I was thanking him, I reached out and he reached out thinking I was about to shake his hand—but instead I gave him a bear hug. This was a few weeks before we knew what the word "COVID-19" would mean.

Mandy and I were allowed to go to his hospital room immediately, since he required no recovery time. Mark was an eyewitness to the surgery, so he gave us a detailed account of the operation, which I will now try to capture:

"At 2:30 a.m., he inserted the catheter. He told me he would put in a contrast dye that would make it easier to see, which would allow him to remove more of the clot. Every ten minutes or so, he would have me hold my breath for ten to fifteen seconds while he used a syringe from a stack on his table to remove some of the blood clot, and then he put in more contrast dye. He kept repeating this cycle for a very long time. Finally, he inserted an IVC filter into the artery, turned, and said he was done, and I was going to be fine. He inserted the IVC filter because there still were some small blood clots in my leg, and he did not want them to get back up into my lungs. He finished the surgery at 4:25 a.m. He told me he got all the blood clot out of my lungs. He held both hands out with them cupped and said that was the

amount of blood he removed from the clot. Finally, he said I would need to come back in a few months to have the filter removed."

Mark was in the hospital for six days—three in ICU and three in a regular hospital room. I stayed with him 24/7 the first four days and came home at night the last two. It had been about a week since Linda's knee surgery. She was able to get around in the house with her walker, but getting her in and out of a car was still a challenge. It was far from easy, but we were able to convince Linda that her going to the hospital was not a good idea.

During the days in ICU, they did a good deal of blood work; at one point, they took 57 small vials of blood for testing. The hospital doctor who was seeing Mark told us he would have to be on a blood thinner for the rest of his life. Once a person has a pulmonary embolism, they have a higher chance of having another. After Mark was released from the hospital, he had to go to his family doctor to have his blood tested to see if it was staying within the too thin/too thick range. At first, this was weekly, but once it started staying within the range, they steadily increased the interval between the checking.

Mark was supposed to have the IVC filter removed after three months, but because of the now full-scale COVID-19 pandemic, it took five months. The doctor went in through the artery in Mark's neck. Mark said he was awake, but they covered his head this time, so he was unable to watch during the forty-minute surgery. I told Mark that most normal patients would have preferred not to see, including myself. After the filter was removed, they scheduled Mark to see a hematologist who did more blood work. The results allowed them to change his blood thinner medicine to one that did not require checking. To Linda and me, this was more than an answered prayer; it was a miracle.

Chapter 31

Before starting Part 2, I want to explain how I came up with the name for my publishing company. The first person I worked for was Hess Hall, when I started washing tractor trailer rigs at sixteen; the last person was Lige Hall, the computer center director at TBR. (I do not consider my part-time work for RODP, since Raja and I were considered as self-employed, on one-year contracts with no benefits.) That takes care of the word "Hall." As far "Haven," this came from the name of our subdivision, Hanes Haven, where Linda and I have lived for over thirty years. Putting these two together, I named the publishing company "Haven Hall." Also, I will confirm which of these three statements is not true:

- I have never drank a beer or smoked a cigarette.

- No one else has ever cut my lawn.

- No one else has ever washed or detailed my vehicles.

If you can recall the 114-day Firestone strike, Linda cut the grass for that whole summer; therefore, number two is not true.

There was something else I discovered while writing about the strike and my mother's stay in the hospital: Both the strike and my mother's time in the hospital were exactly 114 days. I had never realized this. During the strike, I thought those 114 days were an eternity, but never considered that my mother was in the hospital just as long. While I whined to

Linda about the never-ending strike, my mother never complained: She did not allow her extended illness to steal her joy, amazingly.

I also want to give a last update on my exercise routine, before we move into Part 2. As everyone is aware, the COVID-19 virus wreaked havoc with our very way of life. On March 21, 2020, all Murfreesboro gyms were required to close because of COVID-19. The reason I know the exact date is the same reason I know the exact date Mark was rushed to the hospital with the blood clot; each happened on our birthdays—January 23 for Mark, and March 21 for me. I am totally aware that, compared to Mark's lifesaving surgery, my gym closing was pretty insignificant. But it meant I could no longer exercise and would quickly begin losing my stamina and endurance levels, which are so hard to regain, especially because of "old" age.

After two weeks, and with no end in sight for reopening, Linda saw my misery and suggested we use some money from our emergency fund to buy our own exercise equipment. And this truly was an emergency since I was driving her crazy. That made perfect sense. I quickly researched online, and we ordered a commercial-grade stationary bike, a commercial-grade abs crunch bench, a weight bench, some dumbbells, and an exercise mat. The stationary bike was, by far, the most expensive item and was not actually just a bike. Over the years, after Linda's back, shoulder, knee, and foot surgeries, she would go to rehab to assist in the healing. Rehab used the same exercise bike we ordered, which was a versatile, total-body workout machine, with an upper-body exerciser and lower-body recumbent bike. It utilized upper and lower cranks, which allowed for total-body workouts.

On May 1st, they announced the gyms could reopen but with many restrictions including limited capacity. By then, I had all my equipment but was still in the process of developing a new exercise routine. I decided to continue exercising at home since the continued restrictions were in place. I was excited about our new equipment, but I continued my gym membership. I did not want our gym to close because of circumstances beyond their control. It took a number of weeks of adjusting before I settled on a new routine, but after a couple of months, it was obvious this was working well. As an added benefit, Linda was using the total workout machine also, but to a much lesser scale.

Before beginning Part 2, I want to make a number of points that hopefully will give the reader a better understanding of my reasons and purpose for writing this book. As a child, I always had an eagerness to learn—and not just learn but fully understand. Sometimes I took this to the point of being what my mother would describe as "a little too inquisitive," and Linda would describe as "a little too annoying." If you recall, when I was twelve and asked my mother about salvation, she told me to read the four gospels. Looking back, I think she knew by pointing me to the Bible, I would be hooked, not just on the gospels, but the whole book. As you are already aware, it worked.

At the beginning of this book was the list of items that I consider myself to be an expert, and the Bible is not included. The reason I made the list was to contrast it with how I feel about the Bible. The Bible is the one book that, the more you understand, the more you realize you have only scratched the surface. Looking back, as a young Christian, I thought reading the Bible was the same as studying. Finally, I realized reading alone is not enough to increase your understanding—the Bible is too wide, too deep, and too layered. Plus, there were times when I made my running, school, and work far more important than my Bible. After the Israel tour, studying the Bible became a priority. This has been the key to bringing God into my life on a more personal basis. Now I understand how my mother could keep her joy during her thirteen years in a nursing home. She had a personal relationship with God and took that relationship with her into the nursing home. Her Jesus, her Bible, and her persistent, abiding faith sustained her through the bad times as well as the good.

Since I am not a theologian nor a Bible scholar, and I have never taken a course on theology, I hope to relate to the average person. The only study tool I have ever used besides the Bible was a book written by David Pawson titled *Unlocking the Bible: A Unique Overview of the Whole Bible*. He is a British Christian writer who visited WOC sometime close to my first retirement. After his sermon, we bought two signed copies of his book—one for Linda and one for me. I immediately set out to read all 826 pages, which ended up taking a year-and-a-half. Before you jump to the conclusion that I must be the slowest reader in history, I will explain. I read it in conjunction with reading through the Bible. I read Genesis, then his section on Genesis, and followed this routine all the way through to Revelation. This was very beneficial in expanding my understanding of the scriptures. It inspired me so much that a few years later, I read *Unlocking the Bible* again, but this time standalone.

After reading Part 1, I hope you feel like you know me well enough to hear a bit about what I believe. My intent is not to spend time on basic Christian beliefs, which are summarized in the Apostles' Creed:

I believe in God, the Father Almighty, Maker of Heaven and Earth. And in Jesus Christ, His only Son, our Lord; Who was conceived by the Holy Spirit, born of the Virgin Mary, suffered under Pontius Pilate, was crucified, dead, and buried. He descended into Hades; the third day He rose again from the dead: He ascended into Heaven, and sits at the right hand of God, the Father Almighty; from thence He shall come to judge the living and the dead. I believe in the Holy Spirit, the holy Christian Church, the communion of saints, the forgiveness of sins, the resurrection of the body, and the life everlasting. Amen.

Instead, I want to look at two areas in the Bible: those that had the most impact on my beliefs, and those I struggled to understand. I will give my opinions on what I have come to believe and include the scriptures upon which I base my views. I especially cover the topics that gave me the most insight into understanding God's character and His continuous plan for our redemption and salvation.

Since my first retirement, I developed a process for studying the Bible that worked far better than any of my previous methods. I wanted to call them "logical building blocks of understanding," but using the word "logical" might have caused the reader to think I was basing my beliefs on logic, and that would be so far from the truth. It took a number of years of experiencing Linda's uncanny ability to defy logic and consistently being right, for me to realize that logic is more valuable for arranging your ideas and thoughts, than for developing your beliefs. Therefore, as I worked my way through the Bible, I would look for biblical principles, concepts, and truths from the part of the scripture that I was studying. I would then create a "building block" (for lack of a better term) of information, based on my thoughts and ideas concerning that section. Then I'd move on and repeat the process in the next section of reading. I realized my thoughts and ideas from one section made it easier to understand the next section. This was a very slow process, but for the first time, it felt like I was starting to understand the Bible as a whole, instead of isolated, individual segments. The way I will be presenting my thoughts may seem strange at first, but hopefully as they tie together, you will begin to get a picture of what I am trying to accomplish and will continue reading.

In Part 2, titled "My Beliefs," I begin by looking at basic biblical truths concerning creation, God, the Bible, faith, etc. In Part 3, I focus on God's divine plan of redemption, which is shown through the Old and New Testaments. One point before I start: No two people will agree on everything, — especially when it comes to the Bible — but hopefully we can agree on the fact that Jesus is our only path to salvation.

Part 2

My Beliefs

Chapter 32

Creation and the Light of Jesus

Remember how, during my first two years in college, some science professors and even a few math professors made a point to let their students know their anti-God and anti-creation beliefs? During those classes, not one person ever spoke up to challenge their arrogant assertions, including myself. I always felt it was because it might affect my grade. Looking back, that was partly true, but the main reason was I did not have the confidence to challenge them. I cannot explain why, but it bothered me right up to the point when I took the leave of absence from work to finish college.

That's when I enrolled in a math course that was totally unnecessary for my major (I promised to discuss this class earlier, in chapter 9). This was a graduate-level math course that took a deep dive into the concepts, steps, and formulas derived by inference from scientific data that explains a principle operating in nature. I wanted to get a first-hand glimpse into how my professors went about reaching their arrogant conclusions (although this course was not specifically designed to be anti-creation / anti-God). This class taught the mathematical method for developing any type of hypothesis, theory, or law. First, it's helpful to have a basic understanding of what constitutes a hypothesis, a theory, and a law:

- A hypothesis implies insufficient evidence to provide more than a tentative explanation. It is an assumption; an idea that is proposed for the sake of argument, so it can be tested to see if it might be true. An example would be a hypothesis that explains the extinction of the dinosaurs.

- A theory implies a greater range of evidence and a greater likelihood of truth. It is a principle that has been formed as an attempt to explain things that have been substantiated by data. Examples would be the Theory of Evolution and the Big Bang Theory.

- A law implies a statement of order in nature that has been found to be invariable under the same conditions. It applies to principles so firmly established, they are almost never questioned. An example would be the Law of Gravity.

Now I will attempt to give you my thoughts after finishing this course. My first point is concerning creation, based on the very first verse in the Bible:

Genesis 1:1 — In the beginning God created the heavens and the earth.

This verse does not say God formed all things from something; it says   God created all things from nothing. The word "created" in Hebrew is "Barah," which means "called out of nothing." God didn't start with something and then somehow rearrange it. He started with nothing, and out of nothing, He called the universe into being. God did this through the beyond-our-understanding power of His spoken Word.

In contrast, the most common definition of The Big Bang Theory states all current and past matter in the universe came into existence based on a single point of infinitely-dense matter, containing intense heat that exploded, and thus expanded, and continues to expand, forming the universe. That is quite a mouthful to say, but it is even harder to swallow. It sounds so scientific, but for me (and I assume for all believers) there is a huge problem. If the universe was formed from this single point of "very heavy matter," who or what created that matter to begin with?

To me, the controversy as to the timespan for the creation of the universe is irrelevant. What difference does it make, if one day is like a thousand years to God, and a thousand years is like one day to Him (2 Peter 3:8-9)? The main thing we need to understand is **God created it out of nothing**. Therefore, I believe there is no alternative to Genesis, scientifically or logically.

Secondly, God does not deal in hypothesis or theories; He only deals with laws, like the laws of nature (for example, the Law of Gravity). It's His laws that hold everything together.

Colossians 1:15-17 — The Son is the image of the invisible God, the firstborn over all creation. For in him all things were created: things in heaven and on earth, visible and invisible, whether thrones or powers or rulers or authorities; all things have been created through him and for him. He is before all things, and in him all things hold together.

Hebrews 1:3a — The Son is the radiance of God's glory and the exact representation of His being, sustaining all things by His powerful word.

I want to make a point concerning the Big Bang Theory. While researching the topic, I found an article by an anti-creation / anti-God physicist who was attempting to explain the Big Bang Theory in his own words. There was a spot in his explanation that really caught my attention. Near his conclusion, he stated that everything that had been created came from one single source of light. Let's compare his own words to some scriptures:

John 8:12 — When Jesus spoke again to the people, He said "I am the light of the world. Whoever follows me will never walk in darkness, but will have the light of life."

John 1:1-3 — Through Him (Jesus) all things were made; without Him nothing was made that has been made.

Hebrews 11:3 — By faith we understand that the universe was formed at God's (Jesus) command, so that what is seen was not made out of what was visible.

From these scriptures we see that God's (Jesus: the Light of the world) spoken word created the universe. Therefore, if these believers in the Big Bang Theory would just study the Bible, it might help them in more ways than one.

I have one more point that deals with this concept of light. Early in our marriage, Linda and I toured Tuckaleechee Caverns in Townsend, Tennessee, in the foothills of the Smoky Mountains. Our guide led us on a one-and-a-quarter-mile trip through the caverns, which were full of formations of stalagmites and stalactites. Toward the end of the tour, he led our group into a huge cavern called "The Big Room." It was so large, you could probably fit a football stadium inside.

Throughout the tour, the caverns had handrails and strings of electrical lighting. But once we were settled in "The Big Room," our guide said he was going to turn off the lights and then light a candle. The only way you would ever be able to appreciate what I am about to say, would be to witness it yourself. When he turned out the lights, that huge room was instantly pitch dark—with "pitch dark" meaning the absolute, total, absence of light—and even that does not do it justice. Then he lit the candle. That one little candle illuminated the entire room.

I considered that one of the most amazing things I had ever witnessed—both the intensity of the dark, and the amount of light the candle created. As I have studied the Bible and read where Jesus is the Light of the world, I think back to that little candle in the cavern. It always makes me appreciate the tremendous power the light of Jesus projects on our sinful world.

Chapter 33

Who Is God?

I know you have heard the expression that God is "The Man Upstairs," but this is so far beneath who God really is. God is so immense, so powerful, so awesome, so caring, so understanding that there is nothing we can compare to Him. The only way to get to know God is through His Word (the Bible). From there, we can get a true picture of who He is.

The fourth word in the Old Testament (In the beginning God) introduces us to God, who started it all. So, what do we know about God? In English, that fourth word is spelled "God," but in Hebrew it was "Elohim," which is a plural word. So, the very first line in the Bible addresses God as plural, and in the whole first chapter of Genesis, God is referenced as plural:

Genesis 1:1 — In the beginning God... (Elohim — plural)

God is referred to as plural again in chapter one:

*Genesis 1:26 — Then God said, "Let **us** (God) make man in **our** image..."*

But God is also referred to as one God throughout the Bible:

Isaiah 46:9 — Remember the former things of old; for I am God, and there is no other; I am God, and there is none like me.

Psalm 86:10 — For you are great and do marvelous deeds; you alone are God.

James 2:19 — You believe that there is one God. Good! Even the demons believe that—and shudder.

So, why the seeming contradiction? For Christians, this is not a contradiction because the Triune Godhead is a plurality of three persons: God the Father, God the Son, and God the Holy Spirit (see verses below). God the Father is the first person of the Godhead, God the Son is the second person, and God the Holy Spirit is the third. Since eternity is timeless, by definition, then none of the three persons supersede the other; each has no beginning and no end.

Luke 3:22 — and the Holy Spirit descended on him in bodily form like a dove. And a voice (Father) came from heaven: "You are my Son, whom I love; with you I am well pleased."

John 14:26 — But the Advocate, the Holy Spirit, whom the Father will send in my name (Son), will teach you all things and will remind you of everything I have said to you.

Matthew 28:19 — Therefore go and make disciples of all nations, baptizing them in the name of the Father and the Son, and the Holy Spirit.

1 Peter 1:2 — who have been chosen according to the foreknowledge of God the Father, through the sanctifying work of the Spirit, to be obedient to Jesus Christ (Son) and sprinkled with his blood: Grace and peace be yours in abundance.

First, to think you will fully understand the Godhead (Trinity) is to make the mistake of thinking God is fully understandable. Nothing is further from the truth. God is infinite; He is beyond us. So, to understand that God is too immense for our created minds should actually be comforting, not discouraging. It reminds me of a saying I read: "If God was small enough for me to fully understand, He would not be big enough to save me." Therefore, as a Christian, I believe there is one God made up of three co-equal persons (personalities): Father, Son, and Holy Spirit. And those three persons, as one God together, created everything from nothing. For creation, I like to think that God the Father was the thought behind it; God the Son was the voice that spoke it; and God the Holy Spirit was the power that enabled it.

Here are a few of God's attributes that are so special and unique, only He could possess them.

God is sovereign:

Romans 9:19-21 — One of you will say to me: "Then why does God still blame us? For who is able to resist his will?" But who are you, a human being, to talk back to God? "Shall what is formed say to the one who formed it, 'Why did you make me like this?' Does not the potter have the right to make out of the same lump of clay some pottery for special purposes and some for common use?"

Exodus 33:19 — And the Lord said, "I will cause all my goodness to pass in front of you, and I will proclaim my name, the Lord in your presence. I will have mercy on whom I have mercy, and I will have compassion on whom I have compassion."

He is absolutely sovereign; there is no one above Him. His Word is flawless, perfect, and true. He is unchanging in His character, will, and promises. He can do whatever He wants to do. He is the Creator, and we are the created, and it is not for the human mind to question. Afterall, the scripture tells us, *"His thoughts are higher than our thoughts, His ways are higher than our ways."*

God is omniscient and omnipresent:

Isaiah 46:9-10 — Remember the former things, those of long ago; I am God, and there is no other; I am God, and there is none like me. I make known the end from the beginning, from ancient times, what is still to come. I say, 'My purpose will stand, and I will do all that I please.'

Hebrews 4:13 — Nothing in all creation is hidden from God's sight. Everything is uncovered and laid bare before the eyes of him to whom we must give account.

Psalm 139:7-10 — Where can I go from your Spirit? Where can I flee from your presence? If I go up to the heavens, you are there; if I make my bed in the depths, you are there. If I rise on the wings of the dawn, if I settle on the far side of the sea, even there your hand will guide me, your right hand will hold me fast.

God is omniscient, which means "all knowing." He knew everything before creation. God is omnipresent, which means "all present." He is capable of being everywhere at the same time, encompassing the whole universe.

God is infinite:

Psalm 147:5 — Great is our Lord and mighty in power; His understanding has no limits.

Psalm 113:4-6 — The Lord is exalted over all the nations, his glory above the heavens. Who is like the Lord our God, the One who sits enthroned on high, who stoops down to look on the heavens and the earth?

Revelation 1:8 — "I am the Alpha and the Omega," says the Lord God, "who is, and who was, and who is to come, the Almighty."

God knows no restrictions of space, ability, or power. He is without limits. He is everywhere, and there is no place where God is not supreme, for He governs all.

God never changes:

Psalm 102:25-27 — In the beginning you laid the foundations of the earth, and the heavens are the work of your hands. They will perish, but you remain; they will all wear out like a garment. Like clothing you will change them and they will be discarded. But you remain the same, and your years will never end.

Hebrews 13:8 — Jesus Christ is the same yesterday, today, and forever.

God is immutable, which means He never changes—in fact, it is impossible for God to change. Change requires some increment of time, and eternity is timeless. But God does change how He deals with mankind from generation to generation, based on His continuous effort to redeem humanity and restore them back into a relationship with Him.

God loves mankind:

Genesis 1:27 — So, God created mankind in His own image, in the image of God He made them, male and female He created them.

There appears to be a contradiction as I read this verse, but since I do not believe there are any contradictions in the Bible, then it must be a lack of understanding on my part. First, our Triune God is an invisible Spirit and so are His created angels. So, you would think the angels would be considered to be created in God's image, not mankind. But that is not what God said. So, we need to look deeper.

We know our one Triune God is made up of three persons, with each having their own mind, will, and emotions. Humans also have a mind, will, and emotions. I believe it is our mind, will, and emotions that were created in His own image. Through them, we are more connected to God than the angels. Therefore, God can form a more personal relationship with us. This is the reason we can be called the children of God.

1 John 3:1 — See what great love the Father has lavished on us, that we should be called children of God! And that is what we are! The reason the world does not know us is that it did not know him.

Ephesians 3:18-19 — may have power, together with all the Lord's holy people, to grasp how wide and long and high and deep is the love of Christ, and to know this love that surpasses knowledge—that you may be filled to the measure of all the fullness of God.

Romans 5:8 — But God demonstrates his own love for us in this: While we were still sinners, Christ died for us.

John 3:16 (KJV) — For God so loved the world, that he gave his only begotten Son, that whosoever believeth in him should not perish, but have everlasting life.

So, why does God love us? I want to use my own experience in an attempt to respond. When Linda and I were expecting our first child, we were both excited and began preparing for the blessed event. But the moment I held our son in my arms something happened that I had never experienced before. I immediately felt overwhelming love for this little stranger, to the point that it filled my whole heart. Linda described it the same way. Then, when we had our daughter, we felt the exact same way again. I think this is the way all parents feel about their newborns, and from that point forward, you only want the best for them. This is exactly how I think our Triune God feels about mankind. God has the same love for mankind (His created children) as we have for our newborns.

So, we were created in the image of God, given a free will, and have emotions that match His own. God wants someone He can love and see that love returned, based on our free choice. So, when God extends His love toward us, He expects us to love Him in return. But it is each person's choice; we don't have to love God in return. God extends his love to all of mankind, but to our own eternal detriment, we don't have to respond. God has every right to expect us to love Him back, since He loved us first, but He will never force us.

I want to finish this chapter with one final thought concerning our Sovereign God: He knows you to your very core. He knows your every thought and every deed, both the good and bad. He knew you when you took your very first breath and knows when you will take your very last under the sun. So, my question is: Why would anyone not want to have a personal relationship with our Creator?

Chapter 34

The Holy Bible

This topic is dear to my heart, but the magnitude of its importance and relevance is far beyond my ability to express. Therefore, I am going to approach it based on my own personal quest to better understand the Bible. And the key word that would describe my efforts would be "inconsistent." Looking back, it is easy to see that, despite my best intentions, I let life get in the way. My desire was unwavering, but my priorities were far more important—especially work and running. It was only after my trip to Israel that a light came on that allowed me to see the error of my ways. I had never actually studied the Bible. Read it, yes—cover to cover at times. But actually studying it? Never. After my trip to Israel, I made the decision to make studying the Bible a priority.

I have to say, studying the Bible is much different than college course-work study. It took some time before I began to feel comfortable in what I was doing. I started by buying a parallel Bible that had the two versions (NIV and KJV) side-by-side. This is when I begin to realize how much differences in translation can impact the meaning of a verse. I still read the Bible for enjoyment, mainly the King James Version, since that is what I grew up reading. But when studying, I use parallel versions.

It took a number of years to find a method of study that worked for me. I decided to look at the Bible as one giant, complicated, computer program. The Bible has a beginning and an end. A computer program has a beginning and an end. A computer program starts at the beginning and tracks requirements, conditions, and outcomes from the start to a hopefully successful completion. What if I started at the very beginning of Genesis and tracked God's involvement with mankind, from generation to generation, all the way to the end of Revelation? I would be able to collect information about how God dealt with each stubborn generation. As I collected this data, I would be able to develop a pattern on how God reacted to each generation's acceptance or rejection of His will. This data would allow me to see God's character in action and use it to project how God will react to each and every next generation.

As Christians, we believe the Bible is the divinely inspired Word of God (God-breathed) that comes alive to those who read and seek its truths. Without a doubt, the Bible is our greatest resource in improving our understanding of God, yet it is under-utilized by many. Therefore, is there sufficient evidence to warrant the idea that the Bible is, in fact, a book of divine origin? Yes, there is, and the following offers a sampling of evidence that should lead the reader to that conclusion, too.

2 Peter 1:20–21 — Above all, you must understand that no prophecy of Scripture came about by the prophet's own interpretation of things. For prophecy never had its origin in the human will, but prophets, though human, spoke from God as they were carried along by the Holy Spirit.

In this passage, Peter teaches that when you read scripture, what you are reading does not merely come from a man but also from God. The Bible is the writing of some forty different men over a span of approximately 1,600 years. These men came from a variety of cultural and educational backgrounds, writing in different languages (Hebrew, Aramaic, Greek). They spoke with their own language and style. But Peter mentioned two other dimensions of their speaking: *"spoke from God,"* and *"carried along by the Holy Spirit."*

First, they spoke from God; what they had to say was not merely from their own limited perspective. They did not originate the truth they wrote; they were the passageway. The truth in what they wrote belonged to God, not man.

Second, not only is what they spoke from God, but so was how they spoke; it was moved by the Holy Spirit. God did not simply reveal truth to the writers and then depart, hoping they would express it accurately. Peter said while they were writing, they were moved by the Holy Spirit. Therefore, the writing of our Bible was not left to men's human skills; through the centuries, God used the Holy Spirit to move the process to completion.

What about the New Testament writings?

2 Timothy 3:16 — All Scripture is God-breathed and is useful for teaching ...

John 16:12-13 — "I have much more to say to you, more than you can now bear. But when he, the Spirit of truth, comes, he will guide you into all the truth. He will not speak on his own; he will speak only what he hears, and he will tell you what is yet to come."

1 Corinthians 2:12–13 — We have received not the spirit of the world, but the Spirit which is from God, that we might understand the gifts bestowed on us by God. And we impart this in words not taught by human wisdom but taught by the Spirit.

So, from the written Bible itself, Christians can conclude that God (the Holy Spirit) is the Divine Author of all scripture. Therefore, the implications are so profound and far-reaching that every part of our lives should be impacted by the scripture, *"carried along by the Holy Spirit,"* and *"spoke from God."*

Is there other evidence that the Bible is truly God's Word? The following reasons affirm its divine origin:

It's unified without contradiction:

Although composed of sixty-six books that were written by

a multitude of authors over the ages, it all fits together with amazing unity and order as to be a book of divine origin. From Genesis to Revelation, there is an unfolding of the theme of man's fall, God's plan for his redemption, the atoning death of God's Son, Jesus Christ, and the ultimate salvation of the believer. So, how can one not be awed by the consistent evidence of this being the inspired Word of God?

The scriptures dealt with infectious diseases and quarantining:

Instructions concerning infectious diseases and quarantining were part of the commandments God gave to Moses.

*Leviticus 15:13 (KJV) — And when he that hath an issue is cleansed of his issue; then he shall number to himself seven days for his cleansing, and wash his clothes, and bathe his flesh in **running water**, and shall be clean.*

In 1845, a young doctor in Vienna named Dr. Ignaz Semmelweis was horrified at the terrible death rate of women who gave birth in hospitals; as many as thirty percent died after childbirth. Semmelweis noted that doctors would examine the bodies of patients who died, then, without washing their hands, go straight to the next ward and examine expectant mothers. This was their normal practice because the presence of microscopic disease was unknown. Semmelweis insisted that doctors wash their hands before each examination, and the death rate immediately dropped to two percent.

Until recent years, doctors washed their hands in a bowl of water, leaving invisible germs on their hands. However, the Bible says specifically to wash under *"**running water**."*

Instructions concerning quarantining were also part of the commandments God gave to Moses.

Leviticus 13:46 — As long as they have the disease, they remain unclean. They must live alone; they must live outside the camp.

Laws of quarantine were not instigated by governments until the 17th century, although it has been practiced by Israel for centuries. The law of Moses, given 3,500 years ago, incorporated many aspects of modern public health that have only been discovered in the recent past. How can anyone doubt this foreknowledge concerning infectious diseases and quarantining came from God?

Prophecy in the scriptures:

In order for prophecy to be valid, the following criteria must be obtained:

- Proper timing (significantly preceding the fulfillment)

- Specific details (not vague generalities or possibilities)

- Exact fulfillment (not merely a high degree of probability)

All of the hundreds of prophecies in the scriptures fit these standards exactly. Although there are prophecies concerning people and nations, I want to touch on some of the 300+ concerning Jesus the Messiah.

Jesus' birth:

He would be born of woman (Genesis 3:15; Galatians 4:4); of the seed of Abraham (Genesis 22:18; Luke 3:34); of the tribe of Judah (Genesis 49:10; Hebrews 7:14); of the royal lineage of David (2 Samuel 7:12; Luke 1:32); and to the Virgin Mary (Isaiah 7:14).

The timing of Jesus' First Coming:

Christ was to appear during the days the Romans reigned (Daniel 2:44; Luke 2:1); while Judah still had her own king (Genesis 49:10; Matthew 2:22). Jesus would be killed about 490 years after the command to restore Jerusalem at the end of the Babylonian captivity [457 B.C.], which would be in A.D. 30 (Daniel 9:24f).

Jesus' betrayal, death, and resurrection:

It was foretold that the Lord would be betrayed by a friend

(Psalm 41:9) for thirty pieces of silver (Zechariah 11:12). He would be spit upon and beaten (Isaiah 50:6) and in death His hands and feet would be pierced (Psalm 22:16). He would be killed, yet His flesh would not experience corruption, and He would be raised from the grave (Psalm 16:10; Acts 2:22f).

I want to make a final point to distinguish between God's original authors of the scriptures and the translators who converted the scriptures into other languages. The Bible only refers to the original proclamation of the scriptures as being inspired by God. But this does not mean the meaning and truth contained in the original is lost in translation. Most Bible scholars agree that more than ninety-nine percent of the original meaning is retained in good translations, such as the KJV (King James Version), NASB (New American Standard Bible), the NIV (New International Version), and the ESV (English Standard Version). These translations attempt to communicate the meanings of the God-breathed scriptures accurately, without taking away or adding to what the original authors intended.

As I mentioned before, the Bible is layered, with meaning in each verse. And as I study and peel away (garnish) more, it exposes additional truth missed by casual reading. Without question, there are a number of verses in our translated versions where some of the depth and richness of the original texts is lost in the translation. There are also verses where some of the original meaning may have been lost in translation.

The following is an example where some of the depth and richness of the original texts was lost in the translation:

Genesis 1:2 — Now the earth was formless and empty, darkness was over the surface of the deep, and the Spirit of God was **hovering** *over the waters.*

Genesis 1:2 (KJV) — And the earth was without form, and void; and the Spirit of God **moved** *upon the face of the waters.*

This is one of the cases where I think the NIV captures

more of the meaning *("hovering" versus "moved")* than the KJV. For me, the word *"hovering"* has more of an attachment to what is below (creation), whereas *"moved"* has no concern whatsoever to what is above or below (just getting from point A to point B).

The following is an example where some of the original meaning was lost in translation:

*1 Peter 3:7 — Husbands, in the same way be considerate as you live with your wives, and treat them with respect as the weaker **"partner"** as heirs with you of the gracious gift of life, so that nothing will hinder your prayers.*

*1 Peter 3:7 (KJV) — Likewise, ye husbands, dwell with them according to knowledge, giving honor unto the wife, as unto the weaker **"vessel,"** and as being heirs together of the grace of life; that your prayers be not hindered.*

In this case, I think the KJV captures more of the true meaning *("vessel" versus "partner")* than the NIV. The word "vessel" is associated with the physical body, whereas the word "partner" refers more to the entire person. I want to say from experience, if you are ever in a mixed (men and women) Bible study class, and the lesson is 1 Peter, chapter 3, I would recommend using the KJV for that particular class.

There are a few cases in the Bible where the difference in the translation has a significant impact on the meaning of a verse. In a later chapter, I will discuss one instance in particular. If you are keeping up, it will be easy to spot. Finally, the following is a short list of "don'ts" that should prove helpful when reading or studying scripture:

- Don't just read randomly; always read or study with a purpose.

- Don't use the delete button or cross out sections of scripture that do not conform to your beliefs.

- Don't take scripture out of content; you will miss the true meaning and will come away with the wrong message.

- Don't twist or turn the meaning of scripture so it conforms to your narrative or understanding.

- Don't let anyone lead you down a religious rabbit hole or well-worn path to nowhere.

- Don't depend on anyone's divinely-inspired ideas of what God really meant to say.

- Don't get discouraged and give up. Studying the Bible is not a weekend trip; it is a lifelong journey.

In conclusion, God has given us a gift that is priceless. It is clearly the inspired Word of God that should be revered like the holy ground Moses stood on when God spoke to him from the burning bush.

The Bible is not meant to sit on a shelf, collecting dust and pressing dried flowers, but to be read, searched, studied, digested, and understood. It is a treasure chest of truth. You have heard the term, "the gospel truth." It could also be called "stainless steel truth," since it is truth that does not age, decay, or corrode.

Let the Holy Spirit and what you read in the scriptures guide your beliefs. Your Holy Bible and the Holy Spirit will never fail you.

Chapter 35

Eternity Versus Time Under the Sun

In this chapter, we'll discuss one of the foundations upon which my understanding of the scriptures rest. Once I came to an acceptable understanding of this topic, the rest of my thoughts about the Bible more readily fell into place. I am not claiming to be an expert, and each reader will have their own opinion. But I do think studying and forming your own thoughts on this particular topic is a critical step toward a better understanding of the scriptures.

I need to return to "In the Beginning" and look at God's sovereignty and mankind's free will. This is not very easy to do, since there is such a fine line between the sovereignty of God and the free will of man.

First, we need to define "free will." A strict definition would be, "the power or capacity to choose among alternatives or to act in certain situations independently of natural, social, or divine restraints." That's not quite what I was looking for; we need a more biblical definition. For me, the Bible defines "free will" as "the freedom to make choices within the confines and boundaries set by our Sovereign God, in accordance with His sovereign purpose for each and all individuals."

The following are a few of the many verses in the Bible that support the concept of God granting free will to mankind:

Genesis 2:16-17 — And the LORD God commanded the man,

"You are free to eat from any tree in the garden; but you must not eat from the tree of the knowledge of good and evil, for when you eat from it you will certainly die."

Isaiah 55:6-7 — Seek the LORD while he may be found; call on him while he is near. Let the wicked forsake their ways and the unrighteous their thoughts. Let them turn to the LORD, and he will have mercy on them, and to our God, for he will freely pardon.

Deuteronomy 30:19 — This day I call the heavens and the earth as witnesses against you that I have set before you life and death, blessings and curses. Now choose life, so that you and your children may live.

John 7:17 — Anyone who chooses to do the will of God will find out whether my teaching comes from God or whether I speak on my own.

James 4:7-8 — Submit yourselves, then, to God. Resist the devil, and he will flee from you. Come near to God and he will come near to you. Wash your hands, you sinners, and purify your hearts, you double-minded.

Galatians 6:7-8 — Do not be deceived: God cannot be mocked. A man reaps what he sows. Whoever sows to please flesh, from the flesh will reap destruction; whoever sows to please the Spirit, from the Spirit will reap eternal life.

For me, it is hard to understand how God's sovereignty does not cross over and overrun man's free will. If there is any place in the Bible where I think God came close, it would be Saul's encounter with Jesus. When God body-slammed Saul on the road to Damascus, He definitely got Saul's attention, but it was Saul's free-will choice to believe Jesus.

God is absolutely sovereign, that we know for sure. Before creation, God laid out His plan of redemption and salvation to anyone and everyone born under the sun. Somehow, beyond our understanding, He has never taken free will away from mankind to accomplish His purposes.

Now I want to attempt to give my thoughts on our "time

under the sun," compared to God's eternity. Our Triune God is outside of time. He is, *"... the high and lofty one, who inhabits eternity" (Isaiah 57:15).*

Here's another verse that supports this conclusion:

Psalm 90:2 — Before the mountains were born or you brought forth the whole world, from everlasting to everlasting you are God.

This verse is saying that eternity has no beginning and no end (everlasting to everlasting). Therefore, our Sovereign God is everlasting, with no beginning and no end. So, what does that say about the highly-educated skeptic's question, "If God created the universe, then who created God?" It makes the question irrelevant.

I want to compare this idea of a timeless eternity to our time under the sun. We live and age through time with a past, a present, and a future, whereas for God there is no past, present, and future. It is all present (current). Therefore, before the Triune God created the universe, and before Adam was created, sinned, and was cast out of Eden, God knew every single detail for every individual, every nation, and every empire that would occur, from the beginning (creation) to the end of our time under the sun. For us, this is mind-boggling. But if you study your Bible, that is exactly how it is described.

Jeremiah 16:17 — My eyes are on all their ways; they are not hidden from me, nor is their sin concealed from my eyes.

Proverbs 15:3 — The eyes of the LORD are everywhere, keeping watch on the wicked and the good.

Job 28:24 — for he views the ends of the earth and sees everything under the heavens.

Job 34:21 — His eyes are on the ways of mortals; he sees their every step.

So, prior to creation, with that foreknowledge, the Triune God laid out the plan for our redemption and salvation. He did this, taking into account Adam's sin and fall, the continuous rejection by His chosen people, the coming of Jesus of Nazareth to the Nation of Israel, Jesus' rejection as their king, the crucifixion, resurrection, ascension, and Second Coming. Our Triune God knew all of this before mankind's time under the sun began.

Based on my thoughts concerning God's eternity, there is another topic I was able to understand a bit more deeply. I have always understood the fact that God does not change.

Hebrews 13:8 — Jesus Christ is the same yesterday and today and forever.

Since eternity is timeless, it is impossible for God to change. Change requires an increment of time, whether for one second or a thousand years.

This brings up another verse that, at one point, was difficult for me to understand (and which is referenced in many other verses):

Exodus 3:14 — God said to Moses, "I AM WHO I AM. This is what you are to say to the Israelites: 'I AM has sent me to you.'"

Under the sun, I would say "I was, I am, and I will be" (past, present, and future), but in God's timeless eternity, there is no place for past or future, therefore, he just says "I AM WHO I AM." That may seem trifle to the reader, but for me, it was important to my understanding of eternity.

Chapter 36

God's Foreknowledge Versus Man's Free Will

Why are some saved, and others are not? Even though God is sovereign, how do we reconcile the question, "Is God absolute in whom he calls, thus everyone else does not have a chance?" If we are chosen prior to our birth, we have no say in our salvation. To the other extreme, if God is not involved, it is all up to the free will of each individual. Based on my experience when I was saved, it is not either one or the other; it is a combination of both God and my free-will choice.

I want to look at the idea of being called and incorporate it into this discussion of God's foreknowledge versus man's free will. First, God's plan before creation was to offer salvation to everyone, not just some preselected special type or people group. These are just a few of the numerous verses indicating that:

2 Peter 3:9 — The Lord is not slow in keeping his promise, as some understand slowness. Instead, he is patient with you, not wanting anyone to perish, but everyone to come to repentance.

John 6:40 — "For this is the will of my Father, that everyone who looks on the Son and believes in him should have eternal life, and I will raise him up on the last day."

1 Timothy 2:3-4 — this is good and pleases God our Savior, who wants all people to be saved and to come to a knowledge of the truth.

John 3:16 (KJV) — For God so loved the world, that he gave his only begotten Son, that whosoever believeth in him should not perish, but have everlasting life.

These scriptures show that Christ died for all of humanity and His desire is that none should perish. The following scriptures say we were chosen by the divine council of the Triune God before the foundation of the world:

Ephesians 1:4-5 — For He chose us (believers) in him before creation of the world to be holy and blameless in his sight. In love He predestined us for adoption to sonship through Jesus Christ, in accordance with His pleasure and will—

Romans 8:29-30 — For those God foreknew he also predestined to be conformed to the image of his Son, that he might be the firstborn among many brothers and sisters. And those he predestined, he also called; those he called, he also justified; those he justified, he also glorified.

Maybe some biblical scholars can use additional verses to reconcile this seemingly contradiction in scripture. I surely cannot, but I will attempt to explain how I understand this, based on the fact God exists in a timeless eternity. Since eternity is timeless and God is sovereign, prior to creation, God knew every detail for every individual and every nation that would occur, from the beginning to the end of our time under the sun. God knew Abel would have a believing heart and Cain would not. He knew King David would have a believing heart and King Saul would not. God knows all our hearts. So, prior to creation, God knew all who would believe and all who would not.

I want to look at the following verse and attempt to explain how the combination of these four factors make this possible: Sovereign God, timeless eternity, God's foreknowledge, and man's free will.

1 Peter 1:2 — who have been chosen according to the foreknowledge of God the Father, through the sanctifying work of the Spirit, to be obedient to Jesus Christ and sprinkled with his blood: Grace and peace be yours in abundance.

What is this saying? It says God looked from eternity into time and elected to choose us (the believers) through the work of the Holy Spirit. Again, why is this not predestination? It is because God knew every person who would use their free will to choose Him, therefore our Sovereign God elected to offer salvation to those who would accept the offer. We have to decide for ourselves, and yet the moment we decide to believe, God can say, "I chose you." Without faith, this is beyond our understanding, but this is what the scripture says.

I want to look at the following verse, where Jesus is talking to the twelve disciples:

John 15:16 — You did not choose me, but I chose you and appointed you so that you might go and bear fruit—fruit that will last—and so that whatever you ask in my name the Father will give you.

Jesus told the twelve that they did not choose Him, but He chose them for the purpose of bearing eternal fruit. Now, that lines up with God electing to offer salvation to only those who would believe. And this was the same when God chose Noah, Abraham, Joshua, the Judges, the Prophets, and many others. None chose God first; God chose all of them knowing that, based on His foreknowledge, they would choose Him. Is that unfair to those who will never believe? For me, I say no. And remember, someone may be an unbeliever as they are reading this chapter, and yet as they read these words, they suddenly see the light and believe. What happened? Prior to creation, God knew that person would read these words, and based on their own "free will," they would believe. Therefore, prior to creation God chose them. Is that predestination? I don't think so.

Even at twelve years old, the existence of God, and the creation of all things based only on God's spoken word, was not difficult for me to believe; all you had to do was open your eyes and look around. What I had trouble understanding was how highly intelligent people (like some college professors) could deny God's existence and creation. It took many years of studying before I realized why. It is a not a sin problem; it is a heart problem.

Hebrews 3:15 — As has just been said: "Today, if you hear his voice, do not harden your hearts as you did in the rebellion."

Ephesians 4:18 — They are darkened in their understanding and separated from the life of God because of the ignorance that is in them due to the hardening of their hearts.

Proverbs 28:14 — Blessed is the one who always trembles before God, but whoever hardens their heart falls into trouble.

Before I discuss this "heart issue," I want to use an analogy to an event that happened at Firestone when I was a tire engineer. The production area in a large manufacturing plant is not safe—too many things can go wrong. Normally, no visitors are allowed into the plant, but every so often, a department manager or someone at that level of management would have a guest who wanted to tour the plant. In this case, it was a manager's wife and their two small children, a boy and a girl. Well, I ended up being at the wrong place at the right time and was asked to take them on the tour. This tour did not last long. As soon as we entered the production area of the plant, both kids were holding their nose with one hand and had a finger in one of their ears with the other. To make matters worse, the little girl started crying.

As we rushed back into the office area, the wife asked how could I stand that awful smell and that deafening sound? To be honest, I had never thought about it. My major concern was keeping them from being injured. I told her, "You get used to it," which was somewhat true. But actually, it is not that; you slowly, over time, lose your ability to smell that particular odor. You also slowly lose your ability to hear the deep rumble being produced by those huge rubber-mixing machines. Not all of your hearing diminishes, only the specific pitch (frequency) associated with that deep rumble. I guess that is the reason I now wear hearing aids. When I was in the process of buying hearing aids, during the hearing tests, the doctor mentioned the fact that I had lost the ability to hear certain frequencies or tones, which was caused by the years of the deep rumbling noise from the heavy machinery in the Firestone plant. (As a side note, for many years, Linda told me I had "selective hearing" when it came to hearing her, compared to—say—my brother. She implied I would "tune her out" but give my brother my undivided attention. I was glad when the doctor gave me the perfect response: The noise at Firestone must have caused me to have trouble hearing the higher pitch of a woman's voice!)

I tell you this story because this event contributed to creating my theory about spiritual hearing. An unbeliever's ability to hear the voice of the Holy Spirit is directly proportional to the amount the unbeliever's heart has hardened. In other words, as people harden their hearts toward the things of God, they reach a point of unbelief, based on their free-will choice, where there is no turning back. So, the heart of the matter is **guard your heart!**

Chapter 37

Once Saved, Always Saved?

This topic is one that I would rather skip, but it is too important to my understanding of my relationship with God, and it also serves as the foundation for some of my other beliefs. I do feel somewhat biased, since I was raised in a Baptist church. Most Baptists believe in the doctrine of "eternal security" or "once saved, always saved," which is often referred to as the "perseverance of the saints." This means a person who truly repents and turns toward the cross, trusting Jesus Christ as their Savior, will be saved (John 6:37; John 14:6). That salvation is once-and-for-all, eternal, and secure—nothing can take it away.

Thirty years ago, Linda and I felt guided by the Holy Spirit to leave the Baptist church and join WOC, which is inter-denominational. During my studies of the Bible since that time, I have attempted to look closely at my belief in "once saved, always saved," to find scripture that would make me reconsider. After all these years, I can truthfully say I have found nothing to cause me to believe differently. In fact, I have found more scriptures that reinforce my belief. Therefore, I am going to step through this topic and present my case for continuing to believe "once saved, always saved." But, in this case I am not trying to convince anyone to accept my thoughts on this subject over their own. I just want to explain why I still stand behind this belief. I will begin my case for "once saved, always saved" with the following verse:

John 3:36 — Whoever believes in the Son has eternal life, but whoever rejects the Son will not see life, for God's wrath remains on them.

This verse does not say, "Whoever believes in the Son has eternal life (unless they do not do enough good works, or they commit a really bad sin)." And also, it does not say, "has eternal life, until they don't." It just says "has eternal life." I take this literally; you either have eternal life or you don't. I do not see any wiggle room in the verse. And I think what God the Son (our Lord and Savior Jesus Christ) did on the cross is the reason and the only reason our salvation has been secured for eternity.

1 Corinthians 15:2-4 — By this gospel you are saved, if you hold firmly to the word, I (Paul) preached to you. Otherwise, you have believed in vain. For what I received I passed on to you as of first importance: that Christ died for our sins according to the Scriptures, that he was buried, that he was raised on the third day according to the Scriptures.

So, first, to what gospel does Paul refer? The gospel that your salvation comes from believing Christ died for you, was buried for you, and rose from the dead for you. So, what is a true believer?

Romans 10:9-10 — If you declare with your mouth, "Jesus is Lord," and believe in your heart that God raised him from the dead, you will be saved. For it is with your heart that you believe (true believer) and are justified, and it is with your mouth that you profess your faith and are saved.

For me, this is such an important verse in my understanding of a belief that leads to eternal salvation. The verse says, *"with your heart you believe,"* not, *"with your mind you believe."* For me, this is the key to true belief. You must believe from your heart, so your spirit nature comes alive and provides a place for the Holy Spirit to dwell. Since being a true believer does not remove your carnal nature, we still have to wrestle daily against its influence.

Now, wouldn't it be great if God would rid us of our old

carnal nature as He was giving life to the new spirit nature? But no, it all goes back to creation and God honoring man's God-given ability to choose. So, even though a true believer is saved, signed, and delivered into eternity, he is still left with a free-will choice between living in the flesh or living in the Spirit. I do believe that when a true believer sins, it is always from the flesh, not from the Spirit.

I want to share these following verses (from Paul and from John), since they helped me to continue to believe "once saved, always saved":

Romans 8:35-39 — Who shall separate us from the love of Christ? Shall trouble or hardship or persecution or famine or nakedness or danger or sword? As it is written: "For your sake we face death all day long; we are considered as sheep to be slaughtered." No, in all these things we are more than conquerors through him who loved us. For I am convinced that neither death nor life, neither angels nor demons, neither the present nor the future, nor any powers, neither height nor depth, nor anything else in all creation, will be able to separate us from the love of God that is in Christ Jesus our Lord.

Paul is writing to believers (true believers, as defined above), and is saying that none of this will separate us from the love of Christ. God has guaranteed that, because of what Jesus accomplished on the cross, our salvation is secure. Not because of anything we have done (works), but only because of our belief and faith in what Jesus accomplished on the cross (the gospel).

John essentially presents the same conclusion as Paul:

John 10:27-28 — My sheep (true believers) *listen to my voice; I know them, and they follow me. I give them eternal life, and they shall never perish; no one will snatch them out of my hand.*

I want to compare those who, *"listen to my voice"* (true believers), to those who do not *"listen to my voice"* (unbelievers), by comparing Cain and Abel and then

Esau and Jacob. My goal is to try to see this from God's perspective, not mine.

Genesis 4:3-5 — In the course of time Cain brought some of the fruits of the soil as an offering to the LORD. And Abel also brought an offering — fat portions from some of the firstborn of his flock. The LORD looked with favor on Abel and his offering, but on Cain and his offering he did not look with favor. So, Cain was very angry, and his face was downcast.

Hebrews 11:4 (KJV) — By faith Abel offered unto God a more excellent sacrifice than Cain ...

So, why did Cain disregard God's instructions? Maybe Cain felt that since he did not have a lamb, he would have to barter with his brother for one from his flock. This would not be convenient—and besides, why should the offering be something his brother owned, and he did not? But from God's perspective, what does God look for first and foremost? Faith! Cain's problem was the fact he had no faith. He didn't believe what God said, and his total unbelief later resulted in him killing his brother.

For Esau and Jacob, it was the same. In Genesis 25:29-34, Esau gives up his birthright for what? A single bowl of stew! Esau's problem was the same as Cain's: Esau had no faith! He did not believe a thing concerning what God said. And because of his unbelief, Esau could not please God; it was impossible.

Hebrews 11:6 (KJV) — But without faith it is impossible to please him...

God knew Abel and Jacob had a heart open to His Word, and Cain and Esau did not. Why is this so important? Because this early in the Bible, it shows how seriously God viewed unbelief. The point I am trying to make is that, even in the Old Testament, it is not the sin (Cain killing his brother) that separates us from God and salvation, it is that lack of faith and unbelief. See the following two Old Testament verses:

Genesis 15:6 — Abram believed the Lord, and He credited it to him as righteousness.

Habakkuk 2:4 — See, the enemy is puffed up; his desires are not upright – but the righteous person will live by his faithfulness.

I have one more comparison (King Saul to King David) that gets back to my belief in "once saved, always saved." But first I want to state that I do not believe this idea of "eternal security" gives a true believer license to sin without consequences, which I am about to point out as I compare King Saul to King David. As believers, we need to live with the awareness that we still have that old carnal nature, and therefore, we have to be constantly on guard.

I will look at King Saul first, but I will not take the time to attempt to cover King Saul's life in detail. Instead, I will key in on a few areas that show us King Saul—from both God's perspective and from Samuel's (God's prophet) perspective. The people of Israel asked God to give them a king so they would be like all the other nations.

1 Samuel 8:6-7 — But when they said, "Give us a king to lead us," this displeased Samuel; so he prayed to the LORD. And the LORD told him: "Listen to all that the people are saying to you; it is not you they have rejected, but they have rejected me as their king."

This is a good example of where God permits His people to make a choice that is against His sovereign will. He tells Samuel to go find Saul and tell him that God has chosen him to be King of Israel.

As king, Saul started out listening to Samuel and appeared to be "indwelled by the Holy Spirit," but soon he made a very bad decision (a choice of his carnal nature) that reflected the true condition of his heart. Saul was told to wait for Samuel. But the enemy was approaching, and Saul got impatient. He didn't wait.

1 Samuel 13:9 — So, he (Saul) said, "Bring me the burnt

offering and the fellowship offerings." And Saul offered up the burnt offering.

1 Samuel 13:13-14 – "You have done a foolish thing," Samuel said. "You have not kept the command the LORD your God gave you; if you had, he would have established your kingdom over Israel for all time. But now your kingdom will not endure; the LORD has sought out a man after his own heart (David) *and appointed him ruler of his people, because you have not kept the LORD's command."*

So, Samuel was unaware of the condition of Saul's heart, but as the above verses indicate, God was not surprised. With His foreknowledge, God had already prepared for Saul's unbelief. In fact, God had prepared for this prior to creation. Yet, God allowed Saul to reign as king for about forty years, and in the end, Saul took his own life on the battlefield when the battle turned against him.

Now let's look at King David, and then make some comparisons. Again, I will not attempt to cover King David's life in detail. Instead, I will key in on a few areas that show us David's character from God's perspective.

Acts 13:22 (KJV) — And when he had removed him (Saul), *he raised up unto them David to be their king; to whom also he gave their testimony, and said, I have found David the son of Jesse, a man after mine own heart, which shall fulfil all my will.*

God chose David to replace Saul as king when David was still a young boy tending sheep. Why would God still call David "a man after His own heart," knowing David would commit adultery with Bathsheba and have her husband, Uriah, murdered? The answer is God could see David's heart and knew not only that David was a true believer, but had mountain-moving faith, even as a young boy. He had the same kind of faith that Abram had when God changed his name to Abraham and promised to make him the father of a great nation (Abrahamic Covenant).

But God knew much more about David's character. God

knew that David's faith was absolute, even as a young boy when he slew Goliath and said, *"The Lord who delivered me from the paw of the lion and the paw of the bear will deliver me from the hand of this Philistine."*

And David was always thankful to God.

Psalm 26:6-7 — I wash my hands in innocence, and go about your altar, Lord, proclaiming aloud your praise and telling of all your wonderful deeds.

When confronted by Nathan of his sin with Bathsheba, David admitted his sin, asked for forgiveness, and said a prayer of repentance to God.

Psalm 51:1-2 — Have mercy on me, O God, according to your unfailing love; according to your great compassion blot out my transgressions. Wash away all my iniquity.

David was a man after God's own heart because he not only lived his faith daily, but wore it on his sleeve, where it was in full view to everyone who knew him. He was also totally committed to following the Lord through the peaks as well as the valleys. Without a doubt, David was a believer, but the fact that he was a believer did not prevent David from suffering consequences for his actions for the remainder of his life.

I want to discuss some of my takeaways from how God reacted to these men's (Cain and Abel, Esau and Jacob, and King Saul and King David) faith / belief choices.

For Cain and Esau, their total lack of faith and unbelief immediately separated them from any hope or chance for salvation.

For Abel and Jacob, their faith and belief were counted as righteousness and guaranteed their eternal salvation.

King Saul tasted and gained a bit of enlightenment, and even spent a period of time under the influences of Samuel and the Holy Spirit. But it never registered, and he ended up turning his back on their guidance. I know some may believe Saul did just enough to guarantee his salvation, and others believe he was saved, backslid, and lost his salvation. I do not agree with either; I think he was never a true believer, never had a live spirit nature, and therefore was never saved.

Now let's look at King David. At first glance, it would be easy to conclude that David's sins (coveting, adultery, and murder) were far worse than King Saul's. If King Saul was not saved and never gained eternal salvation, then shouldn't King David lose his eternal salvation? Well, I am going to have to say that idea flies in the face of scripture, and therefore makes no sense.

Is the atoning blood of Christ sufficient to not only save us, but also secure our salvation into eternity? Yes, but only for those who have been genuinely saved (true believers). If one is saved and then falls back into living a life of sin, then I question if that person was ever really saved, with King Saul being a good example. For God, there is no question as to whether a person is a true believer since He can see our heart.

In wrapping up this chapter, I want to look at some verses concerning the Book of Life:

Revelation 20:15 — Anyone whose name was not found written in the book of life was thrown into the lake of fire.

John 10:28-30 – "I give them eternal life, and they shall never perish; no one will snatch them out of my hand. My Father, who has given them to me, is greater than all; no one can snatch them out of my Father's hand. I and the Father are one."

So, the Book of Life contains the list of names of all who have eternal security. And I believe that once your name is written there, it is never erased. Who writes a believer's name into the Book of Life? Jesus. And then who is the only one who can remove it? Jesus. So, if Jesus enters it and Jesus removes it, then that would mean Jesus made a mistake. God is sovereign! God cannot make a mistake!

Our eternal security is all about what God does, not what we do. Think of all God does, the moment He saves us and sees our faith. He breathes life into our spirit and puts the Holy

Spirit within us. He forgives us. He places us into the Body of Christ. He redeems us and buys us back. He pays the price for our sins. He justifies us. He sanctifies us. He glorifies us. Now, would God undo all of that?

Chapter 38

Second Chances, Exceptions, God's Will

In this chapter, I want to look at three aspects of God's character, since I see them as being interrelated. All through scripture, we can find examples of God giving us second chances, God making exceptions, and God's sovereign will versus His permissive will. Before I look at some examples, I want to explain this idea of a "sovereign will" and a "permissive will." But first, I must note that this explanation is just my opinion.

Since God is sovereign, He has a perfect will for our lives. But since we have a free will, few follow His perfect will. In fact, the only person born under the sun who continuously followed God's perfect will was Jesus. Therefore, that leaves the rest of us "in a pickle."

The good news is God planned for this prior to creation. Thus, He also has a permissive will, which allows us to "do it our way," extending His love—even when we make choices that are outside His perfect will. In other words, God never forsakes or gives up on us.

I want to start with the Exodus story, since it gives us insight into God's character, as it relates to disobedience and unbelief. Let's start at the point when the Israelites reach Kadesh-Barnea, which borders the Promised Land.

Deuteronomy 1:19-21 — Then, as the Lord our God commanded us, we set out from Horeb and went toward the hill country of the Amorites through all that vast and dreadful wilderness that you have seen, and so we reached Kadesh Barnea. Then I said to you, "You have reached the hill country of the Amorites, which the LORD *our God is giving us. See, the* LORD *your God has given you the land. Go up and take possession of it as the* LORD*, the God of your ancestors, told you. Do not be afraid; do not be discouraged."*

Notice how God is not only telling them to go up and take possession of this land but is also reassuring them with these verses.

Exodus 23:27-30 — I will send my terror ahead of you and throw into confusion every nation you encounter. I will make all your enemies turn their backs and run. I will send the hornet ahead of you to drive the Hivites, Canaanites and Hittites out of your way. But I will not drive them out in a single year, because the land would become desolate and the wild animals too numerous for you. Little by little I will drive them out before you, until you have increased enough to take possession of the land.

The Israelites experienced the miraculous exodus out of their slavery in Egypt. They walked through the Red Sea on dry ground and watched the Red Sea sweep over the Egyptian army and carry them down to their death. They saw the pillar of fire by night, and the pillar of cloud by day. They saw the thunder, lighting, and fire on Mount Sinai. They witnessed miracle after miracle during their journey through the desert and wilderness, and then they finally reached the borders of the Promised Land. This was the land of milk and honey; the land God promised to the descendants of Abraham.

After all these miracles, what was the Israelites' response to God?

Deuteronomy 1:22-23 — Then all of you came to me (Moses) and said, "Let us send men ahead to spy out the land for us and bring back a report about the route we are to take and the towns we will come to." The idea seemed good to me; so I selected twelve of you, one man from each tribe.

This plan to send spies did not directly come from Moses but from the people (the Israelites). God told them to just go up and take possession of the land, but the people suggested this plan to Moses, who in turn presented it to God.

Numbers 13:1-2 — The LORD said to Moses, "Send some men to explore the land of Canaan, which I am giving to the Israelites. From each ancestral tribe send one of its leaders."

Now, this is something that I think can be easily overlooked. Did God intend for those twelve men to go into the Promised Land as spies? No. The sovereign will of God was for the whole nation to go, based on their faith and belief, knowing He would drive out their enemies, because He said He would. All they had to do was go in and occupy their land. But God, based on His "permissive will," permits His people to make a choice that is against His sovereign will, and therefore instructs Moses to allow it. Why? Because throughout scripture, God allows both individuals and nations to exercise their free will, knowing that at times it is to their own detriment. Yet God does not forsake us but continues to extend his love to all of mankind.

They spent forty days spying out the land, and when they returned, this is what they told Moses and the Israelites:

Numbers 13:26-29 — They came back to Moses and Aaron and the whole Israelite community at Kadesh in the Desert of Paran. There they reported to them and to the whole assembly and showed them the fruit of the land. They gave Moses this account: "We went into the land to which you sent us, and it does flow with milk and honey! Here is its fruit. But the people who live there are powerful, and the cities are fortified and very large. We even saw descendants of Anak there. The Amalekites live in the Negev; the Hittites, Jebusites and Amorites live in the hill country; and the Canaanites live near the sea and along the Jordan."

They reported it truly flows with milk and honey. They confirmed everything God had said about the Promised Land was true, but was that enough to convince them to believe they could just go in and take possession of the land? No!

- Despite God's promise, the people who dwell in the land are strong.

- Despite God's promise, the cities are fortified and very large.

- Despite God's promise, we saw the descendants of Anak (a tribe of large men).

- Despite God's promise, they dwell all over the land (there is nowhere for us to live).

This was the report from ten of the twelve; a report that recognizes the faithfulness and truth of God's promise concerning the land, and yet it said, "Despite all that ..." And this was the Israelites' response:

Numbers 14:2 — All the Israelites grumbled against Moses and Aaron, and the whole assembly said to them, "If only we had died in Egypt! Or in this wilderness!"

Of the twelve who were sent out, only Caleb and Joshua expressed faith that, with God's assistance, Israel could occupy the land.

Numbers 14:6-9 — Joshua son of Nun and Caleb son of Jephunneh, who were among those who had explored the land, tore their clothes and said to the entire Israelite assembly, "The land we passed through and explored is exceedingly good. If the LORD is pleased with us, he will lead us into that land, a land flowing with milk and honey, and will give it to us. Only do not rebel against the LORD. And do not be afraid of them because we will devour them. Their protection is gone, but the LORD is with us. Do not be afraid of them."

This was the Israelites' response to Joshua and Caleb's words:

Numbers 14:10 — But the whole assembly talked about stoning them...

This rebellion angered God and brought on His wrath, but Moses interceded on their behalf. Instead of destroying them altogether, God told Moses:

Numbers 14:21-23 — Nevertheless, as surely as I live and as surely as the glory of the LORD *fills the whole earth, not one of those who saw my glory and the signs I performed in Egypt and in the wilderness but who disobeyed me and tested me ten times — not one of them will ever see the land I promised on oath to their ancestors. No one who has treated me with contempt will ever see it.*

And yet, God gave their children a second chance:

Numbers 14:26-32 — LORD *spoke to Moses and Aaron again, saying, "How long shall I put up with this evil congregation who are grumbling against Me? I have heard the complaints of the sons of Israel which they are voicing against Me. Say to them, 'As I live,' declares the* LORD, *'just as you have spoken in My hearing, so I will do to you; your dead bodies will fall in this wilderness, all you numbered men according to your complete number from twenty years old and upward, who have grumbled against Me. By no means will you come into the land where I swore to settle you, except for Caleb the son of Jephunneh and Joshua the son of Nun. Your children, however, whom you said would become plunder — I will bring them in, and they will know the land which you have rejected. But as for you, your dead bodies will fall in this wilderness.'"*

They were standing right on the threshold of the Promised Land, but God told them they would never *"enter my rest."* Why? They had committed many sins of immorality, idolatry (the golden calf), and pagan practices of worship since their exodus from Egypt. God had punished and forgiven them for those sins, as vile as they were. He did not even mention those sins in this passage. So, why did God deny them entrance into His rest? "Unbelief." They could not or would not believe what God had said.

Hebrews 3:19 — So, we see that they (the Israelites) were not able to enter, because of their unbelief.

Let's look at their unbelief more closely. Suppose someone told you something that was absolutely true, and not only true, but was for your benefit. In return, you told them it was a lie. In other words, you called them a liar. Is that not exactly what the Israelites did when they refused to believe God?

Therefore, they wandered through the wilderness for forty years until everyone from that first generation died, except for Joshua and Caleb. After the death of Moses, God called on Joshua to lead the Israelites across the Jordan River and take possession of the Promised Land. But God repeatedly told Joshua to *"be strong and courageous."* Why? God was giving the Israelites a second chance, but this time He did not promise to make all their enemies turn their backs and run. He did not promise He would send hornets ahead to drive them out. They had to fight for the land, but as long as they obeyed, He would be with them and guarantee their victories.

I want to take what we learned about God's character while dealing with the Israelites' disobedience and unbelief and apply it to our relationship with God today. We have a God who gives second chances. These second chances are not something we earn; they are a gift from God, based on His grace and love for mankind. We should never take them for granted. When God gives you a second chance, don't waste it. Embrace it.

Our very salvation is a second chance from God. We are all born sinners, based on our carnal nature, but it is not the sin that prevents us from having eternal salvation. God denied the Israelites entrance into His rest (the Promised Land), not because they were sinners, but because of their "unbelief." Don't reject the gospel. It is the only path to salvation.

A verse I mentioned in the last chapter is relevant here, too:

Romans 10:9-10 — If you declare with your mouth, "Jesus is Lord," and **believe in your heart** *that God raised him from the dead, you will be saved. For it is with your heart that you believe (true believer) and are justified, and it is with your mouth that you profess your faith and are saved.*

We also have a God who makes exceptions. The fact God does not change does not mean that God never changes His mind. We seem to have trouble recognizing that a sovereign God can make exceptions. Both the Old and New Testament are full of examples, and if you do not think that is a very important part of God's character, maybe you will have a change of heart after you read through my examples.

At the time of Noah, God saw that everyone had become wicked and   ungodly. God reached the point where He regretted making man in the first place. Therefore, He made the decision to do something about it.

Genesis 6:6-8 — The LORD *regretted that he had made human beings on the earth, and his heart was deeply troubled. So the* LORD *said, "I will wipe from the face of the earth the human race I have created—and with them the animals, the birds and the creatures that move along the ground—for I regret that I have made them." But Noah found favor in the eyes of the* LORD.

Genesis 6:13 — So God said to Noah, "I am going to put an end to all people, for the earth is filled with violence because of them. I am surely going to destroy both them and the earth."

Before judgment would fall, God had Noah warn that generation of people of the coming judgment—for 120 years—as Noah builds the Ark. But how many listened to Noah? None! Yet, because *"Noah found favor in the eyes of the* LORD,*"* our Sovereign God made an exception and spared a very small remnant of people: Noah and his family.

Starting with Genesis 12 and throughout the Old Testament, God is only dealing with the Nation of Israel, but there were exceptions. For example, He told Jonah to go to the Gentile city of Nineveh. Jonah didn't want to go. He did everything to keep from going because he was under the impression that the God of Abraham was only interested in the Jewish people. He didn't recognize that a sovereign God can make exceptions. So, God told Jonah to go and minister to Nineveh. Jonah said, "They are our enemy. I don't want to see Nineveh saved." But God said, "I do." After God got his full attention, Jonah went to Nineveh.

Another example is when Abraham pleaded with the LORD concerning the inhabitants of Sodom. Why was he so concerned? Lot, his beloved nephew, and his offspring were living there. So, Abraham begins to bargain with God, saying, "Now, Lord, if there are fifty righteous people in Sodom, will you spare it?" God said, "Yes." "Forty?" "Yes." "Thirty?" "Yes." He came all the way down to ten. God said He would make an exception and spare Sodom if there were at least ten believers in the city.

Genesis 18:32 — Then he said, "May the Lord not be angry, but let me speak just once more. What if only ten (righteous people) *can be found there?" He answered, "For the sake of ten, I will not destroy it."*

There were not at least ten; God destroyed Sodom and Gomorrah.

Grace, mercy, and wrath were, are, and always will be co-existing attributes of God's character. What happened to Sodom and Gomorrah is a perfect example. Our nation has experienced His holy grace and holy mercy for centuries, but so far, His holy wrath, not so much!

I have one more example that I saved for last, since it really gives us insight into the character of the man Jesus. Jesus' first miracle was turning water into wine:

John 2:1-5 — On the third day a wedding took place at Cana Galilee. Jesus' mother was there, and Jesus and his disciples had also been invited to the wedding. When the wine was gone, Jesus' mother said to him, "They have no more wine." "Woman, why do you involve me?" Jesus replied. "My hour has not yet come." His mother said to the servants, "Do whatever he tells you."

What just happened? Mary, Jesus's mother let her Son know, *"They have no more wine."* Jesus told his mother, *"My hour has not yet come."* In other words, Mary knew her Son could fix this problem, but Jesus was letting her know that the time for miracles had not yet arrived. Yet, what does

Jesus do? He not only turns water into wine, but it is the finest wine they have ever tasted.

Why am I placing so much significance on this first miracle? Because in performing this miracle, Jesus gives us insight into the character of the man Jesus. Jesus made an exception and made gallons and gallons of wine. Why? Because it was his mother who made the request.

So, this question is for men only: If your mother asked you to turn water into wine, and you had the ability to do it, what would you do? The same as I would do: Make wine by the gallons, just as Jesus did. The point is that Jesus loved and cherished His mother, just like all men should.

Chapter 39

God Is in Control

Everything under the sun since creation and the beginning of human history has been by God's design. So, who is in control of everything? God has absolute control of all things (lock, stock, and barrel). God knows the end before the beginning. I cannot see how any believer would question this, but I have spent much time and thought pondering how in the world does God make everything work together (*Ephesians 1:11 – ...who works out everything in conformity with the purpose of his will*) and still allows us to retain our free will? I have no idea; Without faith it is totally beyond our ability to begin to understand. I think the following poem expresses exactly what I am attempting to say:

The Weaver – author unknown

My life is but a weaving

Between my Lord and me;

I cannot choose the colors

He worketh steadily.

Oft times He weaveth sorrow

And I, in foolish pride,

Forget He sees the upper,

And I the underside.

Not till the loom is silent

And the shuttles cease to fly

Shall God unroll the canvas

And explain the reason why.

The dark threads are as needful

In the Weaver's skilful hand,

As the threads of gold and silver

In the pattern He has planned.

Again, I think we can look at the past and gain insight that can be applied to our relationship with God today *(Romans 15:4 — For everything that was written in the past was written to teach us ...)*. In this chapter, I want to give some specific examples from the Old Testament of "God being in control." I'll include stories about the lives of Joseph, Moses (from his birth to the burning bush), Elijah, Ruth, and finish with the exile of the twelve tribes of Israel.

God's Plan for Joseph:

Now, I am sure everyone who has read the Bible remembers the story of Joseph. Just in case you haven't read the story from Genesis 37, here's a quick summary:

Joseph was his father's favorite, which should have meant his life was easy. Unfortunately, the extra attention made his brothers envious, and they hated him. One night, Joseph had a vivid dream where his brothers, the sun, the moon, and eleven stars bowed down to him. When he told his brothers about the dream, they hated him even more. Later, they seized him and sold him to a caravan of Ishmaelite traders. The traders took Joseph to Egypt and sold him to Potiphar, Pharaoh's captain of the guard. Joseph, the boy who was once cherished by his father, suddenly found himself enslaved.

Despite his circumstances, Joseph prospered in Egypt. But he fell on misfortune again when he was falsely accused of attempting to rape Potiphar's wife and was thrown into prison. While in prison, Joseph accurately interpreted the dreams of two of Pharaoh's servants, who were also prisoners.

Two years later, Pharaoh had two disturbing dreams that no one could interpret. One of the servants Joseph had previously helped suggested to Pharaoh that Joseph could interpret the dreams. Joseph was summoned from prison, and since God was with Joseph, he interpreted Pharaoh's dreams.

Genesis 41:28-30 — "It is just as I said to Pharaoh: God has shown Pharaoh what he is about to do. Seven years of great abundance are coming throughout the land of Egypt, but seven years of famine will follow them. Then all the abundance in Egypt will be forgotten, and the famine will ravage the land."

Pharaoh was amazed and appointed Joseph as second-in-command over Egypt.

Much of what happened to Joseph was challenging and at times exceedingly difficult. But why was this? Because it was all part of God's sovereign plan. God knew that Joseph, as a young boy of seventeen, already had great faith that would never waiver in the face of adversity. So, what did Joseph know as he faced these continuous misfortunes? He knew his God was in control, even if his circumstances looked bleak.

As Joseph's dream prophesied, a great famine hit the land, and Jacob (Joseph's father) sent ten of Joseph's brothers to Egypt to buy food.

Genesis 42:4 — But Jacob did not send Benjamin, Joseph's brother, with the others, because he was afraid that harm might come to him.

The brothers did not recognize Joseph, who was now twenty years older. Joseph treated them harshly and pretended he thought they were spies. We see how the visit ends in this verse:

Genesis 42:19-20 — If you are honest men, let one of your

brothers stay here in prison, while the rest of you go and take grain back for your starving households. But you must bring your youngest brother to me, so that your words may be verified and that you may not die." This they proceeded to do.

At first, Jacob refused to send his youngest son, but finally relented and allowed Benjamin to go with his brothers on their return trip to Egypt. Upon their return, Joseph continued to test their character by placing a silver cup in the sack of Benjamin and falsely accused him of theft. But when Judah offered to stay in place of Benjamin, Joseph knew his brother's character had changed. That's when Joseph revealed to the men that he was actually their brother.

Genesis 45:4-8 — Then Joseph said to his brothers, "Come close to me." When they had done so, he said, "I am your brother Joseph, the one you sold into Egypt! And now, do not be distressed and do not be angry with yourselves for selling me here, because it was to save lives that God sent me ahead of you. For two years now there has been famine in the land, and for the next five years there will be no plowing and reaping. But God sent me ahead of you to preserve for you a remnant on earth and to save your lives by a great deliverance. So then, it was not you who sent me here, but God."

Joseph was exactly where he needed to be for his divine appointment, and when his brothers arrived, Joseph understood this was all according to God's will. Through Joseph's abiding faith and God's sovereign plan, some seventy descendants of Abraham, Isaac, and Jacob escaped the famine and ended up in Egypt.

God's Plan for Moses:

Now let's look at the life of Moses, from his birth to his divine appointment. Moses was the son of Amram and Jochebed of the tribe of Levi. Miriam and Aaron were his brother and sister. He was born in Egypt during the period when the Israelites had become a threat to the Egyptians, simply because of their large population. Pharaoh had ordered that all newborn male Israelite children be cast into the Nile to drown. Amram and Jochebed took their newborn son, placed him in a reed basket, and hid him in the tall grasses of the Nile. Meanwhile, his sister, Miriam, hid and watched over him from a distance. Then, Pharaoh's daughter, who was bathing with a group of women, heard a baby crying and rescued Moses from the river. She named him "Moses," which means "drawn from the water." With her desire for a son fulfilled, she made certain he had the best of everything, including education.

Moses was brought up in the splendor of the Egyptian court as the Pharaoh's daughter's adopted son. As he grew to manhood, he was aware of his Israelite roots and shared a deep compassion for his own people. He became furious while witnessing an Egyptian master brutally beating an Israelite slave, and he impulsively killed the Egyptian. Fearing the Pharaoh's punishment, he fled into the desert of Midian, becoming a shepherd for Jethro, a Midianite priest, and he later married the priest's daughter, Zipporah. While tending the flocks on Horeb Mountain in the wilderness, he saw a bush burning that was not turning to ashes.

*Exodus 3:2-7,10 — There the angel of the L*ORD *appeared to him in flames of fire from within a bush. Moses saw that though the bush was on fire it did not burn up. So Moses thought, "I will go over and see this strange sight—why the bush does not burn up." When the L*ORD *saw that he had gone over to look, God called to him from within the bush, "Moses! Moses!" And Moses said, "Here I am." "Do not come any closer," God said. "Take off your sandals, for the place where you are standing is holy ground." Then he said, "I am the God of your father, the God of Abraham, the God of Isaac and the God of Jacob." At this, Moses hid his face, because he was afraid to look at God. The L*ORD *said, "I have indeed seen the misery of my people in Egypt. I have heard them crying out because of their slave drivers, and I am concerned about their suffering ... So now, go.   I am sending you to Pharaoh to bring my people the Israelites out of Egypt."*

From the burning bush, God told Moses it was now time to deliver the children of Israel out of bondage. He also said he had chosen Moses to lead the Israelites from their life of slavery in Egypt to the Promised Land (the land of milk and honey). So, from the point of the birth of Moses to his divine appointment, who was in control? Our Sovereign God, the God of creation.

God's Plan for Elijah:

Now let's look at another example from the life of Elijah. Israel had gone more than three years without rain, as a judgment for their idolatry and pagan worship. On Mount Carmel, Elijah confronted the evil king, Ahab, and challenged the 450 prophets of Baal to prepare a bull as an offering for their god and Elijah would do the same. Neither one would be allowed to light a fire on their altar. The God who answered with fire from the sky would be considered the true God. The pagan prophets cried out and danced around their altar all day, but they could not get their "gods" to send fire down to burn the sacrifice on their altar. Finally, Elijah had his altar doused in water and then prayed to the Lord to send fire.

1 Kings 18:36-37 — At the time of sacrifice, the prophet Elijah stepped forward and prayed: "LORD, the God of Abraham, Isaac and Israel, let it be known today that you are God in Israel and that I am your servant and have done all these things at your command. Answer me, LORD, answer me, so these people will know that you, LORD, are God, and that you are turning their hearts back again."

Fire immediately consumed the altar, the sacrifice, the wood, stones, soil, and even the water that had overflowed into the trenches around the altar.

1 Kings 18:39 — When all the people saw this, they fell prostrate and cried, "The LORD—he is God! The LORD—he is God!"

Elijah immediately instructed that all the prophets of Baal be seized and put to death. Queen Jezebel heard about what Elijah had done and sent a messenger to tell Elijah, *"By tomorrow at this time you'll be just as dead as my prophets."* Fire had descended from Heaven. The people of Israel had acknowledged God. The false prophets had been put to death. Yet Elijah was afraid and ran for his life. Why? Maybe Elijah was despondent because he felt like he was the last man left who trusted God. Or maybe he just did not understand that "God is in control."

1 Kings 19:10 — He replied, "I have been very zealous for the LORD God Almighty. The Israelites have rejected your covenant, torn down your altars, and put your prophets to death with the sword. I am the only one left, and now they are trying to kill me too."

What was God's answer?

1 Kings 19:18 – "Yet I reserve seven thousand in Israel—all whose knees have not bowed down to Baal and whose mouths have not kissed him."

So, God told Elijah, "You're not the only one; I have reserved for myself a remnant of 7,000 people." This is another example of the recurring theme throughout the Old Testament where the majority of the Nation of Israel, time after time, turned its back on God and succumbed to idolatry and pagan worship. And yet, God is in control and always maintains His remnant of believers. God would chastise the nation as a whole and use His few believers to bring the nation back under the blessing of God. No matter the amount of unbelief or disobedience, God is in control.

God's Plan for Ruth:

Now, I want to look at the Book of Ruth. Through a divine appointment (inspired by God), Ruth had to make a choice— one so significant, it was recorded in scripture. The Book of Ruth gives an account of a Jewish family of Elimelech, Naomi, and their two sons, Mahlon and Chilion, who had moved to Moab to escape a famine in Judah. Once they settled in Moab, tragedy occurs.

Ruth 1:3 — "Now, Elimelech, Naomi's husband died..."

Suddenly, Naomi was left alone with her two sons.

Ruth 1:4-5 — They married Moabite women, one named Orpah and the other Ruth. After they had lived there about ten years, both Mahlon and Kilion also died, and Naomi was left without her two sons and her husband.

Contrary to all the laws and traditions of Israel, both had married Moabite women, and after ten years, both of her sons had died.

Ruth 1:6, 8-10 — When Naomi heard in Moab that the LORD had come to the aid of his people by providing food for them, she and her daughters-in-law prepared to return home from there ... Then Naomi said to her two daughters-in-law, "Go back, each of you, to your mother's home." ... Then she kissed them goodbye and they wept aloud and said to her, "We will go back with you to your people."

Naomi saw fit to go back to her homeland, with the idea that she would leave her daughters-in-law in Moab. This was the point where Ruth had a choice to make (her divine appointment).

Ruth 1:14, 16-18 — At this they wept aloud again. Then Orpah kissed her mother-in-law goodbye, but Ruth clung to her ... Ruth replied, "Don't urge me to leave you or to turn back from you. Where you go I will go, and where you stay I will stay. Your people will be my people and your God my God. Where you die I will die, and there I will be buried. May the LORD deal with me, be it ever so severely, if even death separates you and me." When Naomi realized that Ruth was determined to go with her, she stopped urging her.

Ruth made her choice, and ultimately, her story ended well. She became the wife of Boaz, a relative to Naomi's late husband, Elimelech. Their son, Obed, was the father of Jesse, and Jesse was the father of David. Ruth, based on her free-will choice, became a part of the genealogy of Jesus Christ. Amazing! So, who was in control?

God's Plan for Israel:

There is one more example I want to look at since, for me, it not only allows us to see how God weaves His control from generation to generation, but it is also invaluable in gaining a deeper insight into God's character.

After Solomon's reign, there was a 200-year period where the Nation of Israel was divided into two: the Southern Kingdom (Judah), containing the tribe of Judah and the tribe of Benjamin, and the Northern Kingdom (Israel), containing the other ten tribes. The Israelites formed their capital in Samaria, and the Judaeans kept their capital in Jerusalem. They each had their own line of kings, but they were both still part of the Nation of Israel and Abraham's Covenant promises.

It had come to the point where both kingdoms were regressing morally and spiritually. The Temple in Jerusalem was still the center of all religious activity, but the nation was again succumbing to idolatry and pagan worship and forgetting about their God.

But the Kingdom of Israel was far ahead in their race back into idolatry and pagan worship. God had sent prophets into Judah and up into Israel to warn the people that if they continued to forsake Him, they faced invasion by an enemy who would annihilate many and exile the rest. It was the prophets of the Kingdom of Israel who addressed this danger as being imminent, since the Northern Kingdom had forsaken God and were worshipping other gods.

Consequently, God caused the Assyrians to invade the Kingdom of Israel. They captured most of the Israelites living in the Northern Kingdom (the ten tribes of Israel) and scattered them among cities in their Assyrian Empire.

More than a hundred years later, God told the prophet Jeremiah what would happen if they did not turn from their idolatry. Jeremiah warned the Kingdom of Judah that if they did not repent, the city would be destroyed and they would be carried away captive. But did they listen? No! They threw him in a dungeon, which was where the Babylonians found him during their invasion. They besieged Jerusalem, destroyed the Temple, and took a large remnant of the Jews back to Babylon.

So, Israel's ten tribes went into Assyrian captivity and Judah's two tribes into Babylonian captivity. Seventy years later, God moved the heart of King Cyrus of Persia to allow the Israelites living in Babylon to return to Jerusalem. But those ten tribes who went into Assyrian captivity did not return. Consequently, now some theologians refer to them as "the lost ten tribes of Israel." But this name does not line up with the scripture—and remember "God is in control."

Why was the Northern Kingdom exiled more than 130 years before the Southern Kingdom? They had forsaken God much more quickly and in far greater numbers than the Southern Kingdom. This meant they had a much smaller remnant of believers. The Temple in the Southern Kingdom acted like a magnet, pulling many of the remnant of believers back into the Southern Kingdom. Therefore, when the Assyrians invaded, there were some believers from each of the ten northern tribes living in the Southern Kingdom. After nearly 130 years, those believers from each of the ten tribes must have grown in number. Therefore, when the Babylonians invaded and took their captives back to Babylon, it wasn't just the two tribes, it was all twelve tribes. Seventy years later, they returned to Jerusalem. So, a few theologians might have lost those ten tribes, but you can rest assured, prior to creation, our Almighty God had accounted for every one of them.

This would be a good place to call attention to the way God counts events related to the Nation of Israel compared to the way He counts events related to all other nations. Old Testament prophecy said Israel's exile in Babylon would be seventy years.

Daniel 9:1-2 — In the first year of his reign, I, Daniel, understood from the Scriptures, according to the word of the LORD given to Jeremiah the prophet, that the desolation of Jerusalem would last seventy years.

The following are three examples of how God counts, when dealing with all other nations:

Genesis 15:16 — In the fourth generation your descendants will come back here, for the sin of the Amorites has not yet **reached its full measure.**

Approximately seventy descendants of Abraham went into Egypt. After being in slavery for a number of generations, the Israelites were without any form of identity as a people or a nation. But when the "cup of iniquity" of those living in their Promised Land was full, God spoke to Moses from the burning bush and told Moses to lead His chosen people out of the land of Egypt.

Luke 21:24 — Jerusalem will be trampled on by the Gentiles **until the times of the Gentiles are fulfilled.**

In this verse, the "*times of the Gentiles*" are signified by an increase in wickedness and ungodliness during a period of time in which the Gentiles would have dominion over Jerusalem and the Jewish people. Another way of saying "*until the times of the Gentiles are fulfilled*" would be to say, "until their wickedness and ungodliness has filled this cup of iniquity."

Romans 11:25 (KJV) — ... that blindness in part is happened to Israel, **until the fulness of the Gentiles be come in.**

The "*fulness of the Gentiles*" is the Body of Christ (the Church). As Gentiles are being saved, they are being placed into the Body of Christ.

So, for these last three examples, God is counting an amount instead of counting time. Now, the question is why? This is my opinion: For the two examples that deal with "filling the cup of iniquity," the cup is being filled based on their free-will choices. Therefore, they are determining the time, not God. God knows the exact day and hour, but it is their evil deeds that fill the cup. Therefore, they determine their day of God's wrath.

For the last example, God is again counting an amount instead of counting time. However, this time He is counting the number of believers who are entering the Body of Christ (the Church). This count is ongoing as I am writing this book. When the count reaches the predetermined level set by our Almighty God, the period of grace will end, and the Rapture will occur. What does this mean? It means we, as believers, are actually determining the time of the Rapture. The more we witness and bring new believers into the Body of Christ, the sooner the Rapture will occur.

I want to make one additional point about those seventy years the Israelites spent in exile: It cured them of idolatry, once and for all. They continued to struggle with many issues where they were disobedient to God, but idolatry was no longer one of them. After the exile, there is nothing in scripture that associates the Jewish people with idolatry.

This is so significant that it must have been part of God's plan, when the exile occurred. The reason I think it is so significant is that, after Jesus died on the cross, the Romans overran Jerusalem, Israel was no longer a nation (until 1948), and the Jewish people were scattered into every nation on earth. This means they were among many nations that worship everything but their God of Abraham, Isaac, and Jacob. Their ability to retain their identity as a people, while scattered all over the earth for nearly 2,000 years, is the most miraculous miracle in the Bible. How much more difficult would it have been for these scattered, chosen people to maintain their identity, if at the time they were scattered, they were still falling into idolatry? Nothing surprises God. He is always in control.

Man operates based on his own free will, and the unbelievers are clueless that God has anything to do with it. Yet, He has **everything** to do with it. He is bringing His purposes to fruition in His own way, in His own time.

Isaiah 14:24 — "The Lord Almighty has sworn, 'Surely, as I have planned, so it will be, and as I have purposed, so it will happen.'"

It is amazing! God is behind it all, and today it is no different. God's sovereign design did not stop at the end of the Old Testament. God is aware of every facet of our lives today—just as He was with Joseph, Moses, Elijah, Ruth, and the people of Israel who were exiled.

Always remember God continues to allow man to have free will, and mankind continues to throw roadblocks into His plan of redemption. But does it affect God's schedule? No! Despite all of mankind's missteps, God's plans are right on time. But how? From the peaks of the highest mountain tops to the depths of the deepest valleys, God is in control.

Part 3

Redemption

Chapter 40

Adam's Fall to Abraham

After returning from my tour of Israel in the summer of 2000, I began working on developing a method for studying the Bible. This was far more difficult than I imagined. In the past, studying for school or work was not a problem. More effort would always result in a better outcome. It did not take long for me to realize this was not the case for studying the Bible. I needed a structured method of study that would allow me to build logical blocks of understanding, one upon the other. To do that, I needed a point of focus that I could key on, from Genesis to Revelation. It took a few long training runs, but once it came to me, I knew that my point of focus had to be redemption.

Redemption is God's plan to buy back what He lost in the Garden of Eden. God's plan of redemption unfolds throughout the Bible, based on His sovereign will. From Genesis to Revelation, God has woven within the fabric of scripture a divine strand. This strand is God's divine plan of redemption. It is mankind's lifeline to eternal salvation. God is continually casting it out from generation to generation. It is available to all those who were born under the sun, with no exceptions. Therefore, no one has an excuse to ignore it. Yet, from generation to generation, based on our God-granted free will, only a remnant reaches out and latches on.

In Part 3, I want to focus on this plan of redemption. Prior to creation, the Triune Godhead laid out a master plan for the reconciliation and salvation of fallen humanity. In doing so, God took into consideration the free-will choices of each and every nation, and each and every individual, from generation to generation. Still, from the beginning to the end of time under the sun, all things have and will fall in place, exactly as God predetermined. This included Jesus' first coming, His death on the cross, His burial, and His resurrection.

Acts 2:23 — This man was handed over to you by God's deliberate plan and foreknowledge; and you, with the help of wicked men (Gentiles), *put him to death by nailing him to the cross.*

Everything that was prophesied concerning Jesus' first coming was fulfilled according to His exact timetable. And finally, at the End of the Age, Jesus will return to establish His Kingdom—not as a sacrificial lamb—but as our King. All of this would be totally unimaginable except for our Sovereign God.

I want to look at this plan of redemption in three distinct phases: from Adam's fall until God calls out Abraham; from Abraham until the cross; and from the cross until the end of the ages.

For this first phase, God is dealing with all of humanity. Starting back in Genesis with Adam and Eve's first two sons, Cain and Abel, we see the first example of two requirements for salvation. God gave them specific instructions on how to bring an "offering to the Lord." Faith and shed blood were two basic requirements for their offerings to be accepted by God. Abel came by faith and brought a blood sacrifice. But Cain came, making excuses, and instead of relying on faith, attempted to reason and justify his bloodless offering. Abel's offering was accepted; Cain's was not. Cain was self-willed and did not believe what God said. These following two verses confirm why Abel's offering was accepted and Cain's was not.

Hebrews 9:22 — "...and without the shedding of blood there is no forgiveness."

Hebrews 11:6 — "Without faith it is impossible to please God ..."

From this point until Abraham, everyone had the same opportunity to have a knowledge of God, based on the format given to Cain and Abel. If they would bring a blood sacrifice when their conscience convicted them of having committed a wrong, God would accept them on the basis of their faith. Keep in mind, this was before Moses and the Law. Even so, God gave all mankind a moral compass (conscience) that allowed each to know right from wrong.

Unfortunately, for the most part, the human race rejected God and His offer of salvation. From Adam's fall until the flood—a period of about 1,600 years—the world was in a spiritual darkness that was caused by the willful sin, disobedience, and unbelief of mankind. So, the vast majority of the human race was in a state of rebellion, with little or no concern for the ways of God. At this point, God spoke to Noah.

Genesis 6:13 — So God said to Noah, "I am going to put an end to all people, for the earth is filled with violence because of them. I am surely going to destroy both them and the earth."

But because of Noah's faith, God spared Noah and his family and had Noah build the ark. For the 120 years it took to build, Noah preached of the oncoming judgment. But when the time came, only eight people entered the ark: Noah and his wife, his three sons, and their wives. So, out of all the people on the earth at the time of the flood, how many had remained true to God? A precious few!

Matthew 7:13-14 — "Enter through the narrow gate. For wide is the gate and broad is the road that leads to destruction, and many enter through it. But small is the gate and narrow the road that leads to life, and only a few find it."

This verse reminds me of one of the most famous poems in American literature. Here's an excerpt:

The Road Not Taken - Robert Frost.

Two roads diverged in a wood, and I –

I took the one less traveled by,

And that has made all the difference.

After the flood, God blessed Noah:

Genesis 9:1, 9:7 — Then God blessed Noah and his sons, saying to them, "Be fruitful and increase in number and fill the earth. ... As for you, be fruitful and increase in number; multiply on the earth and increase upon it."

But within 200 years, the people again had an attitude of unbelief and rebellion, with little or no concern for obeying God. What had God told Noah to do after the flood? Be fruitful, increase in number, and fill the earth. But they intended to do just the opposite and went about building the Tower of Babel:

Genesis 11:4 — Then they said, "Come, let us build ourselves a city, with a tower that reaches to the heavens, so that we may make a name for ourselves; otherwise we will be scattered over the face of the whole earth."

God did not like their pride, arrogance, and disobedience. He caused the people to speak different languages so they could not communicate with each other. This confusion caused the people to scatter across the land. But for the next 200 years, nothing changed; the human race continued to turn its back on God and succumb to disobedience and unbelief. This is the point when God would shift the focus of his plan of redemption from all of humanity to a chosen people: the descendants of Abraham.

Chapter 41

God Calls Out Abraham

For 2,000 years, God gave the opportunity for salvation to all of humanity. The only requirement was to listen to their God-given moral conscience when they sinned, then provide the proper blood sacrifice, confess their sin, and God would accept them. They all understood this was what God required, and yet what did they do? All but a precious few rejected it. You can see this story repeat, in generation after generation, as you read the first eleven chapters of the Bible. God, in His foreknowledge, knew this story would not change, so He did something different. He shifted the focus of His plan of redemption from all of humanity to the descendants of a man named Abram (Abraham). From that point until the cross, God's plan of redemption focused on this nation of people.

That leads us to ask the question, what about the rest of humanity? For me, the answer was difficult to grasp, but it is something I cannot sugarcoat, skip over, and ignore. The Bible is perfectly clear that, from Abraham until the cross, God allowed the rest of humanity to follow their wicked hearts and continue in their wicked ways toward their eternal doom. I know this sounds unfair, but humanity had lived continuously in rebellion to God. The world was steeped in wickedness and violence, although they all had an awareness of what God expected of them. Yet only a precious few believed and obeyed God.

During this time from Abraham until the cross, God did make some exceptions:

Rahab and Ruth were both Gentiles, yet are in the genealogy of Christ. When Joshua sent the two spies into Jericho, Rehab demonstrated her faith by hiding and protecting them.

Ruth, by faith, went with Naomi, her mother-in-law, to Bethlehem, and through God's grace, she married Boaz.

During His earthly ministry, Jesus commanded the disciples to go only to the Nation of Israel. Jesus limited His ministry to the Nation of Israel, but with some exceptions. He healed the Canaanite woman's demon-possessed daughter and the Roman centurion's servant.

These exceptions had two things in common: Each dealt with a Gentile who had faith, and each was recorded in the scriptures.

In Genesis, chapter 12, God called out Abram and told him a nation of people would come from him—the Nation of Israel.

Genesis 12:2-3 – "I will make you into a great nation, and I will bless you; I will make your name great and you will be a blessing. I will bless those who bless you and whoever curses you I will curse; and all peoples on earth will be blessed through you." (Abrahamic Covenant)

A few chapters later, God again repeats His covenant and tells Abram that his name will now be Abraham.

Genesis 17:4-7 — As for me, this is my covenant with you: You will be the father of many nations. No longer will you be called Abram; your name will be Abraham, for I have made you a father of many nations. I will make you very fruitful; I will make nations of you, and kings will come from you. I will establish my covenant as an everlasting covenant between me and you and your descendants after you for the generations to come, to be your God and the God of your descendants after you.

From this point through the rest of the Old Testament and the four gospels, God's plan of redemption almost totally dealt with God's chosen people. So, the question is: Why Abraham? What did God see in this man that caused Him to choose Abraham, prior to creation, to be the father of the Nation of Israel?   Amazing faith! God saw Abraham's tremendous faith. By his faith, Abraham recognized that God was real, and Almighty, and that His Word demanded obedience.

Genesis 15:6 — Abram believed the LORD, *and He credited it to him as righteousness.*

Romans 4:3 — What does Scripture say? "Abraham believed God, and it was credited to him as righteousness."

It doesn't say that Abraham offered sacrifices to God. It doesn't say he repented and was baptized. It doesn't say Abraham believed in God. It says Abraham **believed God**. There is a huge difference in believing there is a God and believing God. Most people believe there is a God, but that is a far cry from truly believing God and placing your trust in Him. By his faith Abraham believed what God said, and because of his faith, he took God at His Word and was obedient.

In order for us to fully appreciate the depth of Abraham's faith, I want to look ahead approximately fifty years. God told Abraham to take his son, Isaac, up to Mount Moriah and offer him upon the altar as a sacrifice.

*Genesis 22:1 — Some time later God **tested** Abraham. He said to him, "Abraham!" "Here I am," he replied.*

*Genesis 22:1 (KJV) — And it came to pass after these things, that God did **tempt** Abraham, and said unto him, Abraham: and he said, Behold, here I am.*

The KJV uses *"tempt"* whereas the (NIV) uses *"tested."* In this case, I think the (NIV) has the better translation by far. Satan has been tempting humanity starting with Eve and is still tempting us today. God will test believers to strengthen their faith by showing them He will provide. We see this all through scripture, and Abraham was no exception.

Genesis 22:2 — Then God said, "Take your son, your only son, whom you love—Isaac—and go to the region of Moriah. Sacrifice him there as a burnt offering on a mountain I will show you."

Do you think Abraham would have ever offered his son if he was not a man of tremendous faith? Never! I want to step through some of the verses so we can see Abraham's faith in action.

Genesis 22:5 — He said to his servants, "Stay here with the donkey while I and the boy go over there. We will worship and then we will come back to you."

When Abraham tells his servants to wait, he does not say, "I will return to you." He says, "We will return to you." Now, if that does not give us insight into his faith, nothing does.

Genesis 22:7-8 — Isaac spoke up and said to his father Abraham, "Father?" "Yes, my son?" Abraham replied. "The fire and wood are here," Isaac said, "but where is the lamb for the burnt offering?" Abraham answered, "God himself will provide the lamb for the burnt offering, my son." And the two of them went on together.

How could Abraham feel in his heart that God himself will provide? By his faith! This is the reason his belief was credited to him as righteousness. This is the reason God chose Abraham to be the father of the Nation of Israel.

Abraham obeyed God and offered his son on the altar, but at the last moment, God provided the sacrifice. With God providing the ram for sacrifice in place of Isaac, it was a perfect reflection of what would happen on the cross.

Genesis 22:12-13 — "Do not lay a hand on the boy," he (God) said. "Do not do anything to him. Now I know that you fear God, because you have not withheld from me your son, your only son." Abraham looked up and there in a thicket he saw a ram caught by its horns. He went over and took the ram and sacrificed it as a burnt offering instead of his son.

God did not test Abraham so He could see Abraham's tremendous faith in action. His testing showed Abraham that, because of his faith, God would provide. To fully appreciate what Abraham did, think of this as being your only son, daughter, or someone very close to you. If you can think of it in those terms, it should make you realize the depth and scope of Abraham's faith.

Chapter 42

The Exodus and the Law

In a previous chapter, I looked at Joseph's divine appointment with his brothers, when he saved the descendants of Abraham, Isaac, and Jacob from the famine by bringing them into Egypt. We also looked at Moses' divine appointment when God spoke to him from the burning bush about rescuing His people from Egypt.

While in Egypt, God's chosen people steadily increased in number until they were so numerous, the Pharaoh feared they would turn against the Egyptians, so he forced them into slavery. Yet all this happened as part of God's plan. During their time in Egypt, they grew into a nation of people, which is exactly what God promised Abraham.

Approximately seventy descendants of Abraham went into Egypt. After being in slavery for 400 years, the Israelites were without any form of identity as a people or a nation. But when "the cup of iniquity" of those living in their Promised Land was full, God spoke to Moses from the burning bush and told him the following:

Exodus 3:8 — So I have come down to rescue them from the hand of the Egyptians and to bring them up out of that land into a good and spacious land, a land flowing with milk and honey—the home of the Canaanites, Hittites, Amorites, Perizzites, Hivites and Jebusites.

Moses led them out of the land of Egypt. They walked

through the parted Red Sea and assembled around Mount Sinai, then God gave Moses a message to tell the Israelites:

Exodus 19:5-6 – "'Now if you obey me fully and keep my covenant, then out of all nations you will be my treasured possession. Although the whole earth is mine, you will be for me a kingdom of priests and a holy nation.' These are the words you are to speak to the Israelites."

The people responded:

Exodus 19:7-8 — So Moses went back and summoned the elders of the people and set before them all the words the LORD had commanded him to speak. The people all responded together, "We will do everything the LORD has said." So Moses brought their answer back to the LORD.

God gave the Israelites a promise, but it was a conditional promise. If they would be obedient to His commands and keep His covenant, they would be God's special people and His Kingdom of priests.

These verses reflect and provide some insight into God's plan regarding the redemption of both the Jewish and non-Jewish people. God was offering them an opportunity: Be faithful and obedient, and you will be blessed and will become a nation of priests. Why a nation of priests? God would use them to take His plan of redemption to the rest of the world.

At this point, God gave Moses the Ten Commandments. They were God's moral laws—a moral code of conduct that was based on God's own holy nature. But this was only the first part of the Law of Moses. The Israelites were also given the Civil Law and the Ceremonial Law.

The Civil Law covered every aspect of Israel's daily living, with guidelines for dealing with disputes between themselves, as well as regulations for enforcing the morals of the people.

The Ceremonial Law was related to Israel's worship and became the foundation for the Jewish religion of Judaism— the beliefs and practices of the Jewish people. It gave protocols for establishing the priesthood of Israel, Temple worship, feast days, sacrifices and offerings, and food and purity laws and regulations.

When God gave the Law of Moses to mankind, it was a significant event in His divine plan for our redemption. But why was the Law given? From Adam until the Law, there was no written law and no defined system for worship. Mankind only had their conscience to make them aware of right from wrong. The laws were given to ensure the people of Israel were made aware of their sins—and with that knowledge, they had a choice to make. Based on their faith, they could be convicted, confess their sin to the priest, and follow the prescribed steps of sacrifice to have the sin covered. Based on their lack of faith, they could fail to be obedient to God.

Abraham was saved based on his faith only. Once the Law was given, the people of Israel were saved based on their faith plus confessing their sin and following the prescribed steps of sacrifice.

The Law had been given on Mount Sinai and the people of Israel all responded together, *"We will do everything the Lord has said."* Yet, as soon as they reached the border to the Promised Land, what happened? Since I already covered this in detail in a previous chapter, the answer is simple: They broke their promise. Once they broke it, what did God do? He punished their unbelief by sending them back into the wilderness to wander for forty years, until everyone from that first generation died except for Joshua and Caleb.

Based on the second generation's faith, Joshua led the Israelites into the Promised Land. This was another pivotal event in God's divine plan for our redemption. It is a pattern that was repeated by the people of Israel, over and over, from generation to generation, right up until the cross. A generation would slowly lose sight of God and slip away into unbelief and idolatry. Then God's wrath would fall on them, and they would repent and come back under His blessing.

Later, during the time of Judges, when the Israelites turned their back on God, they would be overrun by their enemies.

Then, God would raise up a judge who would bring them back. The process would begin all over again until the people of Israel begged God for a king so they would be like all the other nations.

1 Samuel 8:20 – "Then we will be like all the other nations, with a king to lead us and to go out before us and fight our battles."

Once God granted the Israelites' request for a king, He used His holy prophets to warn the people of His impending wrath, each time they fell back into unbelief and idolatry. This cycle continued, with the ten tribes of Israel in the Northern Kingdom being taken into exile by the Assyrians. Then later, the two remaining tribes in the Southern Kingdom were taken into exile by the Babylonians. So, the people of Israel went from blessings to curses, based on their obedience and disobedience. During all these cycles, God maintained a remnant of believers.

This all occurred, even though they were given this warning as they entered the Promised Land:

Deuteronomy 28:1-10 — If you fully obey the LORD *your God and carefully follow all his commands I give you today, the* LORD *your God will set you high above all the nations on earth. All these blessings will come on you and accompany you if you obey the* LORD *your God:*

You will be blessed in the city and blessed in the country.

The fruit of your womb will be blessed, and the crops of your land and the young of your livestock—the calves of your herds and the lambs of your flocks.

Your basket and your kneading trough will be blessed.

You will be blessed when you come in and blessed when you go out.

The LORD *will grant that the enemies who rise up against you will be defeated before you. They will come at you from one direction but flee from you in seven.*

The LORD will send a blessing on your barns and on everything you put your hand to. The LORD your God will bless you in the land he is giving you.

The LORD will establish you as his holy people, as he promised you on oath, if you keep the commands of the LORD your God and walk in obedience to him. Then all the peoples on earth will see that you are called by the name of the LORD, and they will fear you.

Deuteronomy 28:15-20 — However, if you do not obey the LORD your God and do not carefully follow all his commands and decrees I am giving you today, all these curses will come on you and overtake you:

You will be cursed in the city and cursed in the country.

Your basket and your kneading trough will be cursed.

The fruit of your womb will be cursed, and the crops of your land, and the calves of your herds and the lambs of your flocks.

You will be cursed when you come in and cursed when you go out.

The LORD will send on you curses, confusion and rebuke in everything you put your hand to, until you are destroyed and come to sudden ruin because of the evil you have done in forsaking him.

Deuteronomy 30:19-20 — This day I call the heavens and the earth as witnesses against you that I have set before you life and death, blessings and curses. Now choose life, so that you and your children may live and that you may love the LORD your God, listen to his voice, and hold fast to him. For the LORD is your life, and he will give you many years in the land he swore to give to your fathers, Abraham, Isaac and Jacob.

As you can see, God warned Israel, time and time again, that if they were obedient, they would be blessed, and if they were disobedient, they would be chastised. They had the Ten Commandments—God's moral laws. They had His civil and ceremonial laws. Yet they were so quick to fall away from His blessings and so slow to return. God knew, prior to creation, that Abraham, Isaac, and Jacob's descendants would struggle with their faith. But this did not stop God from making the Nation of Israel an essential part of his divine plan of redemption.

Chapter 43

The First Coming of Christ

In this chapter, we will continue discussing God's divine plan of redemption by focusing on the gospel, starting at the time of the First Coming of Christ. After studying the Bible for a number of years, this was one of the areas that remained a struggle for me. The many contradictions and issues that seemed to crop up between the gospel preached before and after the cross always seemed to be a challenge to reconcile in my mind.

I think one of the reasons there is so much confusion on this issue is that we fail to understand that the gospel preached **before** the cross was focused directly on the Nation of Israel. **After** the cross, the main focus shifted to the Gentiles. In the book of Acts, Luke records this period of transition, and this is one subject that generates many differing beliefs and opinions. We would not have so many different Christian denominations if that were not the case. I intend to rely on the scriptures in expressing my views; hopefully you readers will do the same. Being in agreement is not my aim or purpose. My hope is that this will give each reader a hunger for a better understanding of the Bible.

Jesus fulfilled Old Testament prophecies:

The Coming of Christ fulfilled the promises made to the Nation of Israel, based on the Abrahamic Covenant and the prophecies of many Old Testament prophets. It is the centerpiece of God's divine plan of redemption. All the purposes of God pivot around this event. God's prophet, Isaiah, spoke repeatedly about the coming Messiah, who would establish a future earthly Kingdom with Jerusalem as its capital. The following are just a few of the many verses that discuss this:

Isaiah 2:2-4 — In the last days the mountain of the LORD's temple will be established as the highest of the mountains; it will be exalted above the hills, and all nations will stream to it. Many peoples will come and say, "Come, let us go up to the mountain of the LORD, to the temple of the God of Jacob. He will teach us his ways, so that we may walk in his paths." The law will go out from Zion, the word of the LORD from Jerusalem. He will judge between the nations and will settle disputes for many peoples. They will beat their swords into plowshares and their spears into pruning hooks. Nation will not take up sword against nation, nor will they train for war anymore.

Isaiah 7:14 — Therefore, the Lord himself will give you a sign: The virgin will conceive and give birth to a son, and will call him Immanuel (meaning: God is with us).

One of the better known of Isaiah's declarations concerning this future Kingdom is his prophecy of Christ's birth:

Isaiah 9:6-7 — For to us a child is born, to us a son is given, and the government will be on his shoulders. And he will be called Wonderful Counselor, Mighty God, Everlasting Father, Prince of Peace. Of the greatness of his government and peace there will be no end. He will reign on David's throne and over his kingdom, establishing and upholding it with justice and righteousness from that time on and forever. The zeal of the LORD Almighty will accomplish this.

The following is one of the most extensive passages by Isaiah. It refers to Jesus' coming and the characteristics of His reign as King over His earthly Kingdom:

Isaiah 11:1-9 — A shoot will come up from the stump of Jesse; from his roots a Branch will bear fruit. The Spirit of the LORD will rest on him — the Spirit of wisdom and of understanding, the Spirit of counsel and of might, the Spirit of the knowledge and fear of the LORD— *and he will delight in the fear of the* LORD. *He will not judge by what he sees with his eyes, or decide by what he hears with his ears; but with righteousness he will judge the needy, with justice he will give decisions for the poor of the earth. He will strike the earth with the rod of his mouth; with the breath of his lips, he will slay the wicked. Righteousness will be his belt and faithfulness the sash around his waist. The wolf will live with the lamb, the leopard will lie down with the goat, the calf and the lion and the yearling together; and a little child will lead them. The cow will feed with the bear, their young will lie down together, and the lion will eat straw like the ox. The infant will play near the cobra's den, and the young child will put its hand into the viper's nest. They will neither harm nor destroy on all my holy mountain, for the earth will be filled with the knowledge of the* LORD *as the waters cover the sea.*

All through the Old Testament, the people of Israel were looking for this coming King who would rule over his glorious earthly Kingdom. But God did not just send His Son. He also sent John the Baptist, who was prophesied by Old Testament prophets Isaiah, Malachi, and others.

Isaiah 40:3 — A voice of one calling: "In the wilderness prepare the way for the LORD; make straight in the desert a highway for our God."

Malachi 3:1 — "I will send my messenger, who will prepare the way before me. Then suddenly the Lord you are seeking will come to his temple; the messenger of the covenant, whom you desire, will come," says the LORD *Almighty.*

The gospel proclaimed before the cross:

Now I want to examine the gospel that was proclaimed prior to the cross, starting with John the Baptist. This is what Jesus said about John the Baptist:

Matthew 11:11 — Truly I tell you, among those born of women there has not risen anyone greater than John the Baptist...

John the Baptist was God's first prophet since Malachi. After the Book of Malachi was written—the last book of the Old Testament—about 400 years elapsed until God had any further dealings with the Nation of Israel. After those 400 years, He sent the angel Gabriel to speak to Zechariah, the father of John the Baptist.

Luke 1:11-16 — Then an angel of the Lord appeared to him, standing at the right side of the altar of incense. When Zechariah saw him, he was startled and was gripped with fear. But the angel said to him: "Do not be afraid, Zechariah; your prayer has been heard. Your wife Elizabeth will bear you a son, and you are to call him John. He will be a joy and delight to you, and many will rejoice because of his birth, for he will be great in the sight of the Lord. He is never to take wine or other fermented drink, and he will be filled with the Holy Spirit even before he is born. He will bring back many of the people of Israel to the Lord their God."

John the Baptist was sent to be the forerunner to the Messiah. His mission was to announce the good news: The King is here, and He's ready to set up the Kingdom. His purpose was to usher in Jesus' earthly ministry to the Nation of Israel; to prepare the way, baptize, and preach to the people of Israel the baptism of repentance.

Matthew 3:1-2 — In those days John the Baptist came, preaching in the wilderness of Judea and saying, "Repent, for the kingdom of heaven has come near."

John the Baptist had a miraculous birth. It was similar to Isaac's birth in that his parents were advanced in age. But this is not the reason his birth was so special. While still in the womb, John the Baptist was filled with the Holy Spirit:

Luke 1:41-44 — When Elizabeth heard Mary's greeting, the baby leaped in her womb, and Elizabeth was filled with the Holy Spirit. In a loud voice she exclaimed: "Blessed are you among women, and blessed is the child you will bear! But why am I so favored, that the mother of my Lord should come to me? As soon as the sound of your greeting reached my ears, the baby in my womb leaped for joy.

John spent his life preparing for and completing his God-inspired mission, which ended with him baptizing Jesus. Then He was arrested and ultimately beheaded by King Herod. After John the Baptist was arrested, Jesus began proclaiming the same message as John the Baptist: The good news of a glorious Kingdom over which He would be the King.

Matthew 4:12 — When Jesus heard that John had been put in prison, he withdrew to Galilee.

Matthew 4:17 — From that time on Jesus began to preach, "Repent, for the kingdom of heaven has come near."

After Jesus had chosen His twelve disciples, He gave them this same message to proclaim:

Luke 9:1-2 — When Jesus had called the Twelve together, he gave them power and authority to drive out all demons and to cure diseases, and he sent them out to proclaim the kingdom of God and to heal the sick.

So, for the three years of Jesus' earthly ministry, this gospel of the Kingdom was preached—but not to the Gentile world. It was a gospel of good news for the Nation of Israel.

Matthew 10:5-7 — These twelve Jesus sent out with the following instructions: "Do not go among the Gentiles or enter any town of the Samaritans. Go rather to the lost sheep of Israel. As you go, proclaim this message: 'The kingdom of heaven has come near."

When the Canaanite woman brought her demon-possessed daughter to Jesus, he said this:

Matthew 15:24 — He answered, "I was sent only to the lost sheep of Israel."

But Jesus made an exception when He saw the woman's great faith, and He healed her daughter.

I have quoted a number of verses to establish my belief that the gospel before the time of the cross—the gospel of the Kingdom—was specifically directed to the people of Israel. It was promised in fulfillment of God's Old Testament Covenants and was prophesied throughout the Old Testament. Its purpose was to show the Nation of Israel that Jesus of Nazareth was the Christ, the Son of God, and the promised Messiah.

Along with this gospel, there was another aspect of Jesus' earthly ministry that provided additional confirmation of His claim to be the promised King: During His three-year ministry, Jesus performed many signs and miracles, including healing the sick and curing diseases.

Matthew 9:35 — Jesus went through all the towns and villages, teaching in their synagogues, proclaiming the good news of the kingdom and healing every disease and sickness.

These signs and miracles were as important to His ministry as proclaiming the gospel of the Kingdom, since it validated who He was. He was God's Son, their promised Messiah, their promised King who would establish an earthly Kingdom. Yet they rejected him in unbelief. They just could not comprehend that this was the One promised throughout the Old Testament as their Messiah. How could this be their King, who had come to give them their glorious earthly Kingdom? In spite of the many miracles He performed during those three years, how could a mere carpenter's son from Nazareth be the Promised One?

Let's put this together:

It's time to tie some loose ends together to make sure I am getting my points across, concerning God's plan of redemption. I want to compare the Abrahamic Covenant in

Genesis 12:1-3, to the conditional promise God gave the Nation of Israel as they entered the Promised Land.

Let's discuss the conditional promise first. We already looked at Deuteronomy 28:1-10 and Deuteronomy 28:15-20. If you obey the Lord your God, you will be blessed. If you do not obey the Lord your God, you will be cursed and chastised. And that is exactly what happened. When Israel obeyed God, they were blessed as a Nation, but when they disobeyed, they felt His wrath. So, this conditional promise was a two-way street; God's promises were totally dependent on Israel's responses.

But God's covenant with Abraham was one-way—from God to Abraham and his descendants. Even more importantly, it was unconditional. Since this covenant was spoken by our Sovereign God, it was not just a promise; it was set in stone and guaranteed.

Genesis 12:2-3 — "I will make you into a great nation, and I will bless you; I will make your name great, and you will be a blessing. I will bless those who bless you, and whoever curses you I will curse; and all peoples on earth will be blessed through you."

My point is this: No matter how many times the Nation of Israel turned their back on God, His covenant with Abraham was still binding and irreversible. Therefore, God's declaration that, *"all peoples on earth will be blessed through you,"* was still valid. But it would occur after the cross, since Israel had rejected Jesus of Nazareth as their Messiah. After Israel's rejection, God's divine plan focused directly on the most significant and consequential moments in the history of mankind: the cross and Jesus' death, burial, and resurrection.

Have you ever thought about why God's Son, in complete obedience to His Father, was willing to be tortured and crucified on a cross, where all the sins of mankind were laid on His shoulders? He didn't have to redeem mankind, but He went to the cross to purchase our redemption because He loved us that much. Because of His love for mankind, it was and still is His will that we be saved.

Luke 19:10 — "For the Son of Man came to seek and to save the lost."

This is such a simple verse, yet it carries such a powerful message. Only Jesus' sinless, divine, perfect, blood sacrifice had the power to forgive all the sins of mankind, from Adam until the End of the Age.

Ephesians 1:7 — In him we have redemption through his blood, the forgiveness of sins, in accordance with the riches of God's grace.

Colossians 1:13-14 — For he has rescued us from the dominion of darkness and brought us into the kingdom of the Son he loves, in whom we have redemption, the forgiveness of sins.

Colossians 2:13-14 — When you were dead in your sins and in the uncircumcision of your flesh, God made you alive with Christ. He forgave us all our sins, having canceled the charge of our legal indebtedness, which stood against us and condemned us; he has taken it away, nailing it to the cross.

So, the Good News is the blood of Christ cleansed us of all sin and bought us back (redemption). His death, burial, and resurrection made salvation available to the whole human race—that is the gospel truth.

1 Peter 3:18 — For Christ also suffered once for sins, the righteous for the unrighteous, to bring you to God. He was put to death in the body but made alive in the Spirit.

Romans 1:16 — For I am not ashamed of the gospel, because it is the power of God that brings salvation to everyone who believes: first to the Jew, then to the Gentile.

Chapter 44

The Church Begins

Prior to creation, God knew the descendants of Abraham would not accept His Son as the Messiah. Yet, even after the cross, God empowered the disciples with the power of the Holy Spirit and had them continue to proclaim the gospel of the Kingdom to the Nation of Israel.

So, my question is: After the cross, why did God continue to pursue a lost cause? The following is the best answer I could come up with.

First, our God is a God of second chances who loves us despite our failures. We see this all through the scriptures—in both the Old and New Testaments. Although the plan of redemption took into account their rejection of Jesus, God still intended to give the Nation of Israel every opportunity to believe, but with one exception: He would not override or nullify their free will.

Jesus told the disciples, in detail, how they would be going to Jerusalem, where He would be put to death and rise again on the third day. But they could not comprehend what He was saying. These twelve disciples, who had been with Jesus for nearly three years, didn't understand anything of what He said because it was "hidden" from them.

Luke 18:31-34 — Jesus took the Twelve aside and told them, "We are going up to Jerusalem, and everything that is written by the prophets about the Son of Man will be fulfilled. He will be delivered over to the Gentiles. They will mock him, insult him and spit on him; they will flog him and kill him. On the third day he will rise again." The disciples did not understand any of this. Its meaning was hidden from them, and they did not know what He was talking about.

Therefore, after Jesus' death, they were like sheep without a shepherd and still lacked understanding. Even so, they were still part of God's plan of redemption. Jesus appeared to them over a period of forty days and continued to speak to them about the Kingdom. Before His ascension, Jesus told the disciples the following:

Acts 1:4-5 – "... Do not leave Jerusalem, but wait for the gift my Father promised, which you have heard me speak about. For John baptized with water, but in a few days you will be baptized with the Holy Spirit."

Luke wrote Acts and one of the four gospels, yet he was not one of the twelve disciples. Have you ever wondered why God chose Luke to write these two books of the New Testament? Prior to the cross, Luke witnessed Jesus' earthly ministry, and after the cross he witnessed the disciples as they continued to preach the gospel of the Kingdom to the Nation of Israel. He also witnessed the miraculous transformation of Saul to Paul—the man God chose as the apostle who would take the gospel to the Gentiles.

Luke also witnessed God's plan of redemption as its focus changed from the Nation of Israel only to include the Gentiles. He gave his account of this transition in the book of Acts, where the first eight chapters deal with the gospel of the Kingdom, which continued to be proclaimed to the Nation of Israel by the twelve disciples. Chapter nine tells us about the conversion of Saul, and from that point to chapter fifteen, Luke shifts the focus from the disciples and their message of the gospel of the Kingdom, to Paul and his message of the Gospel of Grace. The remaining chapters in Acts are predominantly about how Paul took this Gospel of Grace to the Gentiles.

At this point, I want to examine the book of Acts more closely. Hopefully, this will help clear up many of the seeming contradictions and issues between the gospel preached before and after the cross. It was only after I put in the time and effort to dig into Acts, verse by verse, that a light came on that not only helped me in my understanding of Acts, but also cleared up much of my confusion concerning the gospel.

Right after Jesus' ascension, Peter and the other disciples met in Jerusalem and selected a new disciple (Matthias) to replace Judas.

Acts 1:26 — Then they cast lots, and the lot fell to Matthias; so he was added to the eleven apostles.

Have you ever wondered why this was the very first thing the disciples did after Jesus' ascension? Peter said it was to fulfill prophecy:

Acts 1:20 — "For," said Peter, "it is written in the Book of Psalms: 'May his (Judas) place be deserted; let there be no one to dwell in it,' and, 'May another take his place of leadership.'"

But why did another need to take his place so quickly? Jesus told the disciples this right before His crucifixion:

Matthew 19:28 — Jesus said to them, "Truly I tell you, at the renewal of all things, when the Son of Man sits on his glorious throne, you who have followed me will also sit on twelve thrones, judging the twelve tribes of Israel."

Peter surely remembered this statement. There would be twelve thrones, but they had only eleven disciples; they needed that twelfth man. Now they would be ready for Christ's return, and all thought it would be within their lifetimes.

On the day of Pentecost, ten days after Jesus' ascension, the twelve disciples, along with many of the Jewish Christ-believers, had gathered in Jerusalem. I am using the KJV translation, since it has the fuller meaning that indicates the timing was exactly according to God's timetable and plan:

Acts 2:1 (KJV) — And when the day of Pentecost was fully come, they were all with one accord in one place.

Acts 2:2-4 — Suddenly a sound like the blowing of a violent wind came from heaven and filled the whole house where they were sitting. They saw what seemed to be tongues of fire that separated and came to rest on each of them. All of them were filled with the Holy Spirit and began to speak in other tongues (languages) *as the Spirit enabled them.*

Just as Jesus promised, the Holy Spirit came down on the twelve, and they were empowered. This not only gave them the power to continue Jesus' earthly ministry to the Nation of Israel, but also the power to perform signs and miracles as Jesus had done.

Acts 2:5 — Now there were staying in Jerusalem God fearing Jews from every nation under heaven.

Thousands of Jews had been scattered throughout the nations during the Babylonian captivity. Since they had maintained their Jewish identity, many would return to Jerusalem for feast days like Pentecost. It was many generations since the Babylonian exile. Therefore, these devout Jews could only speak the language of the nations where they lived. Yet they each miraculously heard the twelve disciples in their own language.

Acts 2:6-8,12-13 — When they heard this sound, a crowd came together in bewilderment, because each one heard their own language being spoken. Utterly amazed, they asked: "Aren't all these who are speaking Galileans? Then how is it that each of us hears them in our native language?" … Amazed and perplexed, they asked one another, "What does this mean?" Some, however, made fun of them and said, "They have had too much wine."

Peter said to them:

Acts 2:15 — "These people are not drunk, as you suppose. It's only nine in the morning!"

Peter then spoke to the gathered Jews and explained:

Acts 2:22-23 — "Fellow Israelites, listen to this: Jesus of Nazareth was a man accredited by God to you by miracles, wonders and signs, which God did among you through him, as you yourselves know. This man was handed over to you by God's deliberate plan and foreknowledge; and you, with the help of wicked men (Gentiles), *put him to death by nailing him to the cross."*

Peter made it clear they rejected and killed their Messiah, and then continued with the good news:

Acts 2:36 — "Therefore let all Israel be assured of this: God has made this Jesus, whom you crucified, both Lord and Messiah."

What was the result of Peter's direct message? Many believed and were saved. They stayed in Jerusalem because they thought Jesus would return soon.

Acts 2:37-38, 41 — When the people heard this, they were cut to the heart and said to Peter and the other apostles, "Brothers, what shall we do?" Peter replied, "Repent and be baptized, every one of you, in the name of Jesus Christ for the forgiveness of your sins. And you will receive the gift of the Holy Spirit." ... Those who accepted his message were baptized, and about three thousand were added to their number that day.

After Pentecost, Peter and the other disciples relentlessly preached to the Nation of Israel that if they would repent, be baptized, and believe, Jesus would return, and they could have their Kingdom.

Acts 3:17-20 — "Now, fellow Israelites, I know that you acted in ignorance, as did your leaders. But this is how God fulfilled what he had foretold through all the prophets, saying that his Messiah would suffer. Repent, then, and turn to God, so that your sins may be wiped out, that times of refreshing may come from the Lord, and that he may send the Messiah, who has been appointed for you—even Jesus."

But the Sanhedrin religious leaders were greatly disturbed:

Acts 4:2-4 — They were greatly disturbed because the

apostles were teaching the people, proclaiming in Jesus the resurrection of the dead. They seized Peter and John and, because it was evening, they put them in jail until the next day. But many who heard the message believed; so the number of men who believed grew to about five thousand.

Although Peter and John were being persecuted, they continued to proclaim the gospel and performed many signs and wonders:

Acts 5:12, 14-15 — The apostles performed many signs and wonders among the people ... Nevertheless, more and more men and women believed in the Lord and were added to their number. As a result, people brought the sick into the streets and laid them on beds and mats so that at least Peter's shadow might fall on some of them as he passed by.

As a result, many followers were added daily to the Jerusalem church, and the number of believers reached the point that it became difficult for the disciples to administer to the needs of these thousands of Christ-followers.

Acts 6:2-5 — So the Twelve gathered all the disciples together and said, "It would not be right for us to neglect the ministry of the word of God in order to wait on tables. Brothers and sisters, choose seven men from among you who are known to be full of the Spirit and wisdom. We will turn this responsibility over to them and will give our attention to prayer and the ministry of the word." This proposal pleased the whole group. They chose Stephen, a man full of faith and of the Holy Spirit; also Philip, Procorus, Nicanor, Timon, Parmenas, and Nicolas from Antioch, a convert to Judaism.

As more Jews recognized Jesus as their Messiah, the Jewish religious leaders began to persecute them in order to stamp out these followers of Jesus of Nazareth. This persecution steadily increased. Several years later, some zealous members of a synagogue seized Stephen and brought him before the Sanhedrin, based on false charges. Stephen responded:

Acts 7:52-54, 58-60 — "Was there ever a prophet your ancestors did not persecute? They even killed those who predicted the coming of the Righteous One. And now you have betrayed and murdered him — you who have received the law that was given through angels but have not obeyed it." When the members of the Sanhedrin heard this, they were furious and gnashed their teeth at him. ... Meanwhile, the witnesses laid their coats at the feet of a young man named **Saul.** *While they were stoning him, Stephen prayed, "Lord Jesus, receive my spirit." Then he fell on his knees and cried out, "Lord, do not hold this sin against them." When he had said this, he fell asleep.*

Acts 8:1 — And Saul approved of their killing him. On that day a great persecution broke out against the church in Jerusalem, and **all except the apostles** *were scattered throughout Judea and Samaria.*

The Jewish religious leader's persecution of the Christ-followers greatly increased after the stoning of Steven. Though they were convicted by Steven's words, they rejected his message that exposed their evil ways. From that point, their fury compelled them to wipe out this threat to their position of power. The persecution became so intense, thousands of followers were forced to flee Jerusalem and were scattered throughout Judea and Samaria. Because of this persecution, these Jewish Christ-followers spread the gospel of the Kingdom far beyond the city of Jerusalem.

I have looked at two events that had an impact on God's plan of redemption: Pentecost and the stoning of Stephen. Now, I want to compare the response to Peter's message to the Jews at Pentecost, with the response to Stephen's speech to the members of the Sanhedrin.

In order to make this comparison, I am going to repeat one important verse from each event:

Acts 2:37 — When the people heard this, **they were cut to the heart** *and said to Peter and the other apostles, "Brothers, what shall we do?"*

Peter's message cut them to the heart, which means they were convicted. Their response was to believe Peter's message, and about 3,000 became Christ-followers.

Acts 7:54 — When the members of the Sanhedrin heard this, they were furious and gnashed their teeth at him.

*Acts 7:54 (KJV) — When they heard these things, **they were cut to the heart,** and they gnashed on him with their teeth.*

Unfortunately, the NIV left out a key part of the verse *(they were cut to the heart),* which has an impact on the full meaning.

These Sanhedrin religious leaders were also convicted, but their response was to kill the messenger. They stoned Stephen. Both groups were convicted, but only those at Pentecost believed. This is an excellent example that shows being convicted does not guarantee anything; it simply puts you in a position of choice. Based on your free will, you can choose obedience or disobedience, belief or unbelief, eternal salvation or eternal separation from God. We **are not predestined** prior to creation. It is our **God-given choice!** The fact God already knows our choice changes nothing. It is still our choice—to follow God, or not—each time the Holy Spirit convicts us.

Chapter 45

An Invitation to the Gentiles

One year after the death of Stephen, an event occurred that began to shift God's focus from the Nation of Israel to include the Gentiles. The best place to start the discussion would be with the man who witnessed the stoning of Stephen: Saul of Tarsus. First, a question: Why Saul of Tarsus?

My initial thought was, "What was God thinking? This man was a Pharisee; a religious zealous who was intent on eradicating all those who were following Jesus of Nazareth!"

Acts 22:3-5 — "I am a Jew, born in Tarsus of Cilicia, but brought up in this city. I studied under Gamaliel and was thoroughly trained in the law of our ancestors. I was just as zealous for God as any of you are today. I persecuted the followers of this Way to their death, arresting both men and women and throwing them into prison, as the high priest and all the Council can themselves testify. I even obtained letters from them to their associates in Damascus, and went there to bring these people as prisoners to Jerusalem to be punished."

And yet, before creation, God picked Saul of Tarsus to be the apostle to the Gentiles; the one man who would take God's divine plan of redemption to all of humanity. Since God does not make mistakes, my challenge was to see this from His perspective instead of my own.

Over the generations, God chose Noah, Abraham, Moses, Joshua, the Judges, the Prophets, David, the twelve disciples, and others. What did they all have in common, except for one of the twelve? Prior to creation, God saw that each had a heart for God. How in the world did Saul of Tarsus make it into this select group? I cannot base this on specific verses of scripture, but this is my opinion: In addition to having a heart for God, each one was chosen, not based on who they were, but on who they would become after being empowered by the Holy Spirit.

I want to look at a number of verses that will unveil how God transformed Saul into the Apostle Paul, who would take the gospel to the Gentiles. Hopefully then, the reasons God chose Saul will become more evident. Afterall, it was Saul's encounter with Jesus on the road to Damascus that began the transition in God's plan of redemption to include the Gentiles. Here's what happened:

After Saul witnessed Stephen's death, he decided to pursue the believing Jews in Damascus.

Acts 9:1-2 — Meanwhile, Saul was still breathing out murderous threats against the Lord's disciples. He went to the high priest and asked him for letters to the synagogues in Damascus, so that if he found any there who belonged to the Way, whether men or women, he might take them as prisoners to Jerusalem.

But God had a different plan.

Acts 9:3-5 — As he neared Damascus on his journey, suddenly a light from heaven flashed around him. He fell to the ground and heard a voice say to him, "Saul, Saul, why do you persecute me?" "Who are you, Lord?" Saul asked. "I am Jesus, whom you are persecuting," he replied.

Saul of Tarsus was a highly-educated, devout, Jewish man who believed in the God of Abraham, Isaac, and Jacob; the Old Testament; the Mosaic Law; and Judaism. He was a Pharisee of the Pharisees. Yet he did not know Jesus of Nazareth until he was sprawled out in the dirt on the road.

When Jesus asked Saul why he was persecuting Him, Saul did not reply, "Who are you?" He replied, *"Who are you, Lord?"* This shows that Saul instantly recognized the voice of His God—the God of Abraham, Isaac, and Jacob. Jesus responded, *"I am Jesus, whom you are persecuting."*

For Acts 9:6, it's worth looking at both the KJV and the NIV, since the NIV left out a key part of the verse.

Acts 9:6 — "Now get up and go into the city, and you will be told what you must do."

Acts 9:6 (KJV) — And he trembling and astonished said, Lord, what wilt thou have me to do? And the Lord said unto him, Arise, and go into the city, and it shall be told thee what thou must do.

The KJV includes Saul's response, *"Lord, what wilt thou have me to do?"* For me, it is critical in my understanding that, while Saul was still lying in the dirt, he instantly believed that Jesus was God's Son, the Messiah.

Acts 9:7-9 — The men traveling with Saul stood there speechless; they heard the sound but did not see anyone. Saul got up from the ground, but when he opened his eyes, he could see nothing. So they led him by the hand into Damascus. For three days he was blind, and did not eat or drink anything.

While Saul was experiencing this physical blindness in Damascus, a Jewish Christ-follower named Ananias had a vision:

Acts 9:11-12 — The Lord told him, "Go to the house of Judas on Straight Street and ask for a man from Tarsus named Saul, for he is praying. In a vision he has seen a man named Ananias come and place his hands on him to restore his sight."

Ananias tried to explain why this might not be a good idea:

Acts 9:13-14 — "Lord," Ananias answered, "I have heard many reports about this man and all the harm he has done to your holy people in Jerusalem. And he has come here with authority from the chief priests to arrest all who call on your name."

But the Lord meant what He said. He told Ananias, *"Go!"*

Acts 9:15-16 — But the Lord said to Ananias, "Go! This man is my chosen instrument to proclaim my name to the Gentiles and their kings and to the people of Israel. I will show him how much he must suffer for my name."

Notice that God (the Lord Jesus) told Ananias He chose Saul to proclaim the name of Jesus to the Gentiles—and to the people of Israel, as well. So, the gospel that Paul would proclaim was for all humanity—Jews and Gentiles. But what gospel? And what was the very last thing He told Ananias? *"I will show him how much he* (Paul) *must suffer for my name."*

Ananias obeyed the Lord Jesus.

Acts 9:17-19 — Then Ananias went to the house and entered it. Placing his hands on Saul, he said, "Brother Saul, the Lord—Jesus, who appeared to you on the road as you were coming here—has sent me so that you may see again and be filled with the Holy Spirit." Immediately, something like scales fell from Saul's eyes, and he could see again. He got up and was baptized, and after taking some food, he regained his strength.

Saul began to preach in the synagogues in Damascus that Jesus was the Son of God. That's how Saul of Tarsus, the man who had thought Jesus was an imposter, began preaching that Jesus truly was the Messiah.

Acts 9:21-22 — All those who heard him were astonished and asked, "Isn't he the man who raised havoc in Jerusalem among those who call on this name? And hasn't he come here to take them as prisoners to the chief priests?" Yet Saul grew more and more powerful and baffled the Jews living in Damascus by proving that Jesus is the Messiah.

So far, I have been using what Luke wrote in Acts to look at

Saul's conversion, but at this point I need to include some of what Paul wrote in his letter to the Galatians. Without both perspectives, the timing of the next events will become confusing. Paul's life was being threatened, so he had to get out of Damascus.

Acts 9:23-25 — After many days had gone by, there was a conspiracy among the Jews to kill him, but Saul learned of their plan. Day and night they kept close watch on the city gates in order to kill him. But his followers took him by night and lowered him in a basket through an opening in the wall.

Acts 9:26 — When he came to Jerusalem, he tried to join the disciples, but they were all afraid of him, not believing that he really was a disciple.

As you can see in verse 25, he left Damascus. In verse 26, it appears that he went straight to Jerusalem, but that was not the case. There was at least a three-year period between Acts 9:25 and Acts 9:26 that Luke did not record.

At this point, you would think God told him to go straight to Jerusalem to see the disciples, who had been with Jesus for three years and were still proclaiming Jesus' earthly ministry to the Nation of Israel. He could learn from them. Instead, he goes to Arabia. But why? Paul gave us the reason:

Galatians 1:15-16 — But when God, who set me apart from my mother's womb and called me by his grace, was pleased to reveal his Son in me so that I might preach him **among the Gentiles,** *my immediate response was not to consult any human being.*

So, Paul went to Arabia, not Jerusalem.

Galatians 1:17 — I did not go up to Jerusalem to see those who were apostles before I was, but I went into Arabia. Later I returned to Damascus.

It was during this time in Arabia when Saul received from Jesus, *"the mystery that has been kept hidden for ages and generations."*

Colossians 1:25-26 — I have become its servant by the commission God gave me to present to you the word of God in its fullness—the mystery that has been kept hidden for ages and generations, but is now disclosed to the Lord's people.

Galatians 1:11-12 — I want you to know, brothers and sisters, that the gospel I preached is not of human origin. I did not receive it from any man, nor was I taught it; rather, I received it by revelation from Jesus Christ.

So far, I have been looking at God's dealings with mankind, based on His divine plan of redemption. Here are a few key points to help you understand the plan, up to this point:

- God's plan of redemption was originally focused on all nations, but when God called out Abram, the focus shifted to one nation—the descendants of Abraham.

- The gospel of the Kingdom that Jesus and the disciples proclaimed to the Nation of Israel was based on God's covenant and fulfilled Old Testament prophecy.

- The Nation of Israel's rejection of God's Son, Jesus of Nazareth, resulted in the Gentiles being included in God's plan of redemption.

- The revelation of these mysteries to Saul began the shift in focus to include the Gentiles.

Through a series of revelations from Jesus, Saul was given hidden truths concerning the Gospel of Grace, the Church Age, the Body of Christ, and the Rapture. We will explore this more in the next chapter, since they were a vital part in the change in focus of God's plan.

Now, let's continue the journey with Saul. He went to Arabia, back to Damascus, and then to Jerusalem. Unfortunately, there is another timing hurdle to overcome:

Galatians 1:18 — Then after three years, I went up to Jerusalem...

Is Paul saying he went to Jerusalem three years after his

conversion or three years after his return to Damascus? It can be taken either way, but since Paul used Galatians 1 to focus on his conversion, you could make the case that he meant three years after his conversion. In either case, it was at least three years between Acts 9:25 and Acts 9:26, when he returns to Jerusalem:

Acts 9:26-30 — When he came to Jerusalem, he tried to join the disciples, But Barnabas took him and brought him to the apostles. He told them how Saul on his journey had seen the Lord and that the Lord had spoken to him, and how in Damascus he had preached fearlessly in the name of Jesus. So, Saul stayed with them and moved about freely in Jerusalem, speaking boldly in the name of the Lord. He talked and debated with the Hellenistic Jews, but they tried to kill him. When the believers learned of this, they took him down to Caesarea and sent him off to Tarsus.

Chapter 46

The Impact of Peter's Vision

This is a good time to examine something that happened to Peter while Saul was in Arabia. Its importance will not become apparent until some years later, but it was instrumental in paving the way for this shift in focus of God's plan.

At Caesarea, there was a Roman centurion named Cornelius. This man was a God-fearing Gentile who prayed regularly to the God of Abraham. One afternoon he had a vision in which an angel of God told him to send men to Joppa to bring back a man named Simon, who is called Peter.

Acts 10:7-8 — When the angel who spoke to him had gone, Cornelius called two of his servants and a devout soldier who was one of his attendants. He told them everything that had happened and sent them to Joppa.

About noon the following day, as the three approached the city, Peter had a vision. In the vision, a large sheet came down from Heaven containing "unclean animals," according to the Jewish diet and the Mosaic law. A voice told him:

Acts 10:13-15 — ..."Get up Peter. Kill and eat." "Surely not, Lord!" Peter replied. "I have never eaten anything impure or unclean." The voice spoke to him a second time (and a third), "Do not call anything impure that God has made clean."

Peter was still a Law-keeping Jew; he was not about to eat

an unclean animal. But this vision was not about unclean animals; it was about the unclean Gentiles.

Acts 10:19-20 — While Peter was still thinking about the vision, the Spirit said to him, "Simon, three men are looking for you. So, get up and go downstairs. Do not hesitate to go with them, for I have sent them."

Peter, accompanied by some of the believers from Joppa, went back with the three to Cornelius' house in Caesarea. As Peter entered the house, he told Cornelius the following:

Acts 10:28-29 — He said to them: "You are well aware that it is against our law for a Jew to associate with or visit a Gentile. But God has shown me that I should not call anyone impure or unclean. So, when I was sent for, I came without raising any objection. May I ask why you sent for me?"

This was a number of years after Pentecost, yet Peter and the other eleven were still only proclaiming the gospel of the Kingdom to the Jews around Jerusalem.

Cornelius explained he had a vision in which he was told to send to Joppa for Simon, who is called Peter.

Acts 10:33-35 — "... So I sent for you immediately, and it was good of you to come. Now we are all here in the presence of God to listen to everything the Lord has commanded you to tell us." Then Peter began to speak: "I now realize how true it is that God does not show favoritism but accepts from every nation the one who fears him and does what is right."

Peter gave this room full of Gentiles the same good news about Jesus Christ that he did to the Jews at Pentecost.

Acts 10:39-41, 44-45 — "We are witnesses of everything he did in the country of the Jews and in Jerusalem. They killed him by hanging him on a cross, but God raised him from the dead on the third day and caused him to be seen. He was not seen by all the people, but by witnesses whom God had already chosen—by us who ate and drank with him after he rose from the dead. ...

While Peter was still speaking these words, the Holy Spirit came on all who heard the message. The circumcised believers who had come with Peter were astonished that the gift of the Holy Spirit had been poured out even on Gentiles."

Then Peter said:

Acts 10:47-48 — "Surely no one can stand in the way of their being baptized with water. They have received the Holy Spirit just as we have." So he ordered that they be baptized in the name of Jesus Christ. Then they asked Peter to stay with them for a few days.

At Pentecost, the Jews believed, repented, and were baptized, then they received the gift (power) of the Holy Spirit. But these Gentiles in the house of Cornelius, to the astonishment of Peter and the believers from Joppa, received the gift of the Holy Spirit while Peter was still speaking. Not only did they receive it, they received it the moment they believed Peter, not after they repented and were baptized. Therefore, Peter ordered that they be baptized in the name of Jesus Christ. This was not only an indication that God's plan of redemption was shifting to include the Gentiles, but that the gospel itself was also beginning a period of transition.

By the time Peter went up to Jerusalem, the apostles and believers throughout Judea had already heard about him visiting the house of a Roman Centurion. But he had not only entered a house full of Gentiles, he had even dined with them.

Acts 11:2-3 — So, when Peter went up to Jerusalem, the circumcised believers criticized him and said, "You went into the house of uncircumcised men and ate with them."

That's when Peter told them the whole story in detail. Their response showed God was moving in a new way:

Acts 11:18 — When they heard this, they had no further objections and praised God, saying, "So then, even to Gentiles God has granted repentance that leads to life."

As I mentioned earlier, it had been a number of years since

Pentecost, and the message of the gospel of the Kingdom was still only being proclaimed to the people of Israel.

*Acts 11:19 — Now those who had been scattered by the persecution that broke out when Stephen was killed traveled as far as Phoenicia, Cyprus and Antioch, spreading the word **only among Jews**.*

But after the news of Peter's visit to the house of Cornelius had spread throughout Judea, some of those Jewish Christ-followers who had fled to Antioch began to speak to Gentiles (Greeks) of the good news about the Lord Jesus.

Acts 11:20-24 — Some of them, however, men from Cyprus and Cyrene, went to Antioch and began to speak to Greeks also, telling them the good news about the Lord Jesus. The Lord's hand was with them, and a great number of people believed and turned to the Lord. News of this reached the church in Jerusalem, and they sent Barnabas to Antioch. When he arrived and saw what the grace of God had done, he was glad and encouraged them all to remain true to the Lord with all their hearts. He was a good man, full of the Holy Spirit and faith, and a great number of people were brought to the Lord.

When the church in Jerusalem heard about the people in Antioch who were turning to the Lord, they sent Barnabas to check it out. Once Barnabas saw both Jews and Gentiles being saved, he went to Tarsus to find Saul. Why? Here is my opinion:

Remember, it was Barnabas who met Saul in Jerusalem and took him to the apostles. Luke said Barnabas was *"full of the Holy Spirit and faith."* When Barnabas saw these Gentiles being saved, he immediately understood this was inspired by God. Through the Holy Spirit, he was reminded of Saul speaking boldly in the name of the Lord. Therefore, Barnabas did not go back to Jerusalem to report what he saw. Instead, he went searching for Saul so he could bring him back to Antioch to show him how the Lord was moving.

Acts 11:25-26 — Then Barnabas went to Tarsus to look for

Saul, and when he found him, he brought him to Antioch. So, for a whole year Barnabas and Saul met with the church and taught great numbers of people. The disciples were called Christians first at Antioch.

Notice, Saul was still being referenced as Saul, not Paul. It took me awhile in reading the Bible before I realized this name change was not from God, like when Jesus changed Simon's name to Peter:

Matthew 16:17-18 — Jesus replied, "Blessed are you, Simon son of Jonah, for this was not revealed to you by flesh and blood, but by my Father in heaven. And I tell you that you are Peter, and on this rock, I will build my church, and the gates of Hades will not overcome it."

In Acts 13:9, much later than the time of his conversion, the author of Acts (Luke) began and thereafter called him "Paul."

Acts 13:9 — Then Saul, who was also called Paul...

My first question was, why? The idea that the two names were interchangeable could be enough of an answer. This is solely my opinion, but I think Saul started referring to himself as "Paul," and Luke picked up on it and did the same, starting in Chapter 13. The name "Saul" would forever be associated with the persecutor. He had been reborn, by the grace of God, and must have felt like a new person. Therefore, I think he wished to leave the name "Saul" with his prior way of life and replace it with "Paul" to reflect his new life.

Chapter 47

The Beginning of Paul's Ministry

I have reached the point where Paul was in Antioch with Barnabas, and this was the beginning of his ministry. Paul spent the next few years in Antioch, helping Barnabas grow the first Christian church that contained a mixture of Jews and Gentiles. From Antioch, Paul started his first missionary journey to Asia Minor and Europe. Paul and Barnabas preached the Gospel of Grace along trade route towns and many coastal cities, then returned to Antioch about a year later. After Paul's return, a group of Jewish Christ-followers took issue with Gentiles being saved without being circumcised.

Acts 15:1-2 — Certain people came down from Judea to Antioch and were teaching the believers: "Unless you are circumcised, according to the custom taught by Moses, you cannot be saved." This brought Paul and Barnabas into sharp dispute and debate with them. So Paul and Barnabas were appointed, along with some other believers, to go up to Jerusalem to see the apostles and elders about this question.

Accordingly, Paul and Barnabas went to the Council in Jerusalem to present their case.

Acts 15:4-5 — When they came to Jerusalem, they were welcomed by the church and the apostles and elders, to whom they reported everything God had done through them. Then some of the believers who belonged to the party of the Pharisees stood up and said, "The Gentiles must be circumcised and required to keep the law of Moses."

Remember a few chapters ago, when I said the importance of Peter's visit to the house of Cornelius would not become apparent until some years later? Well, it was fourteen years after Paul's first trip to Jerusalem that he returned to meet with the Council in Jerusalem. Now we will not only understand why God sent Peter to the house of Cornelius, but we will be able to see that it was instrumental in paving the way for this shift in focus of God's plan of redemption.

Acts 15:6-11,13,19 — The apostles and elders met to consider this question. After much discussion, Peter got up and addressed them: "Brothers, you know that some time ago God made a choice among you that the Gentiles might hear from my lips the message of the gospel and believe. God, who knows the heart, showed that he accepted them by giving the Holy Spirit to them, just as he did to us. He did not discriminate between us and them, for he purified their hearts by faith. Now then, why do you try to test God by putting on the necks of Gentiles a yoke that neither we nor our ancestors have been able to bear? No! We believe it is through the grace of our Lord Jesus that we are saved, just as they are." ... When they finished, James spoke up. "Brothers," he said, "listen to me. ... It is my judgment, therefore, that we should not make it difficult for the Gentiles who are turning to God."

If he had not been sent by God to the house of Cornelius, would Peter have come to Paul's defense? I don't think so. Though we have free will, we should never forget that God is in control!

Galatians 2:8-9 — For God, who was at work in Peter as an apostle to the circumcised, was also at work in me as an apostle to the Gentiles. James, Cephas, and John, those esteemed as pillars, gave me and Barnabas the right hand of fellowship when they recognized the grace given to me. They agreed that we should go the Gentiles, and they to the circumcised.

With a handshake, twenty-two years after the cross, they

agreed that Paul and Barnabas could continue their ministry to the Gentiles, and they would not be forced to include legalism, circumcision, and Judaism in their message. In other words, they said, "You preach your gospel to the Gentiles, and we will continue dealing with the Jews." But for the rest of Acts, the Nation of Israel continued to fall away from accepting Jesus of Nazareth as their Messiah.

Paul moved forward with his ministry, spreading his Gospel of Grace predominately to the Gentiles, but to a number of Jews as well. From this point until he was martyred some twenty-eight years later, Paul relentlessly proclaimed God's grace through the forgiveness of sin by the sacrifice of Jesus Christ.

During those twenty-eight years, Paul made two more missionary journeys, spreading the gospel in Asia Minor and Europe, and helping to establish churches. At the end of his third missionary journey, he knew he would soon be imprisoned and would likely be killed if he returned to Jerusalem. His final words to the church in Ephesus provide insight into the depth of Paul's faith and his unwavering conviction to complete the mission Jesus entrusted to him, without regard for the relentless hardships he faced:

Acts 20:18-24 — When they arrived, he said to them: "You know how I lived the whole time I was with you, from the first day I came into the province of Asia. I served the Lord with great humility and with tears and in the midst of severe testing by the plots of my Jewish opponents. You know that I have not hesitated to preach anything that would be helpful to you but have taught you publicly and from house to house. I have declared to both Jews and Greeks that they must turn to God in repentance and have faith in our Lord Jesus. And now, compelled by the Spirit, I am going to Jerusalem, not knowing what will happen to me there. I only know that in every city the Holy Spirit warns me that prison and hardships are facing me. However, I consider my life worth nothing to me; my only aim is to finish the race and complete the task the Lord Jesus has given me—the task of testifying to the good news of God's grace."

Paul was right. Once he returned to Jerusalem, his life was in constant danger. He was arrested in Jerusalem, imprisoned in Caesarea, appeared before Festus, appealed to Caesar, sent by ship to Rome, was shipwrecked, and spent two years under house arrest in Rome, where he welcomed all who came to him, teaching about the Lord Jesus Christ.

Acts 28:30-31 — For two whole years Paul stayed there in his own rented house and welcomed all who came to see him. He proclaimed the kingdom of God and taught about the Lord Jesus Christ — with all boldness and without hindrance!

Now, I want to revisit the question, why Saul of Tarsus? What did God see in Saul that caused Jesus to confront him on the road to Damascus? I believe if you study through the book of Acts, focusing on Paul, you will come to realize why God selected him. I am going to list some of the reasons that caused me to acknowledge that God knew exactly what He was doing, and I did not.

First, as I have already stated, God knew Paul had a heart for God; Paul just did not know Jesus of Nazareth.

Paul, like Moses, had the perfect background for the mission God had planned, as part of His divine plan of redemption. The following scriptures show both were in the right place at just the right time, since God is in control:

Acts 7:20-22 — "At that time Moses was born, and he was no ordinary child. For three months he was cared for by his family. When he was placed outside, Pharaoh's daughter took him and brought him up as her own son. Moses was educated in all the wisdom of the Egyptians and was powerful in speech and action."

Acts 22:3 — "I am a Jew, born in Tarsus of Cilicia, but brought up in this city. I studied under Gamaliel and was thoroughly trained in the law of our ancestors. I was just as **zealous** *for God as any of you are today."*

"Zealous" is an attribute of one's character that can be defined as "focused desire, characterized by passion and commitment." That definition fit Paul to a tee. Before his conversion, he was zealous for God and in his persecution of the followers of Jesus of Nazareth. But once he believed that Jesus was the Son of God, the Messiah, he was just as zealous in expanding the knowledge of Christ to the Gentiles and to anyone who would listen.

Paul's ability to explain and record the revelations he received from Jesus Christ had a tremendous influence in spreading Christianity throughout the world. Paul was responsible for at least thirteen, and probably fourteen (if you include Hebrews), of the twenty-seven books in the New Testament. Without Paul's epistles to the Christian churches, the books in the New Testament would be cut in half.

When Jesus confronted Saul on the road to Damascus, you would have thought Saul was about to be put to death. Instead, through His grace and mercy, Jesus offered him salvation. So, the one who persecuted, arrested, and imprisoned the followers of Jesus, received eternal salvation.

When Saul was sprawled in the dirt in his hopeless situation, did he beg for forgiveness? No. He listened to Jesus and believed. Because he believed, God chose him as the apostle who would preach this Gospel of Grace not only to the Jews, but to the Gentiles as well. So, if God's grace could save Saul of Tarsus, then is there anyone so sinful that it would be insufficient to save them? That is a powerful message that should bring hope to us all.

I want to revisit the last thing Jesus told Ananias: *"I will show him how much he must suffer for my name."* Notice that Jesus told this to Ananias, not to Paul. But I don't think it took Paul much time to figure it out. From the day Ananias restored his sight, Paul knew what it was to suffer. Throughout his years of ministry, he suffered one beating after another, imprisonments, and constant opposition. Probably no one born under the sun, except for Jesus, has suffered more for the sake of the gospel than the Apostle Paul. He described it in detail:

2 Corinthians 11:23-28 — Are they servants of Christ? (I am out of my mind to talk like this.) I am more. I have worked much harder, been in prison more frequently, been flogged more severely, and been exposed to death again and again. Five times I received from the Jews the forty lashes minus one. Three times I was beaten with rods, once I was pelted with stones, three times I was shipwrecked, I spent a night and a day in the open sea, I have been constantly on the move. I have been in danger from rivers, in danger from bandits, in danger from my fellow Jews, in danger from Gentiles; in danger in the city, in danger in the country, in danger at sea; and in danger from false believers. I have labored and toiled and have often gone without sleep; I have known hunger and thirst and have often gone without food; I have been cold and naked. Besides everything else, I face daily the pressure of my concern for all the churches.

He suffered one thing after another for the sake of the gospel. Why did Paul have to suffer so much, just so we might receive the gospel? I have no answer. He persevered relentlessly, right up until being put to death. What kept him from giving up and calling it quits? I think one thing that helped him endure was remembering how he had persecuted the Christ-followers prior to his conversion. But these words from Paul show us the main reason:

Romans 8:18 — I consider that our present sufferings are not worth comparing with the glory that will be revealed in us.

With all the sufferings and hardships Paul endured, he said it's nothing compared with what's waiting for us; the glory that will be revealed.

And finally, on a personal note, after returning from the Israel tour over twenty years ago, I made the decision to get serious about studying the Bible. Slowly, the Bible no longer seemed beyond my understanding. As for Paul, I went from wondering what God was thinking to admitting God knew what He was doing. The more I understood about Paul, the more I realized he was the gold standard in finishing a race strong. When I decided to write this book, my first thought was, "How can I come up with a title that captures the essence of what I am trying to say?" The first thought that came to me was "Paul." So that's the origin of my title, **Finishing Strong Under the Sun**.

Acts 20:24 — However, I consider my life worth nothing to me; my only aim is to finish the race and complete the task the Lord Jesus has given me—the task of testifying to the good news of God's grace.

Chapter 48

The Mysteries Revealed to Paul

Prior to looking at these mysteries, I want to discuss an issue that some Christians have had to overcome or still struggle with today, and it deals with Paul and his epistles. Since it could possibly impact a person's salvation, in this case, I do not think it is okay to agree to disagree. When it comes to our eternal salvation, this is the one topic where there is no room for error. It is more than just life or death. It is a matter of eternal life with God or eternal separation from God. This is not like archery, where you receive points for being near the bullseye; almost believing gains nothing!

My intention is not to try to explain Paul's doctrine in depth. Especially, since for much of it, my understanding is still lacking. A good place to begin to understand Paul's doctrine would be studying Romans, but with a word of caution: When you read Paul's epistles, you will need to bring your own periods; they are in short supply in Paul's writings!

Every Christian, sooner or later, is faced with accepting or rejecting the doctrines contained in Paul's epistles, which are based on the revelations he received directly from Jesus. I admit it took many years for me to understand why they were revealed to Paul and not someone else, but I have never questioned his writings. I not only believe that Paul's epistles were inspired, but that Paul received these revelations directly from Jesus.

I think there are two main reasons some Christians struggle

with accepting them, and it has nothing to do with the fact that, prior to his conversion, Paul persecuted the Jewish Christ-followers.

First, he is totally on his own, when it comes to what he writes in these doctrines. There is nothing in Old Testament prophesy nor the four gospels concerning these revelations. So, why should we accept Paul's writings? Because they are in the New Testament. About half of the books in the New Testament were written by Paul. They would not be part of the Bible if they were not inspired by God. Remember, God is in control!

And the second reason is Paul's epistles are not easy-to-read and understand. His doctrines are deep and far-reaching. They require more than casual reading. When I was twelve and my mother told me to read the four gospels, she knew what she was doing. If she suggested I begin with some of Paul's epistles, I would have been as lost as a goose in a new back yard.

As we work through the next few chapters, my hope is that you'll gain an understanding of why Paul's writings are not only trustworthy and foundational to our faith, but they also show a fundamental shift in God's plan for redemption. I want to begin by considering the following three mysteries that had the greatest impact on God's plan of redemption. Let's start with considering why they are called "mysteries."

Deuteronomy 29:29 — The secret things belong to the LORD our God, but the things revealed belong to us and to our children forever...

Romans 16:25 — Now to him who is able to establish you in accordance with my gospel, the message I proclaim about Jesus Christ, in keeping with the revelation of the mystery hidden for long ages past,

Ephesians 3:8-9 — Although I am less than the least of all the Lord's people, this grace was given me: to preach to the Gentiles the boundless riches of Christ, and to make plain to everyone the administration of this mystery, which for ages past was kept hidden in God, who created all things.

Until the revelation of these mysteries was revealed to Paul, they had been kept secret, known only in the mind of our Sovereign God. There is nothing in Old Testament prophecy concerning them. This is when God shifted the focus of His plan of redemption from His chosen people to all people of all nations. The following list and accompanying verses are a part of the doctrines of the Gospel of Grace, which Paul proclaimed in his ministry. These three mysteries are found uniquely in Paul's epistles:

The mystery of the Body of Christ:

I am going to repeat: Only Paul uses the term "The Body of Christ." Only Paul's epistles contain the doctrine that explains how our belief in Jesus Christ places us in the Body of Christ, the Church as we know it.

Colossians 1:25-27 — I have become its servant by the commission God gave me to present to you the word of God in its fullness— the mystery that has been kept hidden for ages and generations, but is now disclosed to the Lord's people. To them God has chosen to make known among the Gentiles the glorious riches of this mystery, which is Christ in you, the hope of glory.

Ephesians 3:4-6 — In reading this, then, you will be able to understand my insight into the mystery of Christ, which was not made known to people in other generations as it has now been revealed by the Spirit to God's holy apostles and prophets. This mystery is that through the gospel (the Gospel of Grace) the Gentiles are heirs together with Israel, members together of one body, and sharers together in the promise in Christ Jesus.

Ephesians 1:22-23 — And God placed all things under his (Christ's) feet and appointed him to be head over everything for the church, which is his body, the fullness of him who fills everything in every way.

The mystery of Israel's temporary blindness:

Israel was God's chosen people, through whom all people of all nations would be blessed. As a nation, they not only rejected their Messiah, they crucified God's Son, Jesus, on a cross. Therefore, this revelation to Paul is saying that, as a nation, they have been temporary blinded (set aside for a period of time) until the fullness of the Gentiles is realized.

Romans 11:25 (KJV) — For I would not, brethren, that ye should be ignorant of this mystery, lest ye should be wise in your own conceits; that blindness in part is happened to Israel, until the fulness of the Gentiles be come in.

The mystery of the rapture:

This revelation concerning the departure of the Body of Christ (the Church), which was revealed to Paul, is an essential part of the Church Age doctrine in Paul's epistles.

1 Thessalonians 4:15-17 — According to the Lord's word, we tell you that we who are still alive, who are left until the coming of the Lord, will certainly not precede those who have fallen asleep. For the Lord himself will come down from heaven, with a loud command, with the voice of the archangel and with the trumpet call of God, and the dead in Christ will rise first. After that, we who are still alive and are left will be caught up together with them in the clouds to meet the Lord in the air. And so we will be with the Lord forever.

1 Corinthians 15:51 — Listen, I tell you a mystery: We will not all sleep, but we will all be changed —

1 Thessalonians 5:9 — For God did not appoint us (Body of Christ believers) to suffer wrath but to receive salvation through our Lord Jesus Christ.

Revelation 3:10 (KJV) — Because thou hast kept the word of my patience, I also will keep thee from the hour of temptation, which shall come upon all the world, to try them that dwell upon the earth.

For the remainder of this chapter, I want to look at this transition from the gospel of the Kingdom to the Gospel of Grace. Beginning with Christ's First Coming, the gospel of the Kingdom was preached by John the Baptist, Jesus, and the twelve disciples before the cross.

Matthew 10:5-7 — These twelve Jesus sent out with the following instructions: "Do not go among the Gentiles or enter any town of the Samaritans. Go rather to the lost sheep of Israel. As you go, proclaim this message: 'The kingdom of heaven has come near.'"

For a number of years after the cross, the twelve disciples continued to preach this gospel to the Nation of Israel. At Pentecost, Peter added to the message, telling them that Jesus, who they had crucified, was the Christ, their promised Messiah, and God had raised him from the dead.

Acts 2:22-24 — "Fellow Israelites, listen to this: Jesus of Nazareth was a man accredited by God to you by miracles, wonders and signs, which God did among you through him, as you yourselves know. This man was handed over to you by God's deliberate plan and foreknowledge; and you, with the help of wicked men, put him to death by nailing him to the cross. But God raised him from the dead, freeing him from the agony of death, because it was impossible for death to keep its hold on him."

After Pentecost, Peter and the other disciples continued to proclaim the gospel of the Kingdom. After Peter had healed a man who had been lame from birth, he spoke to the crowd of onlookers:

Acts 3:17-20 — "Now, fellow Israelites, I know that you acted in ignorance, as did your leaders. But this is how God fulfilled what he had foretold through all the prophets, saying that his Messiah would suffer. Repent, then, and turn to God, so that your sins may be wiped out, that times of refreshing may come from the Lord, and that he may send the Messiah, who has been appointed for you—even Jesus."

This Kingdom message is specifically focused on the Nation

of Israel and not on the Gentiles, since its emphasis concerns the Kingdom. The Gentiles had no idea about a King setting up his Kingdom, but the whole Nation of Israel knew exactly what this meant. The Old Testament is full of prophecy concerning the Messiah coming to Jerusalem to establish His earthly Kingdom in the last days. The following are just a few of those verses:

Jeremiah 23:5-6 — "The days are coming," declares the LORD, *"when I will raise up for David a righteous Branch, a King who will reign wisely and do what is just and right in the land. In his days Judah will be saved and Israel will live in safety. This is the name by which he will be called: The* LORD *Our Righteous Savior."*

Zechariah 8:3 — This is what the LORD *says: "I will return to Zion and dwell in Jerusalem. Then Jerusalem will be called the Faithful City, and the mountain of the* LORD *Almighty will be called the Holy Mountain."*

Micah 4:1 — In the last days the mountain of the LORD*'s temple will be established as the highest of the mountains; it will be exalted above the hills, and peoples will stream to it.*

Therefore, this message, *"Repent, for the kingdom of heaven has come near,"* was not a message for the Gentiles. It was for the lost sheep of Israel. God gave Israel every opportunity to repent and believe, but they continued in their unbelief. Therefore, what was God about to do? He was going to set Israel aside, take away their Temple, scatter them into nations all over the world, and shift the focus of His plan of redemption from His chosen people to the Gentiles. God decided that, through Paul, He would reveal these things that had been kept secret. Therefore, based on these divine revelations, Paul became the apostle who would take the Gospel of Grace to the Gentiles.

Paul gave us the essence of the Gospel of Grace in the following verses:

1 Corinthians 15:1-4 — Now, brothers and sisters, I want to remind you of the gospel I preached to you, which you received and on which you have taken your stand. By this gospel you are saved, if you hold firmly to the word I preached to you. Otherwise, you have believed in vain. For what I received I passed on to you as of first importance: that Christ died for our sins according to the Scriptures, that he was buried, that he was raised on the third day according to the Scriptures,

Since this message (the Gospel of Grace) was revealed to Paul after Jesus was crucified, it states that you are saved by believing that Christ died for our sins, was buried, and was raised on the third day. What Jesus accomplished on the cross set in motion the change in focus of the plan of redemption and this resulting Gospel of Grace.

Chapter 49

The Cross Changed Everything

The cross is, by far, the most important event in the history of humanity. It is the crucial point where everything in God's plan of redemption comes together.

God the Father loved us so much, He sent His Son to be the one sacrifice that would redeem humanity. God the Son willingly shed His sinless blood, died on the cross, and was buried for three days. And through the power of God the Holy Spirit, He was resurrected. What Jesus accomplished on the cross changed everything, including the focus and message of God's plan of redemption.

Let's examine some of the major changes that occurred because of the cross.

From Law to grace:

All the Law can do is condemn and convict, based on our sin. It has no power to point us to salvation. It is impossible to keep the Law well enough to satisfy Almighty God. That is the reason Christ had to die on the cross— to fulfill the Law.

Jesus' earthly ministry was focused on the Nation of Israel, under the condition of the Law. The Nation of Israel had been under the Law ever since God gave the Ten Commandants to Moses on Mount Sinai.

John 1:17 — For the law was given through Moses; grace and truth came through Jesus Christ.

After the cross, the plan of redemption was no longer under the Law, nor was it affiliated with the Nation of Israel, Judaism, or Temple worship. It was totally based on the grace of God, through the finished work of the cross—Christ's death, burial, and resurrection. It is this finished work of the cross that is the backbone of the Gospel of Grace. Therefore, Paul's message is under grace, not Law.

Romans 6:14 — For sin shall no longer be your master, because you are not under the law, but under grace.

No longer are we being weighed down from the condemnation based on the "Thou shalls" and "Thou shall nots." Now, through God's grace, the Holy Spirit brings conviction to the unbeliever, causing him to see the truth of the gospel. Then, those who believe this Gospel of Grace and place their faith in Christ receive eternal salvation and are indwelled by the Holy Spirit.

Galatians 2:19-21 — "For through the law I died to the law so that I might live for God. I have been crucified with Christ and I no longer live, but Christ lives in me. The life I now live in the body, I live by faith in the Son of God, who loved me and gave himself for me. I do not set aside the grace of God, for if righteousness could be gained through the law, Christ died for nothing!"

God's gospel message before Israel was under our moral conscience; through Israel it was under Law; and now, apart from Israel, it is under grace.

Shed blood:

Starting with Cain and Abel, God's gospel message throughout the ages had two absolute requirements for salvation: faith and shed blood.

*Hebrews 9:22 — ..."and without the **shedding of blood** there is no forgiveness."*

*Hebrews 11:6 — "**Without faith** it is impossible to please God..."*

In this Old Testament passage, it says that there is no

forgiveness without the shedding of blood:

*Leviticus 17:11 — For the life of a creature **is in the blood**, and I have given it to you to make atonement for yourselves on the altar; **it is the blood** that makes atonement for one's life.*

I am aware that there are some Christian denominations that want to shy away from this "shed blood" topic, nevertheless we cannot ignore the God-inspired words of scripture. Removing songs like "There is Power in the Blood" from their hymnals seems like a foolish attempt to dilute the "power" of God's written Word.

Starting with Adam and Eve, God introduced animal sacrifice, which only covered the sin. It had no power for forgiveness. Animal sacrifice continued until God the Father sent His Son as the one sacrifice that had the power to redeem all of humanity. Therefore, God the Son willingly shed His sinless blood, died on the cross, and was buried for three days. Through the power of God the Holy Spirit, He was resurrected.

Works:

This has been a topic of disagreement in many Bible study classes I have attended over the years. It deals specifically with works, works, and more works. After hearing this discussed so many times, I feel qualified to at least give my thoughts on this topic. To start, I want to look at the following verses:

James 2:24 — You see that a person is considered righteous by what they do and not by faith alone.

James 2:17 — In the same way, faith by itself, if it is not accompanied by action, is dead.

James 2:20 — You foolish person, do you want evidence that faith without deeds is useless?

James could not make it any clearer. He says, without a doubt, that works are necessary for salvation.

Romans 3:28 — For we maintain that a person is justified by faith apart from the works of the law.

Galatians 2:16 — know that a person is not justified by the works of the law, but by faith in Jesus Christ. So we, too, have put our faith in Christ Jesus that we may be justified by faith in Christ and not by the works of the law, because by the works of the law no one will be justified.

Paul could not make it any clearer. He says a man is justified by faith, apart from works. James says that faith alone cannot save, but Paul says it does. Paul says our justification comes through faith and works play no part. If this does not sound like a contradiction, then nothing does. It cannot be resolved by claiming "bad translations" as the culprit. Therefore, either scripture is contradicting itself, or something else is wrong. Since I absolutely believe that scripture is the divinely inspired Word of God, then something else is wrong.

It took many years before I felt I understood enough to reach my own conclusion on this issue. I want to step through my process, since this is a good example of my method of studying the Bible. In other words, I am not giving this detail in an attempt to just explain my conclusion (although it is one that I am comfortable with). I also want to show you how I got there.

Let's reexamine God's plan of redemption, but this time we'll take into account "works." Prior to Abraham, Moses, and the Law, the focus was on all of humanity. Everyone had the same opportunity to have a knowledge of God (salvation), based on the format given to Cain and Abel. During this time, it was their God-given moral conscience that would condemn and convict them. Then, if they would bring a blood sacrifice, God would accept them, on the basis of their faith and obedience. During this period of time, the salvation message was this: If you believe God and prepare and offer a proper animal sacrifice (shed blood), it would be accepted, and you would be in good standing with God. So, this message contained two basic requirements for salvation: faith and shed blood.

*Hebrews 9:22 — ...“and without the **shedding of blood** there is no forgiveness.”*

*Hebrews 11:6 — “**Without faith** it is impossible to please God...”*

But at this time, the salvation message also contained one additional requirement: works (they had to prepare and offer the sacrifice). Therefore, I had to conclude that this message of salvation is in agreement with James.

James 2:24 — You see that a person is considered righteous by what they do and not by faith alone.

Once God gave Moses the Law, the Nation of Israel not only had their moral conscience to condemn and convict, they were now also under the Law of Moses (moral law, civil law, and ceremonial law). The Law added to man's moral conscience by chiseling into stone the "Thou shalls" and "Thou shall nots."

The salvation message still contained the two basic requirements: faith and shed blood. The ceremonial law designated that, when convicted of sin or wrong doing, based on faith, they had to confess the sin to the priest and follow the prescribed steps of providing the proper blood sacrifice (works).

When Jesus began His ministry to the Nation of Israel, they were still under the Law. The Temple was still operating and sacrifices were being brought to the Priest. Jesus ministered under that Law for the entire period of His ministry. Peter's message at Pentecost was *"Repent and be baptized* (works), *every one of you, in the name of Jesus Christ for the forgiveness of your sins."*

It appears that throughout the Old Testament and during Jesus' earthly ministry, no one came into a right standing (salvation relationship) with God without some form of works. The only exception was Abraham *("Abraham believed God, and it was credited to him as righteousness")*.

Therefore, I had to conclude that this Kingdom message of salvation is also in agreement with James.

After the cross, as the focus of God's plan of redemption began shifting to all people of all nations, Jesus gave Paul these revelations of the mysteries. Paul took this Gospel of Grace to the Gentiles, without circumcision, without sacrifices, and without Temple worship.

Romans 1:16 — For I am not ashamed of the Gospel (of Grace), *because it is the power of God that brings salvation to everyone who believes: first to the Jew, then to the Gentile.*

Now I want to try to reconcile James' position of "faith plus works" versus Paul's stance of justification coming through "faith alone." Before the cross, obedience (works) was a requirement for salvation. After the cross, good works happen as a result of salvation. Therefore, this is not a contradiction in scripture—both James and Paul were spot-on. We are the ones creating this confusion, and I am including myself, since it took me such a very long time to reach this conclusion.

To further explain, let's step through an analogy of two "messages of salvation" jigsaw puzzles. Hopefully, if not justifying my understanding of Law, grace, and works, at least it will show how I got there.

The "before the cross" puzzle was cut from a template of Law, and the "after the cross" puzzle was cut from a template of grace.

The "before the cross" puzzle is scattered with "works" pieces. The "after the cross" puzzle is also scattered with "works" pieces.

Each puzzle fits together perfectly (as God intended). But we create a problem when we attempt to mix and match the "works" pieces between the two puzzles. They were cut from two different templates, so they just will not fit, no matter how hard we try.

But if we leave the "works of obedience" in their Law template puzzle, and the "resulting good works" pieces in their grace template puzzle, there is no confusion, and therefore no problem with the scripture.

Chapter 50

Redemption and a Gracious Gift

As I have stated in a previous chapter, if I had to use one word to describe the purpose of the Bible, it would be "redemption." In the Old Testament, both Job and Isaiah prophesied about the coming redeemer:

Job 19:25 — I know that my redeemer lives, and that in the end he will stand on the earth.

Isaiah 59:20 — "The Redeemer will come to Zion, to those in Jacob who repent of their sins," declares the LORD.

Our redemption occurred on the cross when an exchange took place. Through His sacrificial blood, Christ took all our shame, condemnation, and sin, and in return gave us His righteousness.

2 Corinthians 5:21 — God made him who had no sin to be sin for us, so that in him we might become the righteousness of God.

I want to look at the following verses in detail, since for me they establish the foundation for this Gospel of Grace message:

Romans 3:25 — God presented Christ as a sacrifice of atonement, through the shedding of his blood—to be received by faith. He did this to demonstrate his righteousness, because in his forbearance he had left the sins committed beforehand unpunished—

Romans 3:25 contains the two absolute requirements of the grace salvation message: *through the shedding of his blood,* and *to be received by faith.* Christ's shed blood forgave all sins, including the sins of all past generations *(the sins committed beforehand)* that had been left unpunished.

Ephesians 1:7 — In him (Christ) *we have redemption through his blood, the forgiveness of sins, in accordance with the riches of God's grace*

Ephesians 1:7 adds that we have redemption through His blood, and not only are we redeemed, but we are forgiven. It says we are forgiven in accordance with His grace. We don't deserve it, but because of God's love for mankind it is through His grace that His Son went to the cross.

Romans 3:24 — and all are justified freely by his grace through the redemption that came by Christ Jesus.

What Christ did on the cross is all that God requires; it is the finished work of the cross. We are *justified freely* (God sees the sinner as if he had never sinned) based on His loving, undeserved *grace* and accomplished by *redemption* (Christ paid the price to buy us back).

So, what about our eternal salvation? Through Abraham comes the Nation of Israel. Through the Nation of Israel comes the Messiah. Through the Messiah comes the cross, and through the cross comes the God-given gift of salvation.

Ephesians 2:8-9 — For it is by grace you have been saved, through faith—and this is not from yourselves, it is the gift *of God— not by works, so that no one can boast.*

Paul is saying our eternal salvation is a gracious, undeserved gift of God. There is nothing *(it is finished)* we can add to what Christ accomplished on the cross. Can you work to merit a gift? No! If so, it would no longer be a gift. God has done everything that needs to be done. Through the finished work of the cross, God created this divinely-wrapped gift containing "eternal salvation" and the "indwelling of the Holy Spirit" with a tag that says: *From:* Almighty God *— To:*

A Believer.

I could have said: *From:* Almighty God — *To:* A Person of Faith. But that does not sound right. Either you believe, or you don't; it is yes or no. There are no increments of belief, whereas there are increments of faith, which means it is measurable. So, the question becomes: How much faith is required to believe God and receive eternal salvation? To paraphrase my pastor, "Just how much faith do I need to make it to the Pearly Gates?"

Remember the verse in the Bible where the man said *"Lord, I believe; help thou mine unbelief"?*

Mark 9:24 (KJV) — And straightway the father of the child cried out, and said with tears, Lord, I believe; help thou mine unbelief.

When we reach that point where, instead of saying "I believe, help my unbelief," we can say "I believe," then we have crossed that threshold of moving from "some measure of faith" to "saving faith." So, the answer to our question is "saving faith." Therefore, *"From:* Almighty God — *To:* A **Believer**" and *"From:* Almighty God — *To:* A Person with **Saving Faith** means the same.

How do you receive this divinely-wrapped gift? You don't need to climb Mt. Everest to claim it. You don't need to keep all the Ten Commandments to claim it. Just believe that everything needed was accomplished on the cross, based on Christ's shed blood—on His death, burial, and resurrection. Once you believe, you are indwelled by the Holy Spirit, the Holy Spirit places you in the Body of Christ, and you receive a precious gift from God: eternal salvation. That is the Gospel of Grace!

Chapter 51

The Disciples and the Kingdom Message

The fact the Grace message replaced the Kingdom message takes nothing away from the importance of the disciples' ministry. Jesus selected these twelve disciples for a key mission, as part of God's plan of redemption. The fact it was unachievable is a reflection on the Nation of Israel and takes nothing away from what the disciples endured and accomplished. Imagine spending three years with Jesus leading and teaching you daily, as you followed Him all over Israel. It is from the disciples' three-year ministry with Jesus that we have the four gospels: Matthew, Mark, Luke, and John. The words of Jesus are found primarily in these four gospels, with each giving an independent retelling of His life. As Jesus neared the end of His three-year ministry, He said the following to the disciples:

Matthew 19:28 — Jesus said to them, "Truly I tell you, at the renewal of all things, when the Son of Man sits on his glorious throne, you who have followed me will also sit on twelve thrones, judging the twelve tribes of Israel."

Jesus promised the twelve that when He set up His Kingdom, they would rule the twelve tribes of Israel, from Jerusalem, under his authority. After the cross, the disciples continued to relentlessly preach the gospel of the Kingdom message and perform healing miracles right up until their death (martyred, except for John).

As for Paul, it was Jesus who chose this persecutor of the

Christ-followers to be the apostle who would take the message of salvation to the Gentiles. But what did Jesus say to Ananias about Paul?

Acts 9:16 — "I will show him how much he must suffer for my name."

That quote from Jesus does not lead us to believe Jesus favored Paul over the Twelve. If anything, it shows believing and following the Lord does not eliminate the consequences of your actions; just look at the life of King David. The Twelve had their mission that focused on the Nation of Israel, and Paul had his that focused on the Gentiles. But Peter, like John, had an additional task.

We have already looked at how God sent Peter to the house of Cornelius (a Gentile), which prepared him to come to the defense of Paul at the Jewish Council. Based on Peter's testimony, the Council agreed that Paul and Barnabas could continue their ministry to the Gentiles, and they would not be forced to include legalism, circumcision, and Judaism in their message. But this was not the only way God used this impulsive fisherman as part of His plan of redemption. Peter had spent three years with Jesus and was the first of the twelve to recognize Jesus as the Messiah.

Matthew 16:15-16 — "But what about you?" he asked. "Who do you say I am?" Simon Peter answered, "You are the Messiah, the Son of the living God."

But as he awaited his death, Peter wrote the following near the end of his second epistle:

2 Peter 3:14-16 — So then, dear friends, since you are looking forward to this, make every effort to be found spotless, blameless and at peace with him. Bear in mind that our Lord's patience means salvation, just as our dear brother Paul also wrote you with the wisdom that God gave him. He writes the same way in all his letters, speaking in them of these matters. His letters contain some things that are hard to understand, which ignorant and unstable people distort, as they do the other Scriptures, to their own destruction.

So, what was Peter saying? Peter said that *"our dear brother Paul"* wrote to you in his epistle, based on the wisdom (revelation of the mysteries) God gave him. Peter also says that Paul wrote his other epistles in the same manner concerning these matters (revelations). Peter admits that Paul's epistles contain some things (doctrine) that are hard to understand.

Finally, Peter says, *"as they do the other Scriptures."* With this statement, Peter is comparing Paul's epistles to the other scriptures in the Bible. Why is this so important? Well, for those who have struggled with accepting Paul's writings, is this not an acknowledgement from the Apostle Peter that Paul's epistles are scripture?

Chapter 52

Defining the Gospel

Now I want to discuss the idea of one gospel versus two or more. So many Christians seem to struggle with this issue. It took me a long time and a lot of study before I reached a point that it made sense to me, and my ideas on this subject are 100 percent based on my understanding of scripture. If a twelve-year-old understands this topic enough to be saved, then is it possible we are making it over complicated and thus creating unnecessary confusion?

So, what is the gospel? I will start with this simple definition: It is the good news that proclaims a salvation that God has made available to each and every person born under the sun. It is the centerpiece of God's divine plan of redemption. As I work through this topic, I will expand on this definition.

To start, I want to make the following two statements: You must believe what God says. That sounds so simple, but it is an absolute requirement for your redemption and salvation. But you cannot believe what you do not know. In other words, how can you believe something if God has yet to say it (or has hidden it from your understanding)?

Starting all the way back in Genesis, what did God say to Cain and Abel? God said to prepare and offer a proper animal sacrifice (shed blood), it would be accepted, and you would be in good standing with God. Through faith, Abel believed God, and based on a lack of faith, Cain did not. This was all they knew. They did not know that God's Son would die on the cross, be buried for three days and be resurrected; therefore, it was all God required at that time. It remained the good news message until God gave the Law to Moses.

After the Nation of Israel received the Law, it was still the good news, but was now under the Law, and it now involved Temple worship, which required the sacrifice being brought to the Priest instead of God. This continued to be the gospel message (good news) until Christ's First Coming.

So, now with the First Coming of Christ, what was God's good news message? Jesus said, *"Repent, for the Kingdom of Heaven has come near."* In other words, Jesus of Nazareth, God's Son, the promised Messiah, the promised King, had come to establish His earthly Kingdom. This Kingdom gospel was now the good news message, and it was preached by Jesus and the disciples to the Nation of Israel during His three years of earthly ministry. It was still under the Law, therefore the Temple worship, feast days, sacrifices and offerings, and food and purity laws and regulations still applied. After the cross, the disciples continued to preach this Kingdom message to the Nation of Israel.

At Pentecost, Peter added that Jesus, who they had crucified, was the Christ, their promised Messiah, and God had raised Him from the dead. But still this gospel of the Kingdom did not include believing in Christ's death, burial, and resurrection as part of God's plan of salvation. Why? Because they could only believe what had been revealed to them, not something that had been kept hidden. I have already discussed Jesus telling the disciples about His upcoming death, burial, and resurrection as they were about to go to Jerusalem. The following verses confirm it remained hidden from them, right up until He had arisen:

John 20:6-9 — Then Simon Peter came along behind him and went straight into the tomb. He saw the strips of linen lying there, as well as the cloth that had been wrapped around Jesus' head. The cloth was still lying in its place, separate from the linen. Finally the other disciple, who had reached the tomb first, also went inside. He saw and believed. (They still did not understand from Scripture that Jesus had to rise from the dead.)

I want to recap the gospel of the Kingdom versus the Gospel of grace. The Kingdom gospel was focused on the Nation of Israel and not on the Gentiles, since its emphasis concerns the Kingdom. Its purpose was to show the Nation of Israel that Jesus of Nazareth was the Christ, the Son of God, the promised Messiah who would establish an earthly Kingdom. The Gentiles had no concept of an earthly Kingdom. The good news of the Kingdom excluded Christ's death, burial, and resurrection because God chose not to reveal it until after the cross.

Through a series of revelations from Jesus, Paul was given hidden truths concerning the Gospel of Grace, the Body of Christ (the Church Age), and the Rapture. Paul was chosen to take this message of grace to both the Jews and the Gentiles. Through the cross, the blood of Christ cleansed us of all sin and bought us back (redemption). His death, burial, and resurrection made salvation available to the whole human race. And the only thing that God asks us to do is believe that everything needed was accomplished on the cross. Once you believe, you are indwelled by the Holy Spirit, the Holy Spirit places you in the Body of Christ, and you receive a precious gift from God: eternal salvation. This is the Gospel of Grace!

I want to wrap up my thoughts on this issue of one gospel versus two or more. First, counting the number of gospels is really not relevant. You can call it one, two, or multi-versions. What we do know is God has one and only one plan of redemption, and within that plan of redemption, there is only one way to salvation: through Jesus Christ. It was set in motion by our Triune God, prior to creation. Despite mankind's free-will choices and Satan's constant attempts to interfere, God's plans cannot be altered and will run their intended course.

Matthew 6:10 — your kingdom come, your will be done, on earth as it is in heaven.

Chapter 53

Impact of the Revelation of the Mysteries

As we have discussed, the revelations Jesus gave to Paul began the transition of God's plan of redemption from the Nation of Israel to all nations, including Israel. It also started the transition from the good news message of the Kingdom, which was focused on the Nation of Israel, to the message of grace to the Gentiles. But this is not the only way scripture was impacted by these mysteries.

The revelations to Paul concerning the Gospel of Grace, the Body of Christ (Church Age), and the Rapture blew a gigantic hole in the Old Testament prophecy timeline for Israel. Nothing in Old Testament prophecy (or in the four gospels, for that matter) refers to these revelations. Therefore, the Old Testament prophecy timeline excludes the Age of Grace (the filling of the Body of Christ). The prophets had no concept that there would be 1,900+ years where God would be dealing with the Gentiles while the Nation of Israel would be in a period of spiritual darkness. In the New Testament, the twelve disciples and even Paul thought Christ would return during their lifetime. Therefore, the filling of the Body of Christ (the Church Age) has put an extended pause in the Old Testament prophecy timeline.

We are now 1,900+ years into the Church Age, and new believers are still being added to the Body of Christ. I want to continue to focus on God's plan of redemption, as it weaves through generation after generation as the Body of Christ is being filled. Discussing redemption through this Age of Grace is going to require my thoughts on the timing of the Rapture, which in turn impacts the timing of the Tribulation, the Second Coming, and the Kingdom.

I am going to use a verse from Luke (Luke 21:24), three verses from Daniel (Daniel 9:24-26), and a verse from Romans (Romans 11:25) to give my opinion on the timing and order of these end-times events.

I will start by looking at Luke 21:24 in detail.

Luke 21:24 (KJV) — Jerusalem shall be trodden down of the Gentiles, until the times of the Gentiles be fulfilled.

This verse contains a reference to a period of time *(until)*, meaning there is a start and an end. Keeping up with the beginning and ending of this period of time is a challenge. I am not saying that you will need to be a math major to understand, but you will need to give this your undivided attention.

The *"times of the Gentiles"* are signified by an increase in wickedness and ungodliness during a period of time in which the Gentiles will have dominion over Jerusalem and the Jewish people. The *"times of the Gentiles"* started when the Gentile nation of Babylon invaded Israel.

Jeremiah 27:6a — Now I will give all your countries into the hands of my servant Nebuchadnezzar king of Babylon;

In 606 B.C., Nebuchadnezzar came from Babylon and besieged the city of Jerusalem, destroyed the Temple, and took the Jews captive. For many years I had prayed for "the peace of Israel" thinking this meant that the nations in the Middle East would cease their aggression and allow Israel to live in peace. But this prayer is about far more than security from attack. I have come to understand that, more importantly, it is about the Nation of Israel finally being brought back under God's blessings. I have also come to understand that *"trampled on by the Gentiles"* does not mean continually being physically occupied (underfoot), but instead always under the political pressure and influence of the Gentile nations.

I have established the start of the *"times of the Gentiles"*—or maybe not. This is a little more complicated than it seems, at first. It will require some verses from Daniel before I can establish the actual beginning of the *"times of the Gentiles."* There are a number of verses in Daniel that are critical in our understanding of end-times prophecy. Daniel, chapter 9, contains some of the most amazing and significant prophetic passages in the Bible. In fact, if you were to remove this chapter from the Old Testament, understanding these end-times events and their timing would be absolutely impossible. As I examine these verses, remember that the timing of Daniel's end-times prophecy for Israel does not take into account the revelation of the mysteries to Paul.

Daniel 9:24 — "Seventy 'sevens' are decreed for your people and your holy city to finish transgression, to put an end to sin, to atone for wickedness, to bring in everlasting righteousness, to seal up vision and prophecy and to anoint the Most Holy Place.

Seventy 'sevens' means seventy weeks of years. Since a week is seven days, 70 times 7 is equal to 490 years, as noted in the following verse, which also references seven weeks of years:

Leviticus 25:8 — Count off seven sabbath years—seven times seven years—so that the seven sabbath years amount to a period of forty-nine years.

I want to look at the words *"your people"* in Daniel 9:24, since its meaning has an impact on our *"trampled on by the Gentiles"* timeline. Who were Daniel's people? The people of Israel. Why is God (through the angel Gabriel) saying *"your people"*? If you look back at scripture, starting with Moses, sometimes God would call Israel *"His people"* and other times He would call them *"your people."* Why the difference? When they are in a period of obedience and under His blessing, God calls Israel *"His people."* But when they have been set outside His blessings, then God calls them *"your people."* And this is the case; Israel is still exiled in Babylon, outside of God's blessings. The reason this is important is that all through scripture, while Israel is outside God's blessing, God's prophecy timeline for Israel stops. This means that even though the *"times of the Gentiles"* started with Nebuchadnezzar's invasion of Israel, the seventy-year exile is not counted. Therefore, the 490-year count started when King Artaxerxes gave Nehemiah the decree that allowed their return to Israel.

Nehemiah 2:4-5 — The king (Artaxerxes) said to me, "What is it you want?" Then I prayed to the God of heaven, and I answered the king, "If it pleases the king and if your servant has found favor in his sight, let him send me to the city in Judah where my ancestors are buried so that I can rebuild it."

Now, knowing the beginning of the 490 years, we can look at this next verse:

Daniel 9:25 — Know and understand this: From the time the word goes out to restore and rebuild Jerusalem until the Anointed One, the ruler, comes, there will be seven 'sevens,' and sixty-two 'sevens.' It will be rebuilt with streets and a trench, but in times of trouble.

So, (7 + 62 = 69 weeks). Therefore, it will be (69 x 7 = 483 years) from the king's decree until the cross.

Daniel 9:26 — After the sixty-two 'sevens,' the Anointed One will be put to death and will have nothing ...

Immediately after the expiration of those 483 years, Jesus of Nazareth, the Messiah, was *"put to death"* (crucified). Christ's whole three-year earthly ministry was to prepare Israel for this glorious Kingdom, knowing they would reject it and bring about the crucifixion. Was it a valid offer? Yes, but they turned it down.

And yet, Jesus will be coming back to give them a second chance. This is just like when God offered Israel the Promised Land, knowing they would reject it. But God did not give up on Israel. After forty years in the wilderness, He gave them a second chance. This is no different than today, with our expectation of His Second Coming.

As I write this, there is still a 70th week of seven-years to complete Daniel's prophecy. But I need to look at Romans 11:25 prior to discussing the completion of this 70th week.

Romans 11:25 (KJV) — ...that blindness in part is happened to Israel, until the fulness of the Gentiles be come in.

The *"fulness of the Gentiles"* is the Body of Christ (the Church). As Gentiles are being saved, they are being placed into the Body of Christ. While this filling is occurring, the Nation of Israel will remain in a temporary period (1,900+ years and counting) of spiritual blindness. Although the nation as a whole will be spiritually blind, some individual Jews will also be saved and placed in the Body of Christ.

For the Church Age, this filling of the Body of Christ began after the cross, as God shifted the focus of His plan of redemption from the Nation of Israel to all nations. Knowing the exact time of the start of the filling of the Body of Christ is not critical. It has no impact of the timing of end-time prophesy. It is when the *"fulness of the Gentiles"* (the Church Age) occurs that is important to the timeline.

So, when will this Church Age end? It will end when that last person to be saved by grace becomes part of the Body of Christ. Only our Sovereign God knows the day and hour this will occur, and the exact number who will be saved through grace.

So, if you think that, prior to creation, God set the date for when the Body of Christ would be filled—according to scripture, that is not the case. Although only God knows the exact time, it will be determined based on man's free-will choice of belief or unbelief. Therefore, the more we, as believers, spread the gospel and bring new believers into the Body of Christ, the sooner it will be filled. When the last believer, based on the Gospel of Grace, has been saved and the *"fulness of the Gentiles"* is complete, the Church will be taken out (the Rapture). This will trigger the start of the rest of the Old Testament end-times prophecy, the beginning of the last seven years of Daniel's 490-year timeline, which just happens to be the exact length of time of the Tribulation. The Second Coming will occur at the end of the seven-year Tribulation, with the *"times of the Gentiles"* ending with the glorious return of Christ.

So, what does this all mean? It means I adamantly believe in a Pre-Tribulation Rapture, but I know there are those who do not. There are many scriptures concerning the end times that are difficult to understand, and their meanings range from somewhat to extremely debatable. Therefore, for the remainder of this chapter I am going to explain why I totally, 100 percent, believe in a Pre-Tribulation Rapture, which will trigger the beginning of the Tribulation, then the Second Coming of Christ, followed by the Kingdom. My reasons are not tied to these debatable timing issues, but rather are solely based on my understanding of the following two topics:

The Body of Christ just does not fit in the Tribulation.

As we have discussed, from Abraham until the cross, God's plan of redemption was focused directly on the Nation of Israel, which includes Jesus' three-year earthly ministry. From the time God gave Moses the Law until the cross, Israel was under the Law, which included the Temple worship, feast days, sacrifices, and offerings. The gospel message (good news) to Israel concerned the promised Messiah; the promised King coming to Israel to establish His earthly Kingdom. During Jesus' three-year earthly ministry, the gospel of the Kingdom was preached only to the Nation of Israel by John the Baptist, Jesus, and the twelve disciples.

But after the cross, the Nation of Israel was set outside

God's blessings and placed into an extended period of spiritual blindness. Based on Israel's rejection and crucifixion of Jesus, God's plan of redemption shifted in focus from the Nation of Israel to the Gentiles. This was set in motion when Jesus revealed to Paul hidden truths (mysteries) concerning the Body of Christ (the Church Age), the Gospel of Grace, and the Rapture. For 1,900+ years and counting, the Nation of Israel has remained in a period of spiritual blindness as believers continue to be placed in the Body of Christ, based on the Gospel of Grace.

Trying to put the Body of Christ in the seven-year Tribulation is like trying to put a square peg in a round hole. It will not fit, no matter how hard you try. The Abrahamic Covenant was made with Israel and did not include the Gentile nations. The Kingdom was only promised to the Nation of Israel. Prior to the cross, for generations, God dealt primarily with Israel. For the Church Age, the Body of Christ is being filled primarily with Gentiles. So, God has always dealt with them separately. Why would God change?

The Kingdom gospel message to Israel was under the Law; the grace gospel message during the Church Age is under grace. Law and grace cannot be mixed; it would be like trying to mix water and oil. This Kingdom message is specifically focused on the Nation of Israel and not on the Gentiles, since its emphasis concerns the Kingdom. The Gentiles had no idea about a King setting up His Kingdom. But the whole Nation of Israel knew exactly what this meant. The Old Testament is full of prophecy concerning the Messiah coming to Jerusalem to establish His earthly Kingdom in the last days.

So, what gospel will be proclaimed during the Tribulation?

Matthew 24:14 (KJV) — And this gospel of the kingdom shall be preached in all the world for a witness unto all nations; and then shall the end come.

It does not line up with the character of God.

Having the Body of Christ be part of the Tribulation does not line up with the character of our Sovereign God. During the tribulation, God's wrath will fall on the Nation of Israel, and it is going to be in judgment. Why should He bring judgment on the believing Church? That does not line up with God's character; therefore, it just does not make sense.

1 Thessalonians 5:9 — For God did not appoint us (the Body of Christ, believers) *to suffer wrath but to receive salvation through our Lord Jesus Christ.*

But He is going to bring judgment on unbelieving Israel and the "left behind" unbelieving Gentiles. All members of the Body of Christ have been promised eternal salvation. Each new believer is being counted, and when the count reaches full, the Church Age ends. If the Rapture is after the beginning of the Tribulation, those believers living at the time who "fall away" would be removed from the Body of Christ and lose their salvation. It would be contrary to God's character to place believers in the Body of Christ, give them eternal salvation, test them, and then take it away. The Tribulation is a time of wrath, not testing. So, based on God's character, explain to me why God would subject them to the Tribulation. That makes no sense.

What does God do the moment He saves us? He breathes life into our spirit and puts the Holy Spirit within us. He forgives us. He places us into the Body of Christ. He redeems us; buys us back. He pays the price for our sins. He justifies us. He sanctifies us. He glorifies us. In studying the Bible, is there anything in God's character that would indicate that God would undo all that?

Finally, the Book of Life contains the list of names of all who have eternal security. And I believe that once a name is written, it is never erased. Who writes the names of these Body of Christ believers into the Book of Life? Jesus! And then who is the only one who can remove them? Jesus! So, if Jesus enters a name and then removes that name, that would mean Jesus made a mistake. God is sovereign! God cannot make a mistake.

At this point, I have laid out God's plan of redemption up until the end of the Church Age, using many relevant scriptures. In the following chapters, I will continue to focus on God's plan of redemption and follow it right up to Christ's Second Coming.

Chapter 54

Let's Talk About Miracles

Before we focus on the Tribulation, I want to look at miracles prior to, during, and after the Church Age. Having an understanding of how they differ will help make sense of the miraculous events that will occur, one after the other, during the seven-year Tribulation.

Let's begin with the question, "What is a miracle?" A statistician might say a miracle is any event that has zero percent probability of occurring. A scientist might say any event that contradicts all known natural and scientific laws qualifies as a miracle. But a praying miner, trapped and waiting for rescue as his air supply diminishes, might say each and every next breath is a miracle.

Acts 2:22 (KJV) — Ye men of Israel, hear these words; Jesus of Nazareth, a man approved of God among you by miracles and wonders and signs, which God did by him in the midst of you, as ye yourselves also know:

From this verse, we see scripture refers to three types of supernatural occurrences: miracles, wonders, and signs. All signs and wonders are miracles; all miracles are not signs and wonders. My intent here is not to attempt to distinguish between the three, but to look at the reason for and source of miracles prior, during, and after the Church Age.

During the time God focused on the Nation of Israel, most miracles were on a grand scale—mainly signs and wonders—

to show the people He was their God. If they would believe and be obedient to His commands, they would be blessed; if not, they would be cursed and incur His wrath.

Deuteronomy 29:2-3 — Moses summoned all the Israelites and said to them: Your eyes have seen all that the LORD did in Egypt to Pharaoh, to all his officials and to all his land. With your own eyes you saw those great trials, those signs and great wonders.

Even when Moses led Israel out of Egypt, they witnessed a multitude of incredible miracles like the parting of the Red Sea, the pillar of fire by night, the pillar of cloud by day, and many others. Yet, in spite of all the miracles, the people of Israel continually fell into unbelief. This happened over and over, right up until the First Coming of Christ. Jesus performed supernatural miracle upon miracle during His earthly ministry, while proclaiming the good news that He was the Messiah and had come to establish His Kingdom.

Matthew 9:35 — Jesus went through all the towns and villages, teaching in their synagogues, proclaiming the good news of the kingdom and healing every disease and sickness.

The reason for all His signs and miracles was to prove to the Nation of Israel that He was the Messiah.

John 4:48 — "Unless you people see signs and wonders," Jesus told him, "you will never believe."

Even after three years of performing miracles, signs, and wonders, the Israelites rejected His message and crucified their Messiah because of their unbelief. Yet the disciples continued to preach the gospel and perform miracles until their death.

Acts 2:22-24 — "Fellow Israelites, listen to this: Jesus of Nazareth was a man accredited by God to you by miracles, wonders and signs, which God did among you through him, as you yourselves know. This man was handed over to you by God's deliberate plan and foreknowledge; and you, with the help of wicked men, put him to death by nailing him to the cross. But God raised him from the dead, freeing him from the agony of death, because it was impossible for death to keep its hold on him."

Now, during the Church Age, God still performs miracles—but they are accomplished by the Holy Spirit through our prayers or intercessory prayers, based on God's will. At times, unsolicited miracles can occur as God intervenes, based on His sovereign will. I am sure what a believer considers a miracle, an unbeliever might consider a mere coincidence. But don't tell that to the miner who was rescued just as his air supply ran out.

With the end of the Church Age, the Rapture of the Body of Christ will occur. This supernatural event will end the Age of Grace and will usher in God's various judgments on not only the Nation of Israel, but on all nations on earth. The seven-year Tribulation will be hell on earth, but it will not prevent God from continuing to offer His plan of redemption, right up until the Second Coming of Christ.

Matthew 24:21 — For then (Tribulation) *there will be great distress, unequaled from the beginning of the world until now—and never to be equaled again.*

During the Church Age, many have become skeptical of miracles. But having an understanding of miracles is essential if you have any hope of making sense of the events that will occur during the Tribulation. During these seven years, the supernatural will become commonplace. Even while these terrible, cataclysmic disasters are occurring, God will be performing supernatural signs, wonders, and miracles such that the world has never witnessed.

But Christ will not be the only source of miracles during the Tribulation. The counterfeit Messiah, the Antichrist, is going to perform satanic miracles, signs, and wonders as he attempts to deceive and destroy.

2 Thessalonians 2:9-10 — The coming of the lawless one will be in accordance with how Satan works. He will use all sorts of displays of power through signs and wonders that serve the lie, and all the ways that wickedness deceives those who are perishing. They perish because they refused to love the truth and so be saved.

During these seven years of death and destruction, the Antichrist will be working hand-in-hand with Satan, and God will continue to offer salvation, right up until the Second Coming of Christ.

Chapter 55

The Tribulation and the Second Coming

Now that we have a basic understanding of miracles, it's time to focus on God's plan of redemption through the seven years of the Tribulation. The Gospel of Grace began with the Church and will end with the Church's departure. So, during the Tribulation, it will not be the Gospel of Grace that is preached. Instead, it will be the same gospel of the Kingdom that Jesus and the disciples preached during Jesus' earthly ministry: that Jesus Christ is the promised Messiah, and He is going to usher in the Kingdom. After this gospel is preached for the seven years, He is going to stand on the Mount of Olives and set up His thousand-year Kingdom. That is the "good news" of the gospel of the Kingdom.

Matthew 24:14 — "And this gospel of the kingdom will be preached in the whole world as a testimony to all nations, and then the end will come."

This message is not going to be confined to Israel. It's going to be preached in every tongue, to every tribe and nation, so there will be candidates for the Kingdom from every nation on earth.

After the Rapture occurs, what will be missing besides the believers? All their spiritual influence, which had acted as a shield of resistance to the satanic forces of sin and evil, will have departed with them. This departure will open the floodgates of wickedness as the Tribulation begins.

Although the Tribulation is a time when God's judgment will fall on those "left behind," this does not mean He will close the door on the possibility of salvation. There are three distinct ways God's plan of redemption will be offered during the Tribulation. I want to look at each one in detail, starting with the *"two witnesses."* Remember, prior to the First Coming of Christ, God sent John the Baptist to proclaim the good news that the King (the Messiah) was in their midst, and the Kingdom of Heaven was at hand.

Luke 1:76 — And you, my child (John the Baptist), *will be called a prophet of the Most High; for you will go on before the Lord to prepare the way for him,*

Just as John the Baptist prepared the way for the First Coming of Christ, the "two witnesses" will prepare the way for the Second Coming of Christ.

Revelation 11:3 — "And I will appoint my two witnesses, and they will prophesy for 1,260 days, clothed in sackcloth."

So, for the first three-and-a-half years of the Tribulation, these *"two witnesses"* will stand on the streets of Jerusalem and will be preaching the gospel of the Kingdom—like Jesus, John the Baptist, and the twelve who preached that the King is coming. Their message will be heard all over the world. During this time of immense evil and destruction, how in the world can these two defenseless witnesses do this?

Revelation 11:5-6 — "If anyone tries to harm them, fire comes from their mouths and devours their enemies. This is how anyone who wants to harm them must die. They have power to shut up the heavens so that it will not rain during the time they are prophesying; and they have power to turn the waters into blood and to strike the earth with every kind of plague as often as they want."

As soon the Tribulation begins, and God starts dealing with Israel, the supernatural signs, wonders, and miracles commence with the *"two witnesses."* The two will be empowered by the Holy Spirit to again offer the message that the King is coming. Then, at the end of the three-and-a-half years, God will allow their death.

Revelation 11:7-9 — Now when they have finished their testimony, the beast that comes up from the Abyss will attack them, and overpower and kill them. Their bodies will lie in the public square of the great city—which is figuratively called Sodom and Egypt—where also their Lord was crucified. For three-and-a-half days some from every people, tribe, language and nation will gaze on their bodies and refuse them burial.

In other words, after they are killed, the whole world will see their bodies lying on the streets of Jerusalem. Prior to our generation, this prophesy of people from all nations seeing their bodies as they lay dead on the streets of Jerusalem was beyond understanding. But now, with everyone and his brother owning a cell phone, the whole world will be able to see it in real-time. So, before our generation, this was unbelievable, but now this is well within our understanding. Remember, God is in Control.

Then, after lying there for three-and-a-half days, they stand up on their feet when God brings them back to life and calls them to Heaven.

Revelation 11:11-12 — But after the three-and-a-half days the breath of life from God entered them, and they stood on their feet, and terror struck those who saw them. Then they heard a loud voice from heaven saying to them, "Come up here." And they went up to heaven in a cloud, while their enemies looked on.

So, I have looked at the first of the three ways God will be offering His plan of redemption. Now, I want to look in detail at the second way: the 144,000. Right after the appearance of the *"two witnesses,"* God is going to seal and commission 144,000 young, Jewish men (12,000 from each one of the twelve tribes).

Revelation 7:2-4 — Then I saw another angel coming up from the east, having the seal of the living God. He called out in a loud voice to the four angels who had been given power to harm the land and the sea: "Do not harm the land or the sea or the trees until we put a seal on the foreheads of the servants of our God." Then I heard the number of those who were sealed: 144,000 from all the tribes of Israel.

If you look back in Genesis, chapter 12, at the Abrahamic Covenant, Israel's rebellion to God's commands kept them from becoming a nation of priests. But during the Tribulation, these 144,000 will be God's priests, who will take this gospel of the Kingdom to all the Gentile nations. They will be encircling the globe in a supernatural, miraculous way, telling the world the King is coming. They won't have to learn a language—they will know every language and dialect, everywhere they go. They won't have to fear for their lives—they cannot be taken from them because of the seal on their forehead. They will suffer hardships, hunger, misery, and imprisonment, but their lives cannot be taken.

So, how many are going to be saved by the 144,000? We are not given a number, but we do know from scripture that it will be multitudes, and they will come from every nation.

Revelation 7:9 — After this I looked, and there before me was a great multitude that no one could count, from every nation, tribe, people and language, standing before the throne and before the Lamb. They were wearing white robes and were holding palm branches in their hands.

Revelation 7:13-14 — Then one of the elders asked me, "These in white robes—who are they, and where did they come from?" I answered, "Sir, you know." And he said, "These are they who have come out of the great tribulation; they have washed their robes and made them white in the blood of the Lamb."

But it can't be anyone who, prior to the Tribulation, heard the gospel, considered, and rejected it. Those people are going to come under the complete wrath of God, and in order to justify God's wrath, they are going to embrace the Antichrist.

2 Thessalonians 2:10-12 — and all the ways that wickedness deceives those who are perishing. They perish because they refused to love the truth and so be saved. For this reason God sends them a powerful delusion so that they will believe the lie and so that all will be condemned who have not believed the truth but have delighted in wickedness.

There is one other group of people who will be excluded: anyone who takes the mark of the beast. Scripture tells us those who take the mark of the beast will lose their opportunity for salvation. Even so, the 144,000 are going to have a tremendous response.

Revelation 13:16-17 — It also forced all people, great and small, rich and poor, free and slave, to receive a mark on their right hands or on their foreheads, so that they could not buy or sell unless they had the mark, which is the name of the beast or the number (666) of its name.

Most who are saved by the 144,000 will be martyred immediately because of their belief.

Revelation 6:10-11 — They called out in a loud voice, "How long, Sovereign Lord, holy and true, until you judge the inhabitants of the earth and avenge our blood?" Then each of them was given a white robe, and they were told to wait a little longer, until the full number of their fellow servants, their brothers and sisters, were killed just as they had been.

Some who believe will survive, and some who won't believe will also survive. But all these survivors combined are those who Isaiah calls the *"few men left."*

Isaiah 24:6 (KJV) — Therefore hath the curse devoured the earth, and they that dwell therein are desolate: therefore the inhabitants of the earth are burned, and few men left.

So, what happens to the 144,000?

Revelation 14:1-5 — Then I looked, and there before me was the Lamb, standing on Mount Zion, and with him 144,000 who had his name and his Father's name written on their foreheads. And I heard a sound from heaven like the roar of rushing waters and like a loud peal of thunder. The sound I heard was like that of harpists playing their harps. And they sang a new song before the throne and before the four living creatures and the elders. No one could learn the song except the 144,000 who had been redeemed from the earth. These are those who did not defile themselves with women, for they remained virgins. They follow the Lamb wherever he goes. They were purchased from among mankind and offered as firstfruits to God and the Lamb. No lie was found in their mouths; they are blameless.

The 144,000 will be the most triumphant group of men the world has ever seen. They will redeem and save multitudes of Gentiles from all the nations of the world. Most of those they save will die as martyrs when the Antichrist unleashes his vicious persecution on those who will not worship him. Those who believe and somehow live through the tribulation will enter the millennial Kingdom.

We have looked at the first and second ways God will be offering His plan of redemption during the Tribulation. Now I want to discuss the third way, which will be focused solely on the Nation of Israel. But first, I need to highlight a number of significant events that will occur during the first three-and-a-half years of the Tribulation.

Revelation 6:1-2 — I watched as the Lamb opened the first of the seven seals. Then I heard one of the four living creatures say in a voice like thunder, "Come!" I looked, and there before me was a white horse! Its rider (the first of the four horsemen of the apocalypse) *held a bow, and he was given a crown, and he rode out as a conqueror bent on conquest.*

The seven years of tribulation begins with the opening of that first seal. One of his first major events in the Tribulation will be when the Antichrist goes to Jerusalem and makes a seven-year peace treaty with the Nation of Israel. This will occur right before the appearance of the *"two witnesses."*

Daniel 9:27 — He will confirm a covenant with many for one 'seven.' In the middle of the 'seven' he will put an end to sacrifice and offering. And at the temple he will set up an abomination that causes desolation, until the end that is decreed is poured out on him.

But at the mid-point, after three-and-a-half years, he will suddenly turn on Israel and will cause the sacrifice and offering to stop. In order for something to cease, it has to start. So, this verse is saying that Israel will have sacrificial Temple worship for three-and-a-half years. Then the Antichrist will show his true colors (his evil heart) and not only stop Temple worship but will cause the Temple to be defiled. It will remain that way until the seven years are ended.

Using his satanic powers, the Antichrist is going to turn on the Nation of Israel and unleash all his fury and hatred on them.

Matthew 24:15-16 — "So when you see standing in the holy place 'the abomination that causes desolation,' spoken of through the prophet Daniel—let the reader understand—then let those who are in Judea flee to the mountains."

*Isaiah 10:20-21 (KJV) — And it shall come to pass in that day, that the **remnant** of Israel, and such as are **escaped** of the house of Jacob, shall no more again stay upon him that smote them; but shall stay upon the LORD, the Holy One of Israel, in truth. The remnant* (escaping remnant) *shall return, even the remnant of Jacob, unto the mighty God.*

This "escaping remnant" of Israel is the final way God's plan of redemption will be offered during the Tribulation. So, who will escape *(flee to the mountains)*?

The remnant fleeing into the mountains seems very similar to when the Israelites fled from Egypt. After Israel went through the Red Sea, the Red Sea closed over the Egyptian military and destroyed every one of them without the loss of a single Jew. Then, when they were safely encamped around Mount Sinai, Moses went up the mountain to meet with God.

Exodus 19:3-4 — Then Moses went up to God, and the LORD called to him from the mountain and said, "This is what you are to say to the descendants of Jacob and what you are to tell the people of Israel: You yourselves have seen what I did to Egypt, and how I carried you on eagles' wings and brought you to myself."

This miraculous, supernatural exodus from Egypt was described in scripture as *"on eagles wings."* The same description will be used for this "escaping remnant" at the middle of the Tribulation.

Revelation 12:14-16 — The woman (the escaping remnant) was given the two wings of a great eagle, so that she might fly to the place prepared for her in the wilderness, where she would be taken care of for a time, times and half a time, out of the serpent's reach. Then from his mouth the serpent spewed water like a river, to overtake the woman and sweep her away with the torrent. But the earth helped the woman by opening its mouth and swallowing the river that the dragon had spewed out of his mouth.

Just like during the Exodus, God's fleeing, chosen people will be supernaturally protected by our Almighty God. When Satan and the Antichrist see them escaping, they will send a wave of military forces with the orders to destroy them all. But God will open the earth, and it will swallow the whole group. When the Antichrist sees the destruction of his military force and not the loss of a single Jew, he will turn his anger toward a different remnant of Jews.

Revelation 12:17 — Then the dragon was enraged at the woman and went off to wage war against the rest of her offspring—those who keep God's commands and hold fast their testimony about Jesus.

This is the remnant *"who keep God's commands and hold fast their testimony about Jesus."* So, this is the 144,000 young, Jewish men who will be preaching the gospel of the Kingdom to the nations of the world throughout most of the Tribulation. Satan and the Antichrist will concentrate on these young men for most of the remainder of the Tribulation. But they will be just as unsuccessful as with the "escaping remnant," since the 144,000 cannot be put to death because of the seal. But this is not true for those the 144,000 will be saving. As fast as they become believers during the final three-and-a-half years, most will be martyred.

Revelation 11:13 (KJV): And the same hour was there a great earthquake, and the tenth part of the city (Jerusalem) *fell, and in the earthquake were slain of men seven thousand: and the remnant were affrighted, and gave glory to the God of heaven.*

During this tremendous earthquake, the people in Jerusalem will be terrified, yet this remnant will give *"glory to the God of heaven."* Even though they fled Jerusalem not believing that Jesus is the Messiah, at the time of the great earthquake they will give glory to God (the God of Abraham) and stay under His divine protection. Again, we do not know the exact number, but based on Old Testament prophecy, we know it will be a third of the Jewish population.

Notice that in these prophetic verses in Zechariah, those who give *"glory to the God of heaven"* will be the same ones who *"shall call on my name"* and *"shall say, The LORD is my God."*

Zechariah 13:8-9 (KJV) – And it shall come to pass, that in all the land, saith the LORD, *two parts therein shall be cut off and die; but the third shall be left therein. And I will bring the third part through the fire, and will refine them as silver is refined, and will try them as gold is tried: they shall call on my name, and I will hear them: I will say, It is my people: and they shall say, The* LORD *is my God.*

So, what happens to this "escaping remnant" who flee Jerusalem knowing the God of Abraham, but still not knowing Jesus? They will stay in unbelief, fully protected by God until they see Christ coming, and then they will believe, to the very last person. This will fulfill the following two prophesies:

Isaiah 66:8 — Who has ever heard of such things? Who has ever seen things like this? Can a country be born in a day or a nation be brought forth in a moment? Yet no sooner is Zion in labor than she gives birth to her children.

This will be the case for the "escaping remnant" of Jews when they witness the Second Coming of Christ—all become believers and are saved.

In the Book of John, there are eight sign miracles—seven before Christ's crucifixion, and one after. For Israel, a sign was something that miraculously proved to them that God was responsible. The one that appeared after the crucifixion dealt with the "escaping remnant":

John 21:5-6, 10-11 — He called out to them, "Friends, haven't you any fish?" "No," they answered. He said, "Throw your net on the right side of the boat and you will find some." When they did, they were unable to haul the net in because of the large number of fish ... Jesus said to them, "Bring some of the fish you have just caught." So Simon Peter climbed back into the boat and dragged the net ashore. It was full of large fish, 153, but even with so many the net was not torn.

The nets were not torn, which means not one fish was lost. Yet, in instances during Jesus' earthly ministry, when they had a net full of fish, the net broke. The miraculous part of this sign is the net should have broken, but it didn't. This is the sign to Israel that this remnant, who is going to be spared in those last three-and-a-half years, will all become believers when they see the coming Christ. Not a single one will fail to believe. So, the whole net, full of the escaping Israelites, will be brought into the Kingdom.

Romans 9:27-28 — Isaiah cries out concerning Israel: "Though the number of the Israelites be like the sand by the sea, only the remnant will be saved. For the Lord will carry out his sentence on earth with speed and finality."

Although they go out in unbelief, they will become a saved nation on that day when they see Christ coming, in all His power and glory, as He destroys the Antichrist's armies in the Battle of Armageddon. I want to make one point concerning the word "battle." I consider a battle to be when two opposing forces attempt to impose their will on the other. But in this case, the imposing will be totally one-sided. Therefore, I think "annihilation" would be a more suitable word.

Every last Jew in the remnant will believe that Jesus Christ is the Messiah, the Son of God. If it were not for these survivors (the *"few men left"* and the "escaping remnant"), there would be no one left to enter the thousand-year Kingdom.

Isaiah 1:9 — Unless the LORD Almighty had left us some survivors, we would have become like Sodom, we would have been like Gomorrah.

I am aware of the fact that I have navigated through the seven-year Tribulation without discussing the Letters to the Seven Churches, the Seven Seals, the Seven Trumpets, the Seven Bowls, and more. My focus in Part Two and Three of this book has been twofold: first on my basic beliefs, and then on God's plan of redemption, from Adam's fall to the Second Coming of Christ. Therefore, I will leave end-times prophecy to the end-times experts.

So, who are the survivors that Isaiah 24 identifies as the *"few men left"*?

We have the "escaping remnant" of Jews, who entered God's divine "witness protection plan." After they witness the Second Coming of Christ, all will become believers and enter the Kingdom. We have those few who heard the gospel of the Kingdom from the 144,000, believed, and lived through the Tribulation. But there will still be lost people. The following verses in Matthew 25 confirms there will be unbelievers who survive:

Matthew 25:31-35, 41 — "When the Son of Man comes in his glory, and all the angels with him, he will sit on his glorious throne. All the nations will be gathered before him, and he will separate the people one from another as a shepherd separates the sheep from the goats. He will put the sheep on his right and the goats on his left. Then the King will say to those on his right, 'Come, you who are blessed by my Father; take your inheritance, the kingdom prepared for you since the creation of the world.' ... Then he will say to those on his left, 'Depart from me, you who are cursed, into the eternal fire prepared for the devil and his angels.'"

Each and every Gentile nation of the world will be represented by these survivors. The believers on the right will enter the Kingdom, and the unbelievers on the left will end up in eternal judgment.

God's plan of redemption will conclude with the Second Coming of Christ. Therefore, since Part 3 is titled Redemption, I have reached my destination. But I do not want to leave all these second-chance, flesh-and-blood, believing survivors stranded on the Mount of Olives. So, I will give a brief summary to get them into the Kingdom. This will not be based on specific scriptures, but my thoughts only.

All of the survivors will be gathered and waiting to enter the Kingdom, with probably some apprehension and a lot of expectations. Can you imagine the stories about the great Tribulation they tell their kids and grandkids?

There will be a short period of time (According to Daniel, chapter 12: (30 + 45 = 75 days) from Christ's Second Coming until they enter the Kingdom. Why the wait? After the seven years of God's wrath, the surface of earth will be totally destroyed. The devastation will be comparable to the Flood. Yet, in seventy-five days, God will made it as beautiful as the Garden of Eden.

I want to make a couple more points about these survivors.

First, there will be a small group of Gentile surviving believers who represent each Gentile nation. There will also be a large group (the "escaping remnant") of Jewish believers, whose total will equal one-third of the Jewish population at the time of the Tribulation.

Once in the Kingdom, the Jewish population will again occupy the Promised Land (Israel). The Gentile survivors will return to their homelands all over the earth. During the thousand years, the Jewish people will occupy every square inch of the Promised Land. Since they will start out with a population larger than any of the Gentile nations, they will be the great nation God promised to Abraham. They will be the worship center and the commerce center of the world. From this nation of priests will flow all of God's blessings to each and every Gentile nation. Lest we forget, God's Word is absolute, and every promise contained in the Abrahamic Covenant will be fulfilled during the millennium.

Remember, God is in control!

Chapter 56

Flow Charts and the Bible

Before I wrap up this book (which I am proud to say is totally nonfiction), there is one more topic I want to cover. At the very start, I made a list of things I consider myself to be "an expert." Well, there is one on that list I intentionally skipped, since I wanted to make it part of the conclusion of this book. I could ask you which one, but I do not have confidence you would figure it out. Therefore, I am going to help you: flow charts.

Remember when I took the twelve-month leave of absence from Firestone and went back to college? In my second semester, I took the Advanced Fortran course, and the professor's one assignment for the course was to write a computer program that allowed students to register for courses in EZ College. Prior to writing any actual computer code, I created a sentence-structured, indexed checklist of all the required conditions from my professor's list on the blackboard. In computer terminology, that checklist is called a flow chart. That flow chart for my first complex computer program is the only one I ever wrote. So, how can I claim to be an expert on flow charts? Let me explain.

Since the closing of the Firestone plant in Memphis, I have written hundreds of very complex computer programs. For each and every one, I created a flow chart—but only in my head. I never took the time to write them down. I would read all the requirements for the program. Then, on my next long run, after settling into a comfortable pace, I would concentrate on those specific requirements. With little effort on my part, I could see those requirements in logical blocks, as if they were written on the backside of computer printout paper, with each sheet containing a set of requirements that had to be completed prior to the program reaching the next requirement set. To run successfully, the program had to be coded where it could navigate flawlessly through each requirement set, from the beginning to the end of the computer program.

As an example, when I used Fortran code for the "EZ College" program, the code entered the first set of requirements in a building block that I named "corequisite checking." This building block contained conditional "if" statements, "true and false" statements, and "yes and no" statements that it had to process through to reach the next building block requirement set.

In this example, the student attempted to register for CHEM101, but CHEM101 had a lab called CHEM101L. The program would prevent the student from registering in just CHEM101. Since this chemistry course had a lab, the student had to register for both courses at the same time. The program would not allow the student to take the course in one semester, and then take the lab in a different semester. Thus, the title I gave this building block was "corequisite checking." This is just one simple example. There would be another building block for prerequisite checking, and another for time conflicts, and another to check for max hours exceeded—to name just a few.

Once I could see and line up all the required building blocks in the correct order, then the work was practically done. When I got back in the office, I would punch the computer code directly into the computer and compile the program myself, with no computer lab tech required. Then, I'd test the program for each requirement set. If there were no issues, we'd release the new program to the schools. They, in turn, would do additional testing, and if any issues (bugs) were found, I immediately fixed them and rereleased the program.

I know this sounds so complicated, but in reality it is actually rather simple. The reason I consider it to be "simple" is because the code cannot and will not do anything the programmer does not give it specific instructions to perform. Let's say the code enters a conditional "if" statement that can have five different results, but I, as the programmer, only coded for four of the five. Without a doubt, the code will immediately find the one result that does not have code to support it. The program will become totally confused and give up. Then, I have to go into the code, find the result that was not coded for, and fix it. The code will immediately execute correctly and go on its merry way to completion (hopefully!).

I will add there is new technology that throws a monkey wrench into this method of programming code called "artificial intelligence." I am not going to take the time to attempt to explain how artificial intelligence works. In fact, if anyone could explain it such that you might possibly understand, it would be Babu, since he wrote a technical paper on artificial intelligence thirty to forty years ago. I will just say, based on repetition, the program can be coded to learn trends and build its own database containing this trend data. With no help from the programmer, the computer can use this stored information to make its own decisions and even handle events that the programmer failed to code for. Scary stuff? Not really. A computer does not have a "mind of its own." Unplug the power source, and a computer becomes completely helpless.

Now the question is, why am I finishing this book with a discussion about flow charts? Because after many years of effort, I finally stumbled on a method of studying the Bible that incorporated my God-given gift of using logical visual blocks of a flow chart to navigate through the books of the Bible—from the first verse in Genesis to the last verse in Revelation. This gave me the ability to track and observe God's dealings with mankind from generation to generation.

Part 3 of this book shows the result of this method of study.

To begin, I had to have something to track, so I selected God's divine plan of redemption. Why track redemption? Because it starts in Genesis and weaves its way through every book of the Old and New Testaments. In other words, it is the divine fabric that connects all the "dots." But it not only connects all the dots, it connects them in the exact, correct order so you can see God's interaction with each and every generation. And not just His interaction with the lost and the saved, but also with the Nation of Israel versus all other nations. And finally, I have attempted to learn more and more about God's character, based on how He constantly has to deal with mankind's terrible, free-will choices, and then somehow navigate His divine plan of redemption to the next generation.

So, I have one final question, which is based on the fact you are at the end of this book and still reading: Why in the world should you be interested in my beliefs, thoughts, and opinions about the Bible? My short answer is I am over eighty -years-old, and you are (probably) not! Which means I can see the finish line, and there is nothing left to stop me from finishing strong. In a nutshell, that is the sole reason I have written this second book.

There are several groups of people I hope this book will inspire:

First, for those believers who are entering senior citizen status—my desire is for them to work to improve both their physical and spiritual health, since the best of life is still ahead, just beyond that next hill.

Secondly, for believers of any age who will hopefully be encouraged by my stories of God's grace—both in my own life, and throughout the Bible. I hope seeing my method of Bible study will inspire you to dig more deeply into God's Word.

For all those who are still undecided and continue to straddle the fence, my question is: What on earth are you waiting for?

Finally, if through God's grace and mercy there are unbelievers who read this book, my prayer is that God will use it to soften their hearts so they can hear the voice of the Holy Spirit before it is too late.

Now, here are some final thoughts for you:

- Remember to guard your heart.

- Remember God is in control.

- Remember, in all things, fear God, wait on God, listen to God, and, above all, believe God.

When I say to fear God, there is scripture throughout the Bible that tells us to do so:

Deuteronomy 6:13 — Fear the Lord your God, serve him only and take your oaths in his name.

Trembling and being scared and frightened of God is not the type of fear this verse refers to. The fear it refers to is a reverential awe of God that gives you a wholesome desire to please Him.

Proverbs 14:2 — Whoever fears the Lord walks uprightly, but those who despise him are devious in their ways.

In other words, fearing God means having a desire to humble ourselves before God, rid ourselves of pride, and remind ourselves that our Almighty God is worthy to receive all our praise, honor, and obedience.

What does it mean to wait on God?

Isaiah 40:31 (KJV) — But they that wait upon the Lord shall renew their strength; they shall mount up with wings as eagles; they shall run, and not be weary; and they shall walk, and not faint.

This one was hard for me, especially in my youth. Waiting requires patience, and this is something that I lacked for much of my life. Waiting is only possible within time. God is eternal, and therefore is not limited by time. Just remember that even though God is not bound by time, His timing is always perfect.

How do you listen to God?

Proverbs 8:32 — "Now then, my children, listen to me; blessed are those who keep my ways."

The first step to hearing the words of God is to be still and listen.

Psalm 143:8 — Let the morning bring me word of your unfailing love, for I have put my trust in you. Show me the way I should go, for to you I entrust my life.

Listening to God requires us to have a desire to hear His Word. In order to hear His voice, we must want to do His will and trust that He will direct our paths. That is all that is needed.

And, above all, we must believe God.

Hebrews 11:6 — And without faith it is impossible to please God, because anyone who comes to him must believe that he exists and that he rewards those who earnestly seek him.

Romans 10:9-10 — If you declare with your mouth, "Jesus is Lord," and believe in your heart that God raised him from the dead, you will be saved. For it is with your heart that you believe and are justified, and it is with your mouth that you profess your faith and are saved.

From Genesis to Revelation, God has woven within the fabric of scripture a divine strand. This strand is God's divine plan of redemption—mankind's lifeline to eternal salvation. God is continually casting it out from generation to generation. It is available to all those who were born under the sun, with no exceptions.

Within this divine plan, each of us is given the opportunity to choose. We can believe God and receive the gift of eternal salvation or choose unbelief and eternal separation from God. Remember, God does not deny us eternal salvation because we are sinners, but because of unbelief. It is our choice, but don't reject the good news (the gospel). It is the only path to salvation.

With this in mind, I have to say: It's a crying shame that our eternal salvation is such a serious, personal choice, and yet so many treat it so casually.

Looking back, it is so clear that life is not about finding happiness based on abundance. It is about finding joy based on an inner peace. That inner peace is only attainable through a personal relationship with our Lord, Jesus Christ.

Knowing that God can see my heart is one thing, but writing this book and letting everyone else have an eyewitness view is a different matter. It is not like I made my grand appearance in tattered, worn-out clothes; it's more like I stepped out on the stage, void of any clothing.

I have given this book my all. The sun is slowly setting; there is something in the orange that is telling me I am getting close to Home. Someday, I hope I'll see you there.